ALL THE WAY TO HEAVEN

STEPHEN ALTER

All the Way
to Heaven

AN AMERICAN BOYHOOD

IN THE HIMALAYAS

HENRY HOLT AND COMPANY   NEW YORK

Henry Holt and Company, Inc.
Publishers since 1866
115 West 18th Street
New York, New York 10011

Henry Holt is a registered trademark of
Henry Holt and Company, Inc.

Published in Canada by Fitzhenry & Whiteside Ltd.,
195 Allstate Parkway, Markham, Ontario L3R 4T8

Library of Congress Cataloging-in-Publication Data
Alter, Stephen.
All the way to heaven : an American boyhood in the Himalayas /
Stephen Alter. — 1st ed.
p.   cm.
ISBN 0-8050-5158-9 (hardcover : alk. paper)
1. Alter, Stephen—Childhood and youth.   2. Landour Cantonment
(India)—Social life and customs.   3. Himalaya Mountains Region—
Social life and customs.   I. Title.
DS486.L34A45   1998
818'.5403
[B]—DC21   97-40677

Henry Holt books are available for special promotions and premiums.
For details contact: Director, Special Markets.

First Edition 1998

Designed by Kate Nichols

Printed in the United States of America
All first editions are printed on acid-free paper.

1   3   5   7   9   10   8   6   4   2

For

Jayant and Shibani

*T*he force that through the green fuse drives the flower
Drives my green age; that blasts the roots of trees
Is my destroyer.

—DYLAN THOMAS

*M*y earliest recollections are like everybody else's,
points of light in a long dark tunnel, and to me
as to all others in boyhood the unillumined voids were
just as real as the luminous incidents.

—NIRADH C. CHAUDHRI

*H*er words still filled his mind
As they started their journey,
Just as a mother's voice is heard
Sometimes in a man's mind
Long past childhood
Calling his name, calling him from sleep
Or from some pleasureful moment
On a foreign street
When every trace of origin seems left
And one has almost passed into a land
That promises a vision or the secret
Of one's life, when one feels almost god enough
To be free of voices, her voice
Calls out like a voice from childhood,
Reminding him he once tossed in dreams.

—HERBERT MASON'S *GILGAMESH*

CONTENTS

CONTENTS

ALL THE WAY TO HEAVEN

PROLOGUE

I left my Foss Hill dormitory around nine o'clock on a Saturday morning and walked across to Washington Street. The maple trees were gold and red, dry leaves gusting along the sidewalk. The air was warm for November, an "Indian summer," one of those American expressions that still puzzled me. This was the fall of 1974, my freshman year at Wesleyan. I was carrying a saddlebag in which I'd packed a change of clothes and a couple of my text-books—Robert Graves's translation of *The Golden Ass* and *Light in August* by William Faulkner—as well as my toothbrush and a note-book in which I sometimes wrote poems.

Washington Street cut straight through the center of Middle-town, past the Sicilian church and across Main Street. Woolworth was open and Bob's Surplus, as well as a couple of hardware stores and a corner restaurant serving breakfast. Though I had been down to Main Street several times since I'd arrived at college, it still seemed unfamiliar. The center of town had an empty, run-down feeling about it, deserted except for a few mannequins in the shop windows. Under the clear November sky the colors on the signs were faded and the parked cars looked dusty and abandoned. There were a few bars along the street, the March-In Cafe and John B's, but at that hour of the morning these were closed and even the drunks had disappeared.

I was half a world away from home and my mind was already made up: I didn't like America. As soon as possible, I wanted to go back home to India, where I was born and raised in a hill station called Mussoorie, seven thousand feet up in the mountains of Garhwal. The unhappy, restless feeling in my chest was more than just homesickness, for I was convinced that I didn't belong in this country. Despite the autumn foliage, Connecticut seemed flat and featureless, surrounding me with a sense of dislocation and confinement.

Growing up in the Himalayas I was used to looking out across great distances. From my bedroom window in Mussoorie I could see fifty or sixty miles at least, beyond the Dehra Dun Valley and the Siwalik foothills to the south, across the green mosaic of the Gangetic Plain. Climbing to the top of the ridge above our house my view extended in the opposite direction, northward to the snow peaks of Garhwal. As the crow flies these mountains were forty miles away but they seemed much closer, rising up like the jagged spires and battlements of a celestial city. Their summits were over twenty thousand feet, ascending into the sky above the clouds. The bone white profiles of the high Himalayas were ribbed with ice fields and glaciers, intricate scrimshaw patterns carved by the wind. Each mountain had a name and a mythology reaching back into the earliest epics—Nanda Devi, Trisul, Chaukhamba, Kedarnath, Gangotri, Bandar Punch.

On the far side of Main Street stood an abandoned warehouse with the name Bunce & Co. painted on the high brick walls. One of my friends from India was named Scott Bunce, and the sign had caught my eye when I first arrived in Middletown. The Greyhound station was about a block from Main Street, but I continued walking toward Route 9, which ran along the Connecticut River, a divided highway that would take me out to Interstate 91. I was headed up to Amherst to visit another classmate from India, Tracy Martin, who was studying at UMass. We had talked on the phone once or twice and she had invited me to come up for the weekend.

I had hitchhiked several times before. Soon after arriving in America, before college started, I had been staying in Boston with my father's cousin, Janet Wien. Having nothing better to do, I took off for Montreal, thumbing my way up through Vermont. I wanted to see if I could actually make it all the way to Canada and back. It only took a day and a half in each direction and I got rides without any problems. Nobody hassled me. In Montreal I spent a night at a cheap hotel, walked up to a park overlooking the city, and ate dinner by myself at an Indian restaurant, the Bombay Palace, saag paneer and tandoori chicken, which looked as if it had been dipped in Mercurochrome. The next day I turned around and came back to Boston. I suppose I was testing the limits of this country, going up and crossing the border, then coming back. Janet and her friends had been nervous, and before I set out they kept telling me stories from the newspapers about people getting robbed and killed while they were hitchhiking, but in most of the stories it was the hitchhikers who committed the crimes, and I wasn't really scared.

Now, after two months in college, I was restless again and ready to get out of Middletown. I knew roughly where I was headed though I had never been up to Amherst before. Crossing Route 9, I walked down to the bridge that spanned the Connecticut River, with its high steel arches. There wasn't a lot of traffic but after ten minutes I got my first ride with a middle-aged couple who were headed up to Hartford. As I climbed into the backseat, they seemed overly cheerful and a little nervous. I had a beard in those days and they had probably read the same newspaper stories as Janet and her friends. The couple were relieved to learn that I was a Wesleyan student.

"Where are you from, originally?" they wanted to know.

I hesitated, as I always do when I am asked that question.

"Boston," I said, not wanting to explain too much. This wasn't really a lie because Janet lived there and she was my guardian. I didn't want to admit that my real home was in India, where my parents and brothers still lived, in a section of Mussoorie called Landour. By this time I had learned that it was easier not to tell the truth to strangers, since it meant a lot more questions. Most people probably didn't believe me anyway, when I said that I came from India. Even though I was an American citizen, I had only lived in the United States for two and a half years, off and on.

"You don't have a Boston accent," said the woman, turning around in her seat and squinting at me with curiosity. "You sound British."

"Well . . . you see, my mother's English," I lied. This seemed to satisfy her curiosity.

As we joined the interstate going north, the couple told me that they were on their way to a Bible brunch at the Ramada Inn outside of Hartford and asked if I wanted to go along. I had already noticed the stylized symbol of a fish hanging from their rearview mirror and a copy of *The Living Bible* on the front seat between them. Obviously they'd picked me up in the hope of saving my soul.

I thanked them politely for the invitation but said I had to get to Amherst in time for lunch. The couple kept trying to persuade me to join them and asked if I believed in Jesus, to which I gave an ambiguous reply. I suppose I should have just told them the truth at that point—my parents were missionaries in India, with the Presbyterian Church—but their exit was coming up ahead of us, and reluctantly the husband pulled over into the breakdown lane and let me out.

It was an impossible place to hitch a ride, just a few miles short of Hartford, where the highway divided and went in several different directions. For half an hour I stood there holding out my thumb and nobody responded, the cars going by at seventy miles an hour. I began to wish that I had taken the bus, when I saw a motorcycle slowing down and stopping. The biker looked back over his shoulder and gestured for me to hurry up. He was dressed in scuffed black leather and had a ponytail. I was about to wave him on, when I realized that if I didn't take this ride I would probably be stuck there for another hour.

The Harley-Davidson was chugging like a tractor as I swung my leg up over the back and put the saddlebag on my lap between us. There wasn't much to hold on to but I braced myself the best I could. As we set off, I noticed the emblem on the back of the biker's jacket, "Dark Shadow Riders." After I got over my initial fear of falling off or crashing, I enjoyed the ride. The biker drove fast, weaving in and out of traffic. As we passed through Hartford the oriental dome of the Colt arms factory went by in a blur. There was no possibility of conversation, no need to answer questions, only the rush of air in my face and a hurtling sense of speed.

The Dark Shadow Rider let me off ten or fifteen miles beyond Hartford, near the Massachusetts border, and I thanked him, still windblown and dazed from the ride. There was a lot more traffic on the highway now, and within a couple minutes a large red Buick cut in front of me with its turn signal blinking. At that point I hadn't even put out my thumb, and I was surprised that anyone would stop. The driver was a gray-haired man with glasses, wearing a dark business suit. Opening the front door I slid into the seat beside him and put my saddlebag on the floor.

"Hello, Steve. How are you?"

I looked up at the man in surprise, but didn't recognize him. He knew my name, yet there was nothing familiar about his features or his voice. I tried to remember if I had ever seen him before and thought he might have been the father of one of my classmates in the dormitory, or someone who worked at Wesleyan, but I could make no connection. There was also something threatening about the man that made me hesitate to ask him who he was. The driver did not introduce himself, but the way he talked insinuated that he knew a great deal more about me than just my name. His voice had a flat, unnerving tone, like someone reading from a script.

"I bet you miss India, don't you?" he said after we had gone about a mile.

I hadn't told him that I was from India, but I nodded, confused and frightened. He wanted to know what I was studying in college, and when I told him that I was thinking of majoring in history, he said, "But you want to be a writer, don't you?"

I said I did, afraid to look at him.

"Your mother is a writer, isn't she?" he said.

"Yes, she writes poetry."

I have never believed in mind readers or psychics, and maybe it was my own imagination playing games on me, but as we continued up Route 91, I was absolutely terrified. The man who had picked me up looked like an insurance executive from one of the gleaming towers in Hartford, dressed in an expensive suit and tie, white shirt with cuff links. His hair was thin on top and he was clean-shaven. The glasses he wore were black rimmed, conservative. He could have been any ordinary white man on his way to work, but as he spoke to me I felt that there was something sinister about him. At that moment I would have given anything to be back on the Harley-Davidson, or even to have gone to the Bible brunch at the Ramada Inn, but there was no way that I could get out of the car.

As we neared Springfield I told the man that he could let me off at any of the exits but he said that he was headed farther north and I could ride with him as far as Route 9, which would take me into Amherst. I think he sensed my fear and he was toying with me, dropping hints that he knew other details about my life. I can't remember everything he said but there was a tone of premonition in his voice. I felt completely vulnerable, as if he had gained access to my memories and there was nothing I could hide from him.

In the end he let me off at the Amherst exit and I got out of the car as quickly as I could, relieved to see the Buick drive away. My whole body was shaking even though I kept telling myself that there was no reason to be afraid. Amherst was still about eight or ten miles down the road but I thought about walking the rest of the way rather than taking chances with another ride. A few minutes later a college student stopped and gave me a lift in his pickup truck. He was going to UMass and dropped me at the edge of the campus.

Tracy Martin had a room in one of the high-rise dormitories, which stand like giant silos above the rolling Berkshire Hills. I had her address and room number written down and rode the elevator up to the eighteenth floor. Tracy was there and it was a relief to see her after what had happened to me that morning. I told her about the stranger in the car and we kept trying to figure out who he might have been. I don't know whether Tracy actually believed my story but she could tell that I was shaken.

"Why didn't you just ask him who he was?" she said.

"I don't know. I was too scared."

Later that night we talked about India and friends of ours from Woodstock, the mission school in Landour where my father was the principal. Tracy and I discussed the teachers we had known and hikes we'd taken together, field trips to Rishikesh and Hardwar. For me it was reassuring to be with someone who knew where I was coming from, someone who had actually been there with me. Tracy said that she missed India too though she was reconciled to living in the States. I told her that I was thinking of dropping out of college and going back, unable to resist the constant feeling of nostalgia and loss. I missed my family and the friends with whom I had grown up. I missed the mountains, those white shrouds of snow that seemed to levitate above the lower ridges. In my mind I could trace the silhouette of every mountain near Mussoorie, the peaks which I had climbed—Nag Tibba, with its false summit and cobra temple, Lurntzu and Sirkanda Devi, at the top of which was a shrine to the goddess, Top Tibba, Pepperpot, Flag Hill, and Pari Tibba, which we called Witch's Hill. As I talked about these places I could picture every detail: the cliffs above Kimoin, the leopard's cave, the forests of oak and rhododendron trees, their bloodred flowers hanging like tassels from the branches. I missed the winding hill roads, the Landour bazaar, the clock tower, and Picture Palace. I missed the rivers where I had fished for mahseer and the jungles in which I had hunted for ghoral and barking deer.

All this time, as Tracy and I talked about Mussoorie, I kept thinking of the stranger in the car. Even though I was no longer afraid, I couldn't help but feel unsettled, struggling to figure out how he had known my name and other details of my life. For years afterward I expected to meet this man again and discover who he was, but to this day the driver in the red Buick remains a mystery for which I have no explanation.

PASSIONFLOWERS

One of my earliest memories is of sitting outside the Landour
Community Hospital on the morning when my youngest brother,
Andy, was born. I would have been four years old at the time. My
second brother, Joe, was with me and we were playing in the sun
near the front steps of the hospital. Martha, our ayah, was looking
after us while my mother was upstairs in the delivery room giving
birth. I can't remember if my father was there or not. He was probably on his way up from Etah, the mission compound on the plains
where he was stationed. I have always had a very clear image of that
morning, sitting in the sun with our ayah in front of the hospital.
Martha was chewing paan, her lips and teeth stained red from the
mixture of betel nuts, tobacco, and flavorings wrapped up in a
heart-shaped leaf. Joe and I were picking up gravel with our hands
and making miniature roads and mountains in the dirt as we waited
to hear if we were going to have a new brother or a sister.

Next to the veranda of the hospital was a passionflower vine
climbing up a wooden trellis. Martha picked one of the flowers and

tied it to my hand, as if it were a bright-colored wristwatch. The passionflower was a deep purple and white, its inner petals similar to the markings on the face of a clock, the stamen and pistil like the hour and minute hands. I can still see every detail of that flower in my mind, yet I know that this memory cannot possibly be true, for my brother Andy was born on the first of October and the passionflowers in Mussoorie bloom during May and June.

* * *

All three of us, my brothers and I, were born in the Landour Community Hospital, that gray, unwelcoming structure precariously balanced on the nearly vertical face of the hillside. It was an ugly building, made of concrete and stone, with a sloping asbestos roof. There was a steep driveway that wound its way up from the Tehri Road and a narrow gravel yard surrounded by a wire fence. Next to the entrance was a marble plaque:

FOR THE SERVICE OF JESUS CHRIST
THE CHIEF CORNERSTONE
1938

Inside the hospital it was always dark. The corridors were illuminated by a few dim bulbs, and the small, square panes of glass in the windows filtered out most of the sunlight. A sharp chemical smell of phenyl and formaldehyde penetrated your nostrils the minute you entered the door. Nurses moved about in the shadows, dressed in navy blue sweaters and starched white uniforms, their legs sheathed in pale stockings. They wore little white caps that looked like paper sailboats, attached to their hair with bobby pins. On the ground floor of the hospital was the X-ray room, with a machine that looked like a torture rack and skeletal negatives hanging from clothespins on a wire, opaque images of ribs and broken limbs. Down the hall were the doctors' offices and the laboratory where the technicians in their white coats drew syringefuls of blood from our veins and peered through microscopes at specimens of our stool and urine, searching for amoeba, giardia, and other parasites. In one of the bottles on the shelf of the laboratory was a tapeworm, six or eight feet long, which had been removed from the intestines of a patient. The worm floated in the yellow alcohol solution like an enormous shoelace.

The waiting room in the hospital was also on the ground floor, a spare rectangular lounge with windows along one side. All the years I lived in Landour, the pictures in the waiting room never changed. There was a faded print of a white magnolia on one wall, its petals open and distended. The other picture, above the fireplace, was a painting of Christ in a loose brown robe, knocking at a sinner's door. On the opposite wall there were shelves of evangelical magazines, pious tracts and testimonials, as well as a few pamphlets about health and hygiene—how to find eternal peace in Jesus and protect yourself against TB.

Even though it was my birthplace I hated the Landour Community Hospital. Once or twice a year my brothers and I would go there to get our shots, vaccinations for typhoid, cholera, tetanus, polio, smallpox, and other diseases. Upstairs were the wards and private rooms, as well as the operating theater, which I never saw. The delivery room was on the second floor, equipped with a white metal bed that had stirrups at one end, tall surgical lamps, and a line of stainless steel forceps on the table by the window. There were different wards for different kinds of people. The missionaries got private rooms, and there were isolation wards for hepatitis cases, measles, or chicken pox. The general wards, where most of the Indian patients stayed, villagers and townspeople, remained separate from the rest. When I was thirteen, I spent a night in the hospital after falling off the side of the hill below our house and suffering a mild concussion. Down the hall from me was a man with kidney stones and he groaned and wailed throughout the night like a tormented spirit.

My memories have a way of rearranging themselves and it is

hard for me to recollect each trip I made to the hospital, each illness, each friend or family member that I visited, each physical examination, each shot and blood test. What I remember most is the gloominess of the place, the odor of burnt toast and mutton broth from the kitchens, the brittle sound of the nurses' heels on the hard cement floors, the coughing of patients in the general ward, the faces of villagers waiting outside in the gravel yard, an overwhelming sense of misery and pain.

It was in this same hospital that Martha died of throat cancer when I was fourteen. By then she was no longer working for us; my brothers and I were too old to need an ayah. Occasionally we would meet her on the Landour hillside, where she was employed by another missionary family. Martha would always greet Joe, Andy, and me affectionately and tell us how tall we'd grown. When we heard that she was sick, my mother took the three of us to see Martha in the community hospital and I remember how thin she looked, thinner than she had ever been before. As we stood around her bed, Martha reached out and touched our faces and said our names: "Stevie," "Joey," "Andy." My mother had brought a Kashmiri shawl as a gift for her and we were in tears by the time we left the ward, passing down the dark, grim halls of the hospital and out into the sunlight, where Martha had once tied a passionflower to my wrist.

*   *   *

My birth certificate was issued by the mortuary registrar and medical officer of health, city board, Mussoorie. It is a yellowed sheet of paper, a standard printed form, on which a few cryptic details have been typed:

Date and time of birth: September 15, 1956 at 9:15 A.M.
Name (if any) of Child: Stephen Leslie Alter.
Name of Father or Mother: Robert Copley Alter—Father.
Mary Ellen Alter—Mother.

Mother's age: 30 years, 1st child.

Sex: Male.

Caste: Christian.

Profession of Parent: Missionary.

Name of Mohalla or House or No. of House if any: The
Firs, Landour. Born at Landour Community Hospital.

The year that I was born, my parents had just returned from America and they were studying Hindi at the Landour Language School. My father already knew the language—he too was born in India—though he spoke colloquial Hindustani and needed to practice his reading and writing. My mother had spent three years in India but Hindi was still an unfamiliar tongue, the aspirated consonants, long vowels and short, the nasal tones and gutturals. There were three kinds of *R* sounds and four different *T*s, none of which were similar to English pronunciations. Each day, while I was in her womb, my mother studied her vocabulary, the complex conjugations, the masculine and feminine nouns. As she repeated the words again and again, I was turning somersaults and kicking at her ribs. In the last months of her pregnancy she and my father would walk along the paths in Landour, reciting conversations from the Hindi textbook, as my mother tried to master the key phrases of this foreign tongue. The teachers at the language school, Mr. Sharma, Mr. Massey, and Mr. Dutt, would go over the lessons with her every day as she memorized the words for fruit and vegetables, for household objects, the correct forms of address for servants, children, and husbands, those subtle gradations of politeness that a missionary memsahib was expected to learn.

For my mother India must have seemed strangely disconnected from her childhood home in western Pennsylvania. She grew up in a small town called Utica, tucked into the washboard hills of Venango County, a landscape of undulating fields, deciduous forests, and scattered oil wells. As a girl my mother had never traveled east of Pittsburgh or farther west than Chicago. She met my father while they were students at Westminster College in New Wilmington, Pennsylvania. The two of them fell in love during their senior year and got engaged at the last minute, just before my father returned to India after graduation.

During his three years at college my father was homesick and felt out of place in America. He was eager to get back to Mussoorie, where he had been offered a job at Woodstock School. When my father returned home in the spring of 1947, India was on the brink of independence and the future was troubled and uncertain. The British would soon be leaving and the subcontinent was about to be split into two separate nations, India and Pakistan. He wrote letters to my mother describing the Hindu-Muslim riots and the streams of refugees that were moving in opposite directions across the border. The violence of retribution had spread all over North India and even in Mussoorie there were riots. The town was put under curfew for weeks at a stretch and the British stationed Gurkha soldiers in the bazaar to protect the Muslim residents. During his winter vacation, my father served as a volunteer with the Friends Service Committee, working among the refugees and assisting groups of women and children who were stranded in disputed regions of Kashmir. At this time my grandparents were living in the town of Rawalpindi, which became a part of Pakistan. They too wrote letters to my mother, describing the unrest, but reassuring her that she would be safe when she arrived. Reading these letters, my mother must have had so many doubts and questions, as she prepared to leave her friends and family, setting off on her first uncertain passage to India.

In the fall of 1948 she boarded a freighter called *The Flying Arrow* in New York City, her satin wedding gown packed away in a steamer trunk. My mother didn't know any of the other twelve passengers on the freighter and she was seasick for most of the voyage. When she finally arrived in Bombay my father was there to meet her, but because of a dock strike they had to wait ten days before my mother's luggage was unloaded. The two of them stayed at a mission guesthouse in Bombay, called Raj Mahal, and afterward my parents liked to say they had their honeymoon before their marriage.

Eventually, they traveled north from Bombay by train, aboard the Frontier Mail. It couldn't have been easy for my mother, finding herself so far away from home. None of the descriptions in my father's letters could have prepared her for what she discovered in India. On the train journey she would have seen for the first time women dressed in saris, carrying clay water vessels on their heads, men with turbans and dhotis, mud villages and sandstone forts passing by their carriage window, camel carts and teams of oxen lined up at the level crossings, deformed beggars and bearded sadhus on station platforms. All around her she must have heard the chorus of unfamiliar voices, languages that sounded like gibberish, the cries of hawkers selling tea and sweets, swarms of flies, a rhesus monkey clinging to the bars on the train window, stealing peanuts from her fingers.

When my parents got off the train in Saharanpur it was the middle of the night. They had planned to take the bus from there up to Mussoorie but by that time they had run out of money and couldn't afford the fare. The bus driver, a man named Mathura Das, loaned them a couple of rupees to pay for their tickets and took them up the hill. After that, whenever my parents met him at the bus stand, they would always greet each other with great affection. Many years later I was introduced to Mathura Das, when he had started driving a taxi up and down the road to Dehra Dun. He was a thin, lively man with a starched brown turban that looked twice as large as his head.

My mother and father were married within a week of their arrival in Mussoorie, on the tenth of November, 1948. The wedding was held in Parker Hall, at Woodstock School, and the chapel was decorated with bouquets of wild tree dahlias, large purple blossoms that bloomed around that time of year. After their marriage my parents lived and worked at Woodstock for three years, supervising the boys' hostel and teaching in the high school. Though the surrounding culture of India was unfamiliar, my mother found that the community of American missionaries reminded her of the small-town neighborhoods where she had grown up in Pennsylvania. Landour was a cloistered, tightly knit society and everyone knew each other. Missionaries from different denominations gathered on the hillside every summer and the school and church were the center of their world. Even the discomforts and deprivations of living in Landour, the primitive plumbing and coal stoves, were not too different from what my mother had known as a child.

In 1951 my parents returned to the United States, sailing from Calcutta to Boston. For the next few years they lived in New Haven, Connecticut, where the two of them enrolled at Yale Divinity School, studying theology, church history, and comparative religions. By this time they had decided to become missionaries, and the liberal atmosphere at Yale fostered and reinforced their own commitment to a life of Christian service, free of the dogmas and evangelical fervor of the more conservative denominations. My father's eldest brother, Jim, and his wife, Barry, had already joined the mission, and like them my parents wanted to work among village communities in India. Following my father's ordination my parents were both commissioned by the Presbyterian Board of Foreign Missions, and they left America in the spring of 1956, sailing across the Atlantic on the USS *United States*.

By this time my mother was already pregnant with me, and the combination of morning sickness and rough seas kept her in their cabin for most of the trip. My father read her Agatha Christie novels to keep her spirits up, and one of the stewards finally convinced her to eat a bacon sandwich, after which she felt much better. They stopped over in London for a few days, then boarded the P&O liner *Chusan* on its last voyage to India. The ship was full of British ICS officers, taking a final, sentimental journey to Bombay. The Suez Canal had just been turned over to Egypt, and as the *Chusan* sailed through, the retired colonials kept bemoaning the loss of their empire.

· · ·

Soon after I was born my father took several photographs of me with his Rollieflex camera, black-and-white snapshots in which the shutter opened for a fraction of a second, allowing me to peer in upon my infancy, that narrow aperture through which I now see myself as a newborn baby, fists clenched and eyes crimped tightly shut. I am wrapped in a sweater that is too large for me, the sleeves rolled up around my wrists. For as long as I can remember, my mother kept three of these pictures in a silver frame on her dressing table. Later she added other photographs of my brothers and me, as we grew older, but the newborn images remained in place. Staring at them I would try to recognize something of myself in those squinted features, the shape of my hands, the curved outline of my ear.

Most of my childhood photographs are preserved in an album with a heavy vinyl cover and thick black pages. Between each page is a transparent sheet of tissue paper to protect the pictures. Under the photographs, in white pencil, my mother has written places and dates: "Sept.–Oct., 1956, Mussoorie, 'The Firs'" or "Spring, 1957, Allahabad." In one sequence of photographs I am naked and Martha is bathing me in a tin tub. In another picture my mother holds me to her breast and nurses me. Even without looking at the albums I can picture specific details, the checkerboard of windows at the Firs, the knitted pattern of my sweater, a striped hat and night suit that arrived in a parcel from America soon after I was born. There are pictures of me sitting in a cupboard, playing with a pair of shoes, my blond hair standing straight up like a shock of wheat. These photographs are fragments from a period of my life which I cannot fully piece together, even though the pictures have a surety about them that locates me in a specific time and place. In the background of the photographs I can recognize landmarks, a parapet wall along the Zig Zag path, the rooftops of Sisters' bazaar, fern-draped trees, and in the distance, beyond Landour, the ever-present mountains, shadowy silhouettes of the nearer ridges and the faint white shapes of the higher peaks, almost invisible against the bright exposure of the sky.

Ram Dayal, our cook, is holding me in one of the pictures, while I wave at the camera, a bib around my neck. Further on in the album I am celebrating my first birthday, and after that there are three or four snapshots with my cousin Marty, who taught me how to walk. This album provides me with a series of distinct images and I have difficulty separating my own first memories from the pictures themselves. The photographs are stuck to the pages with triangular corners and over the years the adhesive on many of these came loose, so that the sequence moved about and became confused. In one set of pictures, which appear immediately following my birth, Joe and I are playing with two puppies, one of which is white, the other black. These photographs must have been taken several years after the other pictures on that page but the period of time that separates each image has blurred together in my mind. At other points in the album Andy appears and disappears between my first birthday and our furlough in America, four years later. A loose picture of Martha is tucked into the binding between two pages. She is holding Andy, while Joe and I are leaning against her, my hand clutching at the pleats of her sari. In this way the chronology of my early childhood has become distorted and imprecise, a movable montage of faces, scenes, and incidents.

There is one picture that stands out in my memory, of my mother and me leaving the hospital in a dandie, or sedan chair, carried on the shoulders of four coolies. My mother is smiling at the camera but I am sound asleep. The coolies can't be seen, except for one man's shoulder and the sleeve of his shirt. I have often told the story about my first dandie ride, which almost ended in disaster. As my mother and I were being carried home from the hospital, one of the men lost his footing on the narrow path and the dandie fell to the ground, nearly pitching us over the side of the hill. The place where we fell, as I have visualized it in my mind, was about half a mile above the hospital, at a corner where the cliffs drop more than a hundred feet to the Tehri Road below. Over the years I have often imagined that fatal moment and replayed it in my mind, the coolie losing his balance, our dandie tipping sideways like a canoe, and the look of terror on my mother's face as she clutched me in her arms.

Yet once again, I have to admit that none of this is true. It was my brother Joe who was riding with my mother in the dandie when they fell. I wasn't even there. The two of them were coming home from the hospital after Joe's birth, and I must have been safe at home with Martha. But for reasons that I can't explain, I have always claimed the experience as my own, retelling this story so many times I eventually came to believe that it was mine.

● ○ ■

Mussoorie gets its name from a common Himalayan shrub, mansura (*Coriaria nepalensis*), which has a small purple fruit that tastes something like a black currant. "Mussoorie berries," as we used to call them, attract all kinds of birds and leave a dark stain on your fingers when you pick them. The wood of an old mansura bush is very strong and does not rot when soaked in water. Dairy farmers in the villages around Mussoorie use its branches as stakes for tethering their cattle.

The British had a way of distorting the pronunciation as well as the spelling of most Indian names, so that mansura or mansuri was eventually changed to Mussoorie, which sounds as though it might have been a Welsh hamlet or some castle in Scotland. During the nineteenth century a number of other hill stations were established throughout the Himalayas, summer resorts like Dalhousie, Simla, Kasauli, Nainital, Almora, and Ranikhet. The British came to the mountains in search of a familiar environment, the cold, the mist, the drizzle and rain. Dense forests of oak and pine nurtured their memories of home and the cool climate provided a respite from the hot summer months on the plains. The Himalayas also held a special fascination for the British, perhaps because so many of the peaks remained unconquered.

According to the history books Mussoorie was nothing more than a cluster of shepherds' huts when the first British officers built their hunting lodge near Vincent Hill. By the 1830s several permanent "shooting boxes" had been constructed and a number of regimental sportsmen spent their summers in Mussoorie. The mountains offered an abundance of game: barking deer, ghoral and serow, as well as leopards and Himalayan black bear. There were also plenty of kalij, chir, and koklas pheasant, several species of partridge, and the mountain quail, *Ophrysia superciliosa*, which eventually became extinct.

In 1810 the Dehra Dun Valley and the hills around Mussoorie were ceded by the maharaja of Tehri Garhwal to Major Hyder Hearsey, an Anglo-Indian soldier of fortune. The maharaja was in exile at the time; his kingdom had been conquered by the Ghurkas of Nepal. Hyder Hearsey joined forces with the British East India Company's army and fought bravely to defeat the Ghurkas and drive them out of Garhwal. However, once the Ghurka wars were over, the Honorable Company declared Hearsey's title to Mussoorie illegal and usurped the territory for itself. Throughout the period of British rule, descendants of Hyder Hearsey continued to press for compensation but without success. When I was growing up in Mussoorie, one of the Hearsey family still lived in a tumbledown cottage near Mossy Falls. Virtually destitute, he supported himself by selling flower bulbs and begging in the bazaar.

The Great Trigonometrical Survey of the Himalayas, undertaken by the British during the middle of the nineteenth century, was based in Mussoorie, and the initial benchmark was an observatory on Camel's Back Hill. The first accurate maps of the mountains were produced under the direction of Sir George Everest, after whom the highest mountain in the world was named. Everest had a bungalow built for himself to the west of Mussoorie, near Cloud's End. He also constructed an adjacent building, the "Bibi Ghar," which housed his harem. The Survey of India maintained summer offices at Castle Hill Estate and it was from here, in the late 1800s, that cartographic expeditions traveled back into the hills as far as Tibet and China. The survey parties often disguised them-selves as traders or shepherds to avoid arrest. This was during the period of "the Great Game," when the British were busy mapping out their empire and Kipling's Kim set out on his adventures.

Over the years Mussoorie went through many transformations. Around 1840 a sanatorium for convalescent soldiers was estab-lished, as well as Bohle's brewery and several boarding schools. A number of hotels were built and a flourishing bazaar developed along the Mall Road, the one main street that ran the length of town. By the turn of the century, Mussoorie had become a lively summer resort, known as "Queen of the Hills." While Simla remained the most popular hill station for the British and the seat of colonial government during the summer months, Mussoorie was a seasonal retreat for many of the "Native Princes" and maharajas, who built large estates and threw lavish parties and masked balls. The town developed a reputation for extravagance and scandal, though after independence very few of the maharajas could afford to maintain their properties. Gradually the town attracted a different type of visitor, middle-class tourists and hon-eymoon couples, as well as students from the many boarding schools.

The Landour hillside lay at the eastern end of Mussoorie, a sep-arate ridge, with three rounded summits. The upper half of the hill and most of the northern slope was a military cantonment, where the British convalescent hospital was located. The southern slope was settled by American missionaries who built cottages on the steep hillside. They adopted a pattern of migration similar to the British, women and children retreating to the mountains during the summer months. From mission compounds scattered all over North India the missionaries converged on Landour, as if driven by a flocking instinct. Unlike the town of Mussoorie, with its licentious reputation and gaudy tourist attractions, cinemas, and hotels, the hillside maintained a staid and puritan air.

Situated in the center of Landour, Woodstock School was originally founded in 1854 by a company of British officers and American missionaries. It began as a Protestant girls' school, an alternative to Waverly Convent, which had opened a few years earlier at the opposite end of Mussoorie. Much of Woodstock's heritage reflected a combination of British and American traditions, the vestiges of a colonial past. When I was a student there, some of the townspeople and villagers still referred to Woodstock as the "Company School," even though it had been taken over by the mission societies in 1874. Both my grandfather and my father served as principals of Woodstock, and I studied there from first grade through graduation.

*　　*　　*

Martha and Emmet Alter, my grandparents, first arrived in Mussoorie on April 27, 1917, to spend the summer studying at the Landour Language School. They had landed in India a few months earlier and were posted to Sialkot and Jhelum in the Punjab. My grandmother was from Ohio and my grandfather was born in Oregon, at Warm Springs Indian Reservation. His parents were "home missionaries," working among the Native Americans. The two of them met as students at Westminster—the same college that my parents attended. Soon after their marriage, my grandparents joined the United Presbyterian Mission and were assigned to India. Traveling overland from Ohio to Seattle, they boarded a ship called the *Empress of Russia* and sailed across the Pacific, stopping in Yokohama, Hong Kong, Shanghai, Manila, Hanoi, Saigon, Singapore, and finally Colombo. From Ceylon they took the Jaffna ferry to

Cape Cormorin, the southern tip of India, and traveled the length of the subcontinent by train, eventually arriving at Sialkot.

The generation of missionaries to which my grandparents belonged were dedicated to establishing the church in India. They believed that it was their duty and purpose to convert Hindus and Muslims to Christianity. Socially my grandparents lived quite separate lives from the colonial authorities, but their experience of India was very much a part of the British Raj. For over forty years they lived and worked in the Panjab, spending the summer months in Mussoorie and Kashmir.

In one of her earliest letters home to her family in Ohio, my grandmother described her first impressions of Landour:

My dearest Father, Mother, & Evangeline,

Here we are in our bay window looking out at one high hill upon another out to the snow caps of the Himalayas. We are in a cottage built for three couples and board at the main building down about eighty steps below. We have the middle room with the bay window facing the north so that we really have the best view of all. We are at an elevation of seven thousand feet above sea level where the atmosphere is very cool and bracing after the heat of the Panjab. All the houses up here are situated on the hill sides and are joined together by numerous winding paths and lanes. These hills with their abundant growth of shrubs and trees are a great relief from the sandy plains of the Panjab. . . .

This is the most peculiar weather we are having now. Everyone told us that we should have beautiful sunshine during the months of May and June, but it has rained almost every day this week and looks, so those say who have been here before, as if the summer rains have started in earnest. Do not think, tho, that our view of the mountains has been marred in the least. Rather, it has been enhanced by the everchanging clouds. We are below, above, and in them as they float up and down and across, sometimes hovering over the ravines beneath us in pure white mists, again darkening into the threatening clouds of a thunderstorm, and again casting a pink and lavender hue as they are pierced by the rays of the setting sun. At times we look down to see nothing but the top of the cloud. Then here or there the mist lifts to reveal a village, a river bed, or a clump of trees, standing out more distinctly than usual because of the contrasting shadow around. Yesterday the rain kept up a continual patter until toward evening when the clouds began to ascend from the valleys and the sun came out with a glorious golden glow in the west. To the north the clouds' shadows gradually arose to disclose behind the blue hills the majestic snow-capped range of the Himalayas with the sources of the Ganges and the Jumna piercing the heavens to the west and Badrinath and other peaks sacred to Vishnu to the east. As the detail of crevices and ridges on the snows and glaciers glistened in the radiance of the setting sun we wondered less at the Indian's worship of them as the abode of the gods than at his failing to receive from them a purer spiritual inspiration.

In those days the motor road to Mussoorie had yet to be constructed and my grandparents were transported up the hill in dandies. The walking road from Rajpur climbed almost four thousand feet over a distance of ten miles. At regular stages along the route there were hava ghars, or pavilions, where the sahibs and memsahibs could sit in the shade and enjoy the view, while the dandie bearers caught their breath. These men came from villages in the surrounding hills and during the summer season they worked as coolies in Mussoorie and Landour. There were several designs of dandies but the most common ones were made of wood and canvas, the seat located in the middle like the cockpit of an old-fashioned airplane without the wings or fuselage. The supporting struts tapered to a point at either end and were connected to round crossbars by flexible leather straps, which allowed the coolies to negotiate narrow stretches and sharp corners along the paths. Experienced dandie bearers knew how to walk out of step so that they didn't jostle their passengers.

The motor road, built in the late twenties, was a formidable feat of engineering. There were at least fifty hairpin bends along the road, which followed the twisting contours of the ridges for eighteen miles. Until I was eleven or twelve years old, I used to get carsick while driving to and from Mussoorie. The change in altitude plugged my ears and threw my inner gyroscopes awry. At least once or twice along the route I would have to ask my father to stop the car so that I could throw up at the side of the road. My mother would give me Dramamine or other travel sickness pills, which made me groggy and only added to my discomfort.

Our family car was a Hindustan Landmaster which used to stink of petrol because of a faulty fuel pump, the most claustrophobic vehicle ever built. I only had to sit in it and I would begin to feel carsick. If we were traveling by train to Dehra Dun, the railhead at the foot of the mountains, we would take a taxi up the hill. In the early sixties, many of these taxis were aging Plymouths and Chevrolets. Their low-slung suspension made me feel as if I were on board a ship in a rolling sea. Whenever I got out of the car, I felt an unpleasant sense of vertigo, as if the mountains were still moving beneath my feet.

I don't know how many times I must have traveled up and down the winding road to Mussoorie, bracing myself as the car swerved around a corner, veering close to the parapet wall, and that disoriented, clammy sensation of nausea swelling up inside of me. My father once told me how ballet dancers keep from getting dizzy by fixing their eyes on a static object as they turn a pirouette. I learned to use this technique on the drive to Mussoorie, staring at different landmarks while the car swung back and forth around the corners. It helped a little and even after I stopped getting carsick there were specific landmarks along the road which I would look out for as we made our way up the hill. The first of these was the bridge over "the stone river," near Rajpur, at the foot of the mountain. This river was actually a rock glacier which shifted gradually each year, flowing down from the eroded cliffs above. Staring at the arched pylons of the bridge and the scree of rubble, I could almost see the stones moving as my head began to spin.

Farther up the road, above the Udaseen ashram, was a grassy spur that jutted out at an angle from the main slope of the mountain. We named this ridge "the lone tree hill" because there was a crooked semla tree growing at the top. As a child I used to think of it as Calvary, because of a hymn we often sang in church, "There is a Green Hill Far Away." The semla tree eventually died and its bare branches looked something like a crucifix. As our Landmaster raced around the curves, I stuck my head out of the window for fresh air, trying hard not to lose sight of the lone tree hill.

Halfway up to Mussoorie, at Kulukhet, was a toll barrier where we had to stop and pay road tax. Opposite the toll gate stood a line of tea shops which sold aerated drinks, pakoras, and other snacks. I usually felt so ill by the time we reached Kulukhet that I didn't feel like eating or drinking anything at all. Young boys would come around to the car, selling lemons cut in half and sprinkled with salt and red chili powder. Sucking on a lemon was supposed to cure travel sickness, though it never really worked for me.

Not too far above the toll gate was a corner where the air suddenly became cooler and we got our first clear view of Mussoorie. The town was spread out along the crest of the ridge, a scattering of buildings, all the way from Library bazaar to Gun Hill, from Kulri to Landour. I would pick a building which I recognized and fix my eyes on it, the peaked roofs of Hackman's Hotel or the red-brick structure of the Masonic lodge. By this time the plains were far below us and I could smell the first scent of pines and deodars. The town looked so much closer than it really was, though we seemed to take forever getting there, the road looping back and forth across the mountain. As we turned the hairpin bend below Bhatta checkpoint, I spotted the footbridge at St. George's College high above us. This was another landmark, and I had been told that an Irish priest committed suicide by jumping off the bridge. Fighting back my nausea, I would stare at the bridge and try to imagine the priest, his cassock billowing out like a parachute as he fell to his death.

After almost an hour of driving we finally reached Kin Craig, a flat area which used to be the end of the motor road when my father was a boy. From here on up to the bazaar there was one-way traffic, and we would have to wait for the cars and buses coming down the hill. The policemen, who were stationed at Kin Craig, had a windup telephone, and they would call out the numbers of the vehicles as they passed through the gate. Sometimes we would have to wait for half an hour before the road was clear.

Mussoorie had two bus stands at either end of the town, one at Library bazaar and the other at the Masonic lodge, which was also known as Picture Palace because of a cinema nearby. During the summer season taxis and buses filled the parking area at Masonic lodge, with swarms of coolies unloading baggage. Each of the hotels in Mussoorie had touts stationed at the bus stand, and whenever a vehicle arrived there would be a crush of people calling out the names of different hotels, coolies shouting, ricksha pullers and dandie bearers waiting to transport tourists along the Mall. Peanut hawkers and postcard vendors moved about between the cars and buses, young boys selling soft drinks and street photographers offering to guide honeymoon couples around the town and take their pictures at Mussoorie's many scenic spots.

From the bus stand we would drive on toward the clock tower, which marked the beginning of Landour bazaar. At this point the road narrowed, a line of shops opening onto the street, which was only wide enough for a single car. Blowing his horn my father maneuvered through the crowds of pedestrians and rickshas, dandies, horses, and mules. If there was a vehicle coming in the opposite direction, we would have to stop and back up to a wider point so that it could pass. The worst part of the drive was Mullingar Hill, a treacherous climb at the far end of Landour bazaar. Near the Sikh gurdwara, at the foot of hill, my father would put the Landmaster into the lowest gear and rev the engine before heading up the twisting road, racing around the turns to keep up our momentum and blowing his horn to warn anyone who might get in the way. Halfway up Mullingar was a blind corner that turned sharply to the right, and here I always held my breath, hoping that no cars were coming down the hill. If we ever needed to stop, my brothers and I would jump out and put rocks behind the wheels to keep the car from rolling backward. As the Landmaster roared up Mullingar Hill, bumping over potholes, tires skidding on the slick asphalt and cement, I was never sure if we would make it all the way, the engine straining under the weight of passengers and luggage. All five of us leaned forward in our seats, as if to urge the car upward, until we finally crested the ridge and came to a halt, the radiator steaming like a pressure cooker.

From the top of Mullingar Hill I could see the gray facade of the Landour Community Hospital directly in front of us and the red-roofed buildings of Woodstock School, positioned at different levels on the ridge. Scattered among the trees were many of the cottages where we had lived—Woodside, Hearthstone, Pine Rock. Though I still felt sick to my stomach, the drive up Mullingar helped clear my head. Looking out of the windscreen of our car at the Landour hillside and the blue range of Tehri hills beyond, I was overcome by a disoriented feeling of relief, the giddy pleasure of arriving home.

THE HILLSIDE

If I were to draw a map of Landour from memory, it would look something like a Snakes and Ladders game. The hillside was covered by a network of trails and shortcuts running up and down the ridge. At many places the slope was so steep that there were stone staircases built into the face of the mountain. The longest of these, which we called Jacob's Ladder, ascended from the Tehri Road up to Parker Hall. In many ways our life on the hillside was like a board game, in which we moved from house to house, trying to avoid the serpents which lay in our path. On wet monsoon days, when we were trapped indoors, I used to play Snakes and Ladders with my brothers, throwing the dice and advancing from square to square, climbing the ladders or sliding down the snakes. The rules of the game were controlled by a rigid sense of right and wrong— certain squares had pictures of good little girls carrying gifts or sewing a button on a dress, and bad little boys, kicking a dog or playing in the mud. This simplistic morality governed the mission- ary community in Landour, and each of us grew up with a clear understanding of what was considered naughty and what was nice. Of course the hillside had its share of backsliders, as well as plenty of self-righteous saints, but that was all part of the game we played. Whenever I scrambled up the steps of Jacob's Ladder, I felt a virtuous sense of climbing toward the top of the hill. As a child I had been told the biblical story about Jacob's dream in which he saw the angels ascending and descending a staircase to heaven. In Sunday school we used to sing the song:

> *We are climbing Jacob's ladder,*
> *We are climbing Jacob's ladder,*
> *We are climbing Jacob's ladder,*
> *Soldiers of the cross.*

Other verses followed,

> *Every rung goes higher, higher . . .*
> *Sinner do you love my Jesus? . . .*
> *If you love him why not serve him?*
> *Soldiers of the cross.*

Heading in the opposite direction from the top of the hill, descending Jacob's Ladder with giant steps, or skidding down the khuds and landslides, I had a guilty feeling of being sent all the way back to the beginning once again.

Each mission in Landour had its own cottages, and these were assigned to different families every year. Trails and footpaths connected the scattered houses to the school and the bazaar. Cutting across the middle of the ridge, on a level with the main buildings at Woodstock, was the Tehri Road, which started at the top of Mullingar Hill and wound its way back into the mountains of Garhwal. Running parallel to the Tehri Road, and about five hundred feet above, lay "the Eyebrow," a winding footpath which bisected the hillside from the Landour Community Hospital across to Oakville, the farthest building to the east. The Eyebrow got its name because it was so narrow, no more than a foot in width, where it cut across the cliffs above Pine Point. Descending at right angles from the top of the hill to the Tehri Road was the Zig Zag path, which divided the hillside in half, like a prime meridian. There were dozens of other smaller trails and shortcuts that criss-crossed Landour, a maze of intersecting lines.

At the top of the hill was a level road, formerly a bridle trail, called the Chukkar, which circled the three summits of the ridge, converging at two points in a double helix. The separate loops of the road were known as the first, second, and third Chukkar. This circuitous route led back into itself, without a beginning or an end, like a serpent swallowing its tail. The motor road from Mussoorie joined the Chukkar at St. Paul's Church. This was the old canton-ment sanctuary, built by the British in 1840, a mustard-colored building with a red tin roof and a bell tower. Inside the gate grew two ragged palms and several enormous deodar trees, a species closely related to the cedars of Lebanon. Within the church there were three stained-glass windows with images of the Crucifixion, the Resurrection, and the Ascension of Christ. Memorial plaques on the walls honored British military officers: "Sacred to the mem-ory of Ensign Whitney Robert McCally, 1st Batt. 3rd Reg. 'The Buffs,' who died at Landour on the 15th of May, 1886. This tablet was erected by his brother officers in token of their affection and esteem." St. Paul's Church was one of many landmarks from Lan-dour's colonial past, and the wooden pews still had notches where the British Tommies rested their Enfield rifles when they knelt down to pray.

Outside the gate of St. Paul's was a line of shops and tea stalls called Char Dukan. From here the Chukkar followed the contours of the hill in both directions, twisting its way around the ridges and ravines. Along the outside of the road was a broken fence, and lampposts stood at regular intervals. The Firs Estate, where my par-ents lived when I was born, lay about a quarter of a mile beyond

St. Paul's. Farther on, around the north side of the Chukkar, past Childer's Estate and Alyndale, was the cemetery, which extended above and below the road, a series of shallow terraces lined with weathered tombstones. Some of the graves dated back to the 1830s and contained the remains of British soldiers and their families, many of whom had died at the military hospital in Landour. There was a tall cypress near the entrance, planted in 1870 by the duke of Edinburgh. During the monsoon the terraces and retaining walls were overgrown with ferns and peacock orchids, the graves carpeted in moss. Many of the inscriptions had worn away with time, and the marble crosses were cracked and scarred. The gates of the cemetery were usually locked to keep stray cattle and tourists from toppling the gravestones.

On a level saddle, at the junction of the first and second Chukkar, stood Kellogg Church. This was where most of the American missionaries worshiped during the summer months. A gray castlelike structure, the church was named after Dr. Samuel Kellogg, who helped translate the Bible into Hindi toward the end of the nineteenth century. He was also one of the founders of Woodstock School and wrote a grammar book in Hindi, used by missionaries studying at the Landour Language School, which was housed in an annex behind the church. As a child I was told that Dr. Kellogg died in an accident while riding his bicycle around the Chukkar. He wasn't looking where he was going and rode off the side of the khud. This story was told to my brothers and me as a warning, whenever we strayed too close to the edge.

Just around the corner from Kellogg Church, at the beginning of the second Chukkar, was a flat rock that we used to slide down when we were very small. Walking to church, my brothers and I would insist on stopping at the sliding rock so that each of us could take a turn. Over the years people had carved their names in the rock, and the surface was worn smooth as a schoolboy's slate. Across the road was a larger rock, on top of which grew a crooked oak tree. I used to think of this tree as an octopus; its roots were like tentacles which had wrapped themselves around the boulder and pried it out of the soil. Some years later one of the cantonment board employees claimed to have seen a vision of a Muslim baba, or holy man, who was said to be buried at this spot. The boulder was eventually turned into a shrine and both Hindus and Muslims left offerings of flowers and burned sticks of incense in the knotted roots of the tree.

The second Chukkar circled Lal Tibba, which was the highest point in Mussoorie. During the season, crowds of tourists came to the top of the hill for a view of the Garhwal Himalayas, the line of snow peaks which stood between India and Tibet. Garhwal was known as the "Abode of the Gods" because of the important shrines and temples located at Gangotri, Kedarnath, and Badrinath. Framed by the branches of deodar trees that grew along the Chukkar, the snow mountains looked as if they had been painted against the sky in broad white brushstrokes. Groups of tourists and honeymoon couples would have their pictures taken at Lal Tibba, striking romantic poses, with the Himalayas in the background. At the highest point on the hill stood a pair of binoculars through which we could see the distant mountains magnified to three times their size. Staring into the murky lenses of the binoculars I was able to make out the details of ice fields and rock faces, glaciers and cornices of snow, faintly visible behind a drifting veil of clouds.

During the early seventies a communications tower was built at Lal Tibba and several of the Presbyterian properties nearby were taken over by the government, including the Retreat, a house where my aunt and uncle used to live. The entire area around Lal Tibba became a restricted zone and tourists were no longer permitted to climb to the top of the hill. Around that time I remember hearing rumors that the tower was actually used by the Indian government for monitoring radio frequencies in China, across the border. I doubt if this was true, but Lal Tibba did look like something out of a James Bond film, with large dish antennae and barbed-wire fences.

When he was a boy, my father and his three brothers lived in a house called Fairview, on the north side of the second Chukkar, directly below Lal Tibba. As I was growing up my father would often tell me stories about his childhood—the time his brother Dave, who was five years old, went for a walk with the Fairview chokidar and the two of them came upon a leopard in the forest below the Chukkar. In his panic the chokidar abandoned my uncle and ran back to Fairview to tell my grandmother that the leopard had eaten Dave. Fortunately, by the time she rushed to the spot, the leopard had disappeared and my uncle was happily playing by himself, unaware of any danger. Another story my father often told was about his eldest brother, Jim, throwing a javelin in the yard at Fairview and accidentally punching a hole in Dave's skull. At that time the British surgeon in Mussoorie was a man named T. B. Butcher. (He had an assistant named Nurse Blood.) Dr. Butcher patched the hole in Dave's skull with a metal plate, which I remember tapping with my finger many years later when we visited my uncle in Washington, D.C. These were my father's stories, though sometimes they seemed to be mine as well, memories of Landour shared between us.

Each of the stories had its moral, implicit in the telling, an underlying admonition. From every landmark on the hillside there were lessons to be learned—the waterfall below Fernworth, where one of the chokidars died when he fell over the parapet wall because he was drunk; the house where the boy lived who ate a jack-in-the-pulpit and had to have his stomach pumped; or the corner on the Eyebrow where I almost got bitten by a pit viper that I was trying to catch. Negotiating my way up and down the treacherous trails on the Snakes and Ladders board I came to believe that an element of luck controlled our lives—the rattle and roll of dice (even though there were some missionaries on the hillside who would have objected to any game of chance). Being good Calvinists, my parents believed in predestination, and even as a child I grew up with an unconscious sense of inevitability and fate. At the same time I was reminded of the consequences of my actions, and for the most part I avoided riding bicycles on the Chukkar or throwing javelins at my brothers.

Below Fairview was a house called Cozy Nook, where Mrs. Roberts lived. She was a recluse, and for years most of us didn't even know her name. We referred to her as "the woman with the dogs." She had about forty Pomeranians, and we often heard them barking at night. The only time I saw Mrs. Roberts was when Cozy Nook burned down. My brother Joe and I went to help put out the fire, but there was very little that anyone could do because there was a water shortage in Landour and the pipes were dry. Throughout the day, Mrs. Roberts sat with her dogs, smoking cigarette after cigarette, as she watched the flames consume her house. Her hair was singed and she was wearing an old overcoat which was torn and frayed. Several of the Pomeranians had been killed in the fire and others kept running frantically through the smoke-filled rooms, snapping at our ankles as we threw buckets of dirt on the flames.

After the fire at Cozy Nook we learned more about Mrs. Roberts, who had once been a beauty queen, the most sought-after woman in Mussoorie. During the forties and early fifties she ran a hairdressing salon near Kwality's restaurant in Kulri bazaar. Several maharajas courted her, and those who remembered Mrs. Roberts from those days said that whenever she went out to promenade along the Mall, she carried a parasol to protect her complexion from the sun. Mrs. Roberts (I never learned her maiden name) married an Englishman with some sort of German connections, who went away and left her after independence. One story I heard was that she stayed behind in India because her husband refused to let her take the dogs with them to Europe. She still received a regular amount of money from a bank account in Germany, though nobody knew if her husband was alive or dead. We heard rumors that Mrs. Roberts had drawers full of rupees stashed away inside the house and that the money had been burned up in the flames. After the fire Joe and I helped salvage a few things which remained, and picking through the ashes we found nothing of value: a china vase cracked beyond repair, old shoes, pots and pans which had melted in the heat. There were also stacks of magazines, most of which were badly charred or burned completely. These were beauty magazines from the fifties with faded covers on which blond-haired women in cashmere sweaters flashed bright lipstick smiles.

The only person who had any regular contact with Mrs. Roberts was a man named Ranjit, who lived in a shed behind Cozy Nook. He carried supplies for her from the bazaar and spent the rest of his time smoking bhang and ganja. Ranjit was a threatening-looking character, with long dreadlocks and a tangled beard, though he was actually quite harmless. Whenever I passed him on the Chukkar, he greeted me with a mock salute, the sweet scent of hashish drifting in his wake.

At the junction of the second and third Chukkar was Sisters' bazaar, which got its name from the nursing sisters who used to work at the military hospital. The bazaar consisted of a single tea stall, Munshi Mall's ration shop, and A. Prakash & Co., the general store which provided groceries for most of the missionaries on the hillside. Inder Prakash, the proprietor, had his own canning factory, making jams from different Himalayan fruits—apricots, plums, and wild blackberries. He also produced pickle relish, peanut butter, and cheddar cheese. Prakash's store was not very large and the shelves behind the dusty glass counters were a jumble of tins and bottles, boxes of chocolates and biscuits, jars full of toffees and boiled sweets. When I was eight or nine years old, my brothers and I would buy tins of sweetened condensed milk from Prakash's store and punch holes in the top, drinking the thick, sugary liquid straight from the can.

The hilltop above the third Chukkar was called Prospect Point, a level clearing where we gathered with other families for sunrise picnics on Easter morning. It was also a good place to find beetles during the monsoon. Just below Prospect Point were the buildings that used to house the old military hospital. These had been converted into the Defense Institute of Work Study, a management-training center run by the Indian army. As foreigners we were not allowed inside the gates of the DIWS though we often had to leap out of the way of the military jeeps which came careening around blind corners on the Chukkar.

Rosebank, the house in which my grandparents lived when they first came to Landour in 1917, was about a quarter of a mile beyond Sisters' bazaar, on the north side of the third Chukkar. Though I never went inside Rosebank, I would often look down to see the peaked tin roofs about fifty feet below the road. It was from here that my grandmother looked out of her bay window and saw Bandar Punch and the other mountains for the first time, forty years before I was born. Many things in Landour had changed since then, but the "majestic snow-capped range" that she described in her letters remained the same, stark silhouettes of white against the sky.

At the far end of the third Chukkar lay Elcot Lodge, where the Buchanan sisters lived. They were probably the oldest residents of the hillside, born in India around the turn of the century. Their parents had been Canadian missionaries in Madhya Pradesh. Both sisters, after living and working in India for most of their lives, retired and settled in Landour. When I was in school Miss Ruth was already in her eighties and Miss Edith, her younger sister, was well past seventy. Both of them were spinsters. They lived year round in Elcot Lodge, tending their irises and daylilies, making Scottish marmalade, and keeping a curious and critical eye on the other inhabitants of the hillside. Miss Ruth wrote poems about the snow mountains and tree dahlias, while Miss Edith drew illustrations in India ink. These were printed up as greeting cards, which were sold to support charities at St. Paul's Church.

My parents were good friends of the Buchanan sisters, and on Sunday afternoons we would go to their house for tea. Miss Ruth, who was almost crippled with arthritis, sat in a chair with a shawl over her knees and told stories about her childhood on mission compounds in Bhopal and Indore. I was a little frightened of her because she had piercing eyes, and whiskers on her chin. They had no servants and Miss Edith took care of her elder sister. She was the one who poured the tea and did most of the gardening, a chirpy, energetic woman who always seemed to have something in her hands, dahlia bulbs or a pair of pruning shears. When Miss Ruth finally died, Miss Edith returned to Canada and Elcot Lodge was sold.

•   •   •

Each spring, just as the rhododendron trees began to bloom, the memsahibs started arriving in Landour. They would come up the hill with lines of coolies hauling trunks and boxes, as if they were part of a mountaineering expedition. All of the luggage had to be carried up to the hillside from the bus stand, through the bazaar, and along the trails—quilts and bedding rolls, crockery and cooking pots, ironing boards, sewing machines, pet birds in cages, even pianos. Because of the altitude in Mussoorie it took a couple of weeks to get your "hill legs," and most of the memsahibs were carried to their doorstep in dandies or rickshas. The younger children rode in kandis, a bamboo basket hoisted on a coolie's shoulders.

Throughout the winter the hillside cottages lay empty, doors locked and windows barred, but with the arrival of the memsahibs everything was opened up again. The servants were often sent ahead a few days earlier to set up house. Only the chokidars remained in Landour all year round, to guard the mission properties, while the cooks and ayahs traveled up and down the hill with their employers. The spring semester at Woodstock started around the end of February and most of the older children were put in boarding for a month or two before their mothers arrived in Landour. The first memsahibs began to show up by the end of March but the real migration began in April, once it started to get warmer on the plains. As soon as their mothers came up the hill, students moved out of the dormitories and lived at home.

The memsahibs ruled Landour. For most of the season the hillside remained a community of women and children, except for a few brief weeks in June and July when the men came up to visit their families and escape the worst of the heat. Generally, though, the memsahibs were in charge of the hillside properties and ran the community center and PTA as well as other committees and clubs. A few of the mothers worked at Woodstock or in the community hospital, but most of them were busy looking after children and doing housework, as well as organizing Bible study groups, reading clubs, prayer meetings, square dances, barter sales, and birthday parties.

May Day was the first major event on the hillside, when all of the memsahibs got together. It was celebrated on the playground at Woodstock, with the crowning of the May Queen and her court, as well as a gymnastics display, and stalls selling cotton candy, hot dogs, and ice cream. Each of the classes in the high school organized games and competitions, beanbag throws, shooting galleries, and a tug-of-war. For a number of years the festivities began with a Maypole dance. A group of girls, wearing flowers in their hair and starched white dresses, skipped around in a circle, holding bright-colored ribbons, which they wove in a pattern around the pole. This tradition was finally stopped when some of the more conservative missions objected because the Maypole dance was considered a pagan ceremony.

Besides the school the main focus of activity on the hillside was the community center, which lay along the Eyebrow path. It was a two-story building with a tennis court out front. On the ground floor was a library, and upstairs were a large meeting hall and a kitchen. It was here that the memsahibs congregated for tea parties and other functions, potluck suppers, and annual celebrations like the Fourth of July. Occasionally there would be guest speakers who gave talks or slide show presentations, and some of the memsahibs organized amateur theatrical groups and dramatic readings at the community center. But mostly it was a place for social gatherings, where the women could get together and talk, sharing moments of happiness and melancholy, discussing servant problems, news from family in America, homesickness, gossip, and their children's grades.

The Landour Community Center published a cookbook containing recipes for everything from rhododendron jelly to macaroni casserole. There were instructions on how to substitute for ingredients which weren't available in India and charts that gave equivalent weights and measures, cups and ounces, seers and chataks, recipes for mock apple pie and high-altitude cakes. Much of a memsahib's life involved adapting to the circumstances of the hillside, coping with the frustrations and inconveniences of Landour, dealing with the idiosyncrasies of servants, and catering to the demands of their children and absent husbands. They did all this with a good measure of Christian fortitude and patience which belied their loneliness and isolation.

In many ways Landour was like a small town in middle America—Winesburg, Ohio, transported to the first range of the Himalayas. On the surface it was a quiet, pious world of motherly white women who always smiled at us when we met them on the path. We knew our manners and returned their greetings, then stepped aside to let them pass. A tribal loyalty existed on the hillside, a code of behavior and courtesy which was self-consciously American, reflecting the neighborly attitudes of a mythical world which only existed in story books. Hidden behind this polite facade were acute differences in personality and background, temperament and beliefs. Some of the memsahibs couldn't stand each other and there were feuds that raged from one season to the next. But as children much of the tension in Landour was hidden from our view and we enjoyed a false sense of harmony which the community provided.

For me the hillside was like an extended family and I referred to my mother's friends as "Aunt," even though we weren't related—Aunt Alfie, Aunt Rikki, and Aunt Molly. Everyone knew each other's names. In my first-grade class at Woodstock, there were four boys who had the same first name as myself: Steve Barnhouse, Steve Harper, Steve Rollins, and Steve Sommers. Some of the other names were unusual. For a while there were two families in Landour named the Curries and the Rices, which led to all kinds of jokes at potluck dinners. At Woodstock there was a kindergarten teacher named Miss Goody and a music teacher named Miss Meany, as well as a Mennonite couple whose last name was Nyce. The Beans and the Muttons also lived on the hillside and they were actually related to each other. My dorm supervisor in third grade was called Miss Fluff, and the girls in my class had a housemother named Pearl Treasure. The Getter family, who lived at the top of the hill, had a sign in front of their house, "B. E. Getter," which was a running joke because they had so many children.

Though most of the hillside residents conformed to the social strictures and expectations of the community, there were a few eccentrics in Landour. One of the teachers at the school had a habit of putting eggshells in his sandwiches, and for a while there was a mad Australian who lived at Sisters' bazaar. He used to collect branches in the forest and decorate them with mushrooms and bits of lichen, carrying these around the Chukkar. Some of the Methodist memsahibs, who were the most outspoken, would smuggle whiskey and brandy up to the hillside in empty Dettol tins, supposedly to use for cooking. Another Methodist missionary, George Terry, had an airplane, and I remember one day, while I was playing near their house at Eastwood, he was sitting on the veranda sanding his propeller. Perhaps the most unconventional family were the Hunters, who were Presbyterians and considered beyond the pale by all of the fundamentalists. Dick Hunter was an artist who painted psychedelic murals on Christian themes and even designed the labels for Inder Prakash's "Tangy-ji" jam. He was also a singer and used to stand at the edge of his yard and sing opera into the mist. One year Mr. Hunter came to speak to my seventh-grade Scripture class and showed us slides of his paintings, explaining the symbolism of the colors. He told us that he couldn't understand why the devil was always portrayed as being red, because it was a sacred color. "Jesus is the one who should be painted red," he told us. "The devil is probably the color of snot." Many of the conservative missionaries felt that the Hunters were a bad influence on the hillside, and they were at the center of several controversies. When my brother Andy was in fifth grade, he was supposed to sing the lead in a folk operetta, *Tirakajeet*, that Dick Hunter wrote, but the performance had to be canceled at the last minute. Some of the parents got upset when they learned that their children were going to play the parts of Hindu gods and goddesses.

There weren't any serious scandals that I remember, and if anything had happened it would have quickly been hushed up. An atmosphere of strict propriety hung over the hillside, as pervasive as a monsoon mist. With so many husbands and wives living apart for months on end, one would have thought that there might have been secret affairs, and there probably were, though we never heard about them. Appearances were very important and it was unusual to hear anybody raise his or her voice or carry on an argument in public. Nobody ever got divorced in Landour, though several of the hillside couples split up once they returned to America. Sex was a forbidden topic of conversation, at least within earshot of the children, and there was a chaste, prudish attitude among most of the memsahibs. Very few of them wore makeup and most of them had sensible hairstyles, cropped short or pulled back into a bun. Their clothes were modest, skirts that extended well below the knee and blouses which buttoned to the throat. One or two of the memsahibs wore Indian clothes, mostly salwar kameez, loose tunics with long sleeves and baggy leggings that covered them from head to foot. Some of the Mennonite women wore lace doilies pinned to their hair and dressed in drab colors, sooty grays and muddy browns. Only a few of the more daring memsahibs colored their hair and painted their nails, though this was looked upon with disapproval.

Growing up in Landour I had a sense that everyone was being watched to make sure he or she did not stray from the straight and narrow. Sin was something that lay in wait for us, just beyond the boundaries of the hillside, lurking in the bazaar or hovering in the distance like a dust haze over the plains. Many of the missionaries looked upon India as a country full of sinful heathen who were doomed to hell. As soldiers of the cross they had to set a good example, fighting temptation at every turning of the path, avoiding the snakes and climbing the ladders.

There were so many different missions on the hillside that it was hard to keep track of them all: Methodists and Presbyterians (of which there were two camps), Mennonites and Baptists, Lutherans, Quakers, Disciples of Christ, the Assemblies of God or Pentecostals, who spoke in tongues, the Wycliffe Bible Translators and the leprosy mission; some groups had acronyms like TEAM (The Evangelical Alliance Mission) and BMMF (Bible Medical Mission Fellowship, which we called the Zennana Banana Monkey Mission). Each denomination had its own peculiar theology, and even though all of them were Protestants it seemed as if they could never agree on anything.

Plenty of squabbles erupted between the different groups, conflicts over the behavior of children, rules at Woodstock, the content of church services, films in Parker Hall, and high school dances on the hillside. Every year there were new controversies that stirred up the underlying tensions between one mission and another. Many of these were theological battles which pitted fundamentalists against liberals, arguments over creeds and liturgies or conflicting interpretations of the Bible. But these debates often spilled into other disputes over mundane issues such as property matters, the repair of pushta walls, fights between servants, or the water shortages which plagued the hillside every year.

Despite these fractious differences most of the missionaries shared a common purpose, even if that purpose was interpreted in different ways. Many of the families in Landour had been in India for two or three generations, which added a sense of tradition to our exile. There was a virtuous, self-righteous side to much of what was done and said, traces of manifest destiny that brought us there, the Lord's will, the guiding hand of the Holy Spirit. Most of the missionaries worked among the poor and disadvantaged—tribals, orphans, untouchables, lepers, the sick and diseased—which fostered an aura of selfless altruism and charity. By the mid-sixties the number of missionaries in India had started to decline, partly because the government was refusing to issue new visas and residential permits. This added to a beleaguered sense of persecution among some of the missionaries and perhaps even a touch of martyrdom. The idea of personal sacrifice prevailed on the Landour hillside, with families living apart in remote regions of Assam and Orissa, several days' journey by train, the separation of husbands and wives, children and parents.

Even though my father came up from the plains more often than most of the men, I remember being unhappy because of his absence. My brothers and I awaited his arrival in Landour with eagerness and anticipation. Staring expectantly out of our dining-room window as it grew dark, I would try to be the first to recognize his figure on the path, among the shadows of the oak trees reaching across our yard and the moths flickering around the yellow veranda light. Often my father would arrive late at night, long after we had gone to bed, and I would wake up early the next morning to find him drinking a cup of Nescafé in the living room. For a while he had a Lambretta scooter that he used to drive all the way from Etah, nearly three hundred miles. He would arrive sunburned and exhausted. On one of these trips my father collided with a buffalo in the dark, and his arms and legs were covered with scrapes and scratches.

Most of the time there was a cheerful, animated atmosphere in Landour, but underneath the bustle of activity I sensed a mood of unhappiness, not only in my mother, but in most of the women who were sent up to Landour. Living far away from their homes in America, separated from their husbands on the plains, and looking after children on their own could not have been an easy life. Most of the cottages were spartan and uncomfortable. The electricity often failed and the water supply was unpredictable. There were all kinds of insects and other crawling creatures to contend with, mosquitoes, sandflies, silverfish, scorpions, and spiders. Once or twice a week my mother went around the house with the Flit-gun, pumping a cloud of poisonous gas into the gaps between the cupboards and under the beds to kill whatever bugs were hiding there. The monsoon could be especially depressing, with endless days of rain and mist. Most of the houses were dark and furnished with only the most rustic necessities, tin bathtubs and wood-burning hamams to heat the water, simple charpoys and ancient almirahs, dining chairs that did not match and tables with prosthetic limbs.

Hardly anyone had a telephone in Landour and the most common form of communication was to send "chitties," or notes, which were carried from house to house by coolies. Whenever my mother needed to send a note, one of us would go to the edge of the yard and shout for a coolie at the top of our lungs, "O, Phal-too!" Sounds carried long distances in the mountains, and after one or two calls we would hear a reply from somewhere on the hillside. Within a few minutes a coolie would come running up or down the hill to carry the chittie wherever it needed to go. The word "Phaltoo" could be translated as "idle one" or "unemployed," a demeaning term which was a signal cry for us, standing at the edge of the yard and shouting into the mist:

"O, Phaltoo!"

. . .

The missionaries in Landour initiated a cargo cult, bringing with them sacred objects from America, cookie cutters in the shape of gingerbread men, electric blenders, and waffle irons. Many of the families received food parcels filled with tins of Hershey's cocoa, marshmallows, Kool-Aid, and Tootsie Rolls. These parcels were sent by supporting churches or family members back home and they were delivered by a short, stooped postman in a khaki uniform who made his rounds of the hillside on foot, carrying an enormous canvas satchel. By the time the parcels reached Landour they were crumpled and covered with black sealing wax which the customs officials smeared along the edges after opening them for inspection. The Betty Crocker cake mixes had weevils in them, and the Milky Way and Mars bars were discolored and melted into a congealed brown mass after being transported in a hot railway carriage from Bombay to Dehra Dun. A bottle of maple flavoring would leak into a hoard of jelly beans, leaving a coagulation of amber, green, and red. But no matter how stale or unappetizing the contents of these parcels might be, they were invaluable to us because they came from America. We salvaged whatever we could, licking up the spilled powder from broken Pixie Stix or using our teeth to gnaw the last bits of melted chocolate from the wrinkled foil wrappers.

I remember being jealous of other kids who received more food parcels than we did. Some of the hillside families even got barrels of used clothes which were shipped by sea freight, old sweatshirts and baseball hats, faded blue jeans and well-worn Keds that were sent by church groups in America. My parents discouraged people from sending us parcels because it took so long and exorbitant customs duty had to be paid, usually twice the value of the goods. After a while we stopped getting them altogether, but I remember one of the last packages, sent by my grandparents in Pennsylvania. Among other things was a Duncan Hines blueberry muffin mix. My mother translated the directions on the box for

Ram Dayal but he got confused and threw the blueberries out and mixed their juice in with the batter so that the muffins came out a purplish gray color and had no taste at all.

Food parcels carried a special significance for many of the missionaries because the contents symbolized the land of plenty which they had forsaken, the sacraments of exile. I am sure that many people in Landour prayed for the speedy delivery of these packages and when they arrived it was like receiving manna from heaven. Sometimes the parcels even had miraculous powers. I remember one incident when a teacher at the school, Blake Stevens, was seriously ill in the hospital. Everyone on the hillside was worried about his recovery, and a group of charismatic Christians were praying in shifts at his bedside. They believed in the healing powers of the Holy Spirit and the laying on of hands. Around this time one of the memsahibs got a parcel in which there was a bottle of Oil of Olay. Taking this as a sign, she rushed to the hospital and smeared Blake Stevens's forehead with the lotion, believing that it was sacred oil. Eventually he recovered, but there was a joke on the hillside that the Oil of Olay probably did more for his complexion than his soul.

Landour's cargo cult was perpetuated by the necessity of carrying everything up to the hillside. All of our provisions and supplies were transported in trunks and boxes, baskets and bundles, loaded onto the backs of coolies. During the season there was a constant procession of wallahs, who went door to door selling their wares. The first to arrive in the morning were the bakers, who would open their tin trunks on the front veranda to display an assortment of breads and cakes and cookies. Three different bakers made the rounds of the hillside and all of them were related to each other and came from the same village beyond Tehri. Bhurey Khan was the baker my mother bought things from. A portly man who looked a little like the Hindi film star Raj Kapoor, he always wore a dark suit jacket over a pair of baggy pajamas and carried an umbrella wherever he went. Bhurey Khan's bread was stodgy and

had a mealy texture but his biscuits were more appetizing, ginger-
snaps and coconut macaroons, as well as chocolate cookies with a
drop of frosting in the middle. He also made peanut brittle and
peppermint sticks. The uppermost tray in his trunk was full of pas-
tries with ornate icing, soggy cream horns, and limp éclairs. For special occasions Bhurey Khan baked mince pies and birthday cakes.

The doodh wallahs also arrived early in the morning, delivering milk which they carried from their villages, five or six miles
beyond Landour. The milk was transported in metal containers that
the doodh wallahs carried on their backs. Ram Dayal would bring
an empty pan to the kitchen door as the doodh wallah measured
out a seer or two. Most of the milk in Mussoorie came from buffaloes and had a sour, wet straw smell. It had to be boiled immediately or else it would split. The doodh wallahs were known to add
water to their milk, and one or two of the memsahibs used lactometers, which they brought from America to check the purity of
the milk. Even when it was watered down, buffalo milk produced
a rich cream that Ram Dayal whipped up for us to eat at breakfast
with chapatis and strawberry jam.

Around eight o'clock the clerks from Ram Chander's general
store in Landour bazaar and Prakash's shop at the top of the hill
came by to take our daily order. My mother would have a list prepared for them and later in the afternoon a coolie delivered packets of Brooke Bond tea and Dalda cooking oil, Champion Brand
puffed wheat, Golden syrup, Amul butter, rice, lentils, sugar, and
Kissan's guava jelly. Later in the morning the vegetable and fruit
wallahs arrived, carrying baskets on their heads, loaded with
bananas and mangoes, cauliflowers and green beans. These were
followed by the mutton wallah with his butcher knives and chop-
per to cut whichever piece of meat that Ram Dayal wanted. No
beef was available though we occasionally got buffalo meat from
Dehra Dun. There was also a fish wallah who carried several different kinds in a basket on his head, mostly lanchi and sol but occasionally pomfret and shrimp, which came all the way from Bombay.

Both the mutton wallah and the fish wallah were Muslims, but the pork wallah was a Hindu, a man named Laxmi Chand who made ham and sausages. Pork was the cheapest meat available but it had to be boiled in a pressure cooker for several hours because of the danger of trichinosis. When I was in high school Laxmi Chand won the government lottery and gave up selling pork. With his sudden wealth he built himself a house near the clock tower, bought a truck, and started working as a building contractor. A few years later, in another twist of fate, he was killed in a freak accident when a landslide destroyed his house.

There were so many vendors who came to our door that the procession continued all morning: the egg wallah, who also delivered chickens, dead or alive, the cheese wallah, the newspaper wallah, the charcoal wallah, and the razai wallahs, who came to fluff our mattresses and quilts. Over their shoulders they carried instruments that looked like giant harps with which they teased the cotton into feathery mounds. When they were fluffing quilts on the veranda it looked like snow, their strings twanging rhythmically.

Once a week, Om Prakash, the dhobi or washerman, would arrive at our house, carrying an enormous bundle of laundry on his back. He reminded me of a character in John Bunyan's moral tale, *The Pilgrim's Progress*, who is forced to shoulder the burden of his sins. Coming up the hill, Om Prakash was bent double under the weight of all those clothes. The Dhobighat, where the washermen lived, was right at the bottom of the valley near the stream. Whenever Om Prakash came to the house my mother would count the pieces of laundry with him: twelve shirts, six drawers, eight socks, three jerseys, five half-pants. All of these were piled together, wrapped up in a sheet, and carried away. The following week they came back washed and ironed. To avoid confusion each of our clothes was marked with a tiny symbol drawn with indelible ink, usually on the inside of a collar or waistband.

On Saturday mornings the barbers did their rounds of the hillside, and every two weeks or so my brothers and I would have to sit outside in the yard, on one of the dining chairs, while our hair was cut. There were five or six different barbers in Landour but the one who came to our house most frequently was Sambhu. He had several fingers missing on his right hand though it didn't seem to stop him from using his scissors. On his rounds of the hillside he carried a small attaché case with "Woodstock Barber" painted on the front. Inside were scissors and combs, straight razors and clippers that pulled the hair on my neck. Sambhu also had a shop on Mullingar Hill with a sign that advertised "Crew Cuts and Brush Cuts," which were his specialty. Whenever my father got his hair cut the barber gave him a head massage, kneading and rubbing his scalp for several minutes in an elaborate finger ballet.

On weekends the Kashmiri wallahs came around with handicrafts to sell, papier-mâché boxes, bookends made of carved walnut wood, embroidered shawls and cushion covers. There were also a silver wallah, who sold jewelry, and the lace wallah, from Madras, as well as Mr. Abhinandan, who had a fabric shop in Landour bazaar. Two coolies accompanied him from house to house, carrying bolts of cloth as well as swatches of fabric from which the memsahibs could choose material for clothes and curtains. Mr. Abhinandan was a prominent member of the Jain community in Mussoorie and he was always dressed in immaculate kurta pajama with a Gandhi cap on his head. There were tailors who went from house to house measuring the memsahibs and children for clothes. Budhoo Ram, the shoemaker, would arrive with samples of leather and a large notebook, on the pages of which he traced our feet to get the exact measurements. The tailors and shoemakers carried with them old copies of Sears Roebuck or J. C. Penney catalogs from which they could copy almost anything we wanted, even hunting jackets or basketball shoes.

Another familiar face on the hillside was Doma, a Tibetan woman who sold antiques and reproductions of Buddhist ornaments. She was strikingly beautiful, dressed in a long choga, with a brightly colored apron, and a necklace of amber and silver beads around her throat. Doma's boxes were filled with an assortment of jewelry and semiprecious stones, smoky topaz and amethyst, jade and lapis lazuli. The only woman among all of the wallahs, she carried her wares on her back, trudging up and down the path as if she had just walked all of the way from Tibet. Each year my mother bought Christmas presents from Doma and gifts to send back to our extended family in America, brass spoons encrusted with pieces of turquoise and coral, ornamental daggers, flower vases, copper bells, and Tibetan prayer wheels.

Following after the procession of vendors came the kabadi wallahs, junk dealers who went from house to house and purchased used items which the memsahibs wanted to get rid of, such as empty bottles, old newspapers, and rags. The kabadi wallahs bought broken toys and burned-out hair dryers, torn knapsacks and rusted buckets, anything that could be recycled or resold. What they wanted most of all were discarded clothes or appliances that had been imported from America. For these items the kabadi wallahs were willing to pay a lot of money, and the missionaries kept them well supplied. Each of the junk dealers had his own shop in the bazaar, and these were filled with relics of our cargo cult, fetish objects which the kabadi wallahs scavenged from the hillside homes: old Kodak cameras, warped tennis rackets, Hula Hoops, comic books, broken lactometers, bathroom scales, and dented cupcake trays.

ITHACA

The asthmatic roar of the airplane's engines droned in my ears as I watched the dusty fields and villages slide beneath our wings. Taking off from Delhi we flew across the Punjab, over the border into Pakistan, and farther on, high above the Khyber Pass. Through my window I could see the snow-covered ranges of the Hindu Kush, a mountain barrier which once protected India against invaders. From that height the peaks and ridges looked small and insignificant, wrinkled into folds and creases like strips of pleated muslin. Crossing over the mountains, our airplane shuddered and dipped in the turbulence, as if it were a kite on a string. Whenever my ears popped with a change in pressure, the sound of the engines grew suddenly louder, a menacing growl. I was four and a half years old and I had never been in an airplane before. Peering down at the earth below, I felt my stomach clench into a fist. We flew for hours—it seemed like days—far beyond the mountains of Afghanistan, across the deserts of Iran and Turkey, over Syria, Lebanon, and Cyprus, hovering above the Mediterranean, then plunging into Europe. It was a long, uncomfortable flight, and when we finally landed in Zurich I felt the same dizziness and vertigo that I used to get after driving up the hill road to Mussoorie. Stumbling down the steps from the airplane as we disembarked, I vomited on the tarmac.

Every five years my parents were entitled to a twelve-month furlough in America, a time to visit family and supporting churches, as well as an opportunity for my father to continue his education. On previous furloughs my parents and grandparents had always traveled by ship, and I have often regretted that I was born too late for the era of ocean voyages. In the summer of 1961, we went to America by air instead, stopping over in Europe for a couple of weeks. Leaving India for the first time I kept feeling the uncertain emotions of going home to a country that I had never seen before.

We were on our way to Ithaca, a college town in upstate New York. My parents had explained that we were going to live there for a year. This was all I knew or understood, though gradually, as we journeyed to Ithaca, the place began to represent all kinds of things in my imagination: a sheltered, familiar home, a world of unknown possibilities, the beginning or the end of an odyssey. My parents must have been conscious of the Homeric ironies buried in that name, but I was too young to have these things explained to me. Seven or eight years later my mother would give me a poem to read called "Ithaca," by the Alexandrian poet C. P. Cavafy:

> . . . Always keep Ithaca fixed in your mind.
> To arrive there is your ultimate goal.
> But do not hurry the voyage at all.
> It is better to let it last for long years;
> and even to anchor at the isle when you are old,
> rich with all you have gained on the way,
> not expecting that Ithaca will offer you riches.
> Ithaca has given you a beautiful voyage.

Without her you would never have taken the road
But she has nothing to give you now.

And if you have found her poor, Ithaca has not
    defrauded you.
With such great wisdom you have gained, with
    so much experience
you must surely have understood by then what
    Ithacas mean.

Memorizing this poem as a teenager I could only think of the
Ithaca that I remembered from our furlough in 1961. Cavafy's wan-
derer arrives home as an old man, exhausted and world-weary, full
of regrets and tortured memories. But for me this was the first long
journey of my life, and when I eventually got to Ithaca, by a circuitous route, I was still a young boy, entirely innocent and naive.

*   *   *

Our first stop was Switzerland, perhaps because my parents had
decided that we should revisit our roots. The Alter family originally came from somewhere in the Alps, before emigrating to the
United States toward the end of the eighteenth century. We didn't
know any of our distant relatives in Switzerland, not even the
name of an ancestral village or canton that we could visit. At the
small hotel in Zurich, where we stayed for a couple of nights,
nobody spoke English or Hindustani. The city was foreign to me
and totally disconnected from Landour and Etah. I had never seen
buildings like these before, stacked one against the other along the
street, like a shelf of library books. Everything seemed orderly and
neat, unlike the chaotic streets in India. When we left Delhi, the
temperature had been 110 degrees in the shade and the plains were
scorched and dry. Switzerland was green and cool. The mountains
reminded me of Mussoorie, though the snow peaks of the Alps
weren't quite the same as the Himalayas and the forests were not as
wild and overgrown.

I have only fragments of memory from our stay in Switzerland—Joe and me jumping about on a feather bed in our hotel
room, sinking deep into the goose down comforter, eating breakfast in the dining room, the waitress trying to talk to us in German,
and Andy in a high chair, only eight months old. The morning
after we arrived my father took Joe and me to the zoo, where we
saw tigers, leopards, elephants, and monkeys in a cage. These
Indian animals seemed familiar but out of place in Switzerland. A
few days later we took a train to Geneva and in the dining car I ate
ravioli for the first time in my life. There were clocks at all the stations and my parents kept remarking on the punctuality of Swiss
trains, compared to the Indian railways.

From Geneva we flew on to West Berlin, where my mother
and father had German friends, the Von Hammersteins. We stayed
in a guesthouse near their home and ate our meals with them. The
first night at dinner, I remember, one of their sons, who was about
my age, didn't finish the food on his plate. Mr. Von Hammerstein,
who was very strict, refused to let him eat the strawberries and
cream that the rest of us had for dessert. This punishment seemed
unfair and cruel to me but later my parents explained that Mr. Von
Hammerstein had been imprisoned in a concentration camp during the war for being a member of the German resistance. He had
almost starved to death, which was why he didn't like to see his
own children wasting food. Despite this explanation, I was already
afraid of our host, who took us on a tour of East Berlin the following day. The wall had not yet been built and we passed through
Checkpoint Charlie, a name that has stayed in my mind. A short
while later, as we were driving over a stretch of cobblestones, Mr.
Von Hammerstein told Joe and me that the road was paved with
the heads of naughty little boys. For the rest of the drive, as the car
bumped along, I clung to my mother in absolute terror.

We flew on to London from Berlin but I have no memory of
England, where we stayed for a couple of days before flying across
the Atlantic. This journey was like a dream in which there are no

transitions. One minute I was riding over a cobblestone road in East Berlin and the next thing I remember was waking up in Franklin, Pennsylvania. I have erased the intervening stages of the trip and can't even recall our arrival at Idlewild Airport in New York, or the flight to Youngstown, Ohio, where Grandma Stewart met us and drove us on to Greenville. My grandfather was ill with emphysema and we visited them for a day or two before moving to Franklin, where we stayed with my mother's aunt Gladys for several weeks.

Franklin is my first real memory of America, a small town in the upper reaches of Appalachia, not far from Oil City. At this point my conceptions of this country were still unformed, and the first things I saw when I got out of bed that morning were the flowered wallpaper all around me and a window with lace curtains. Outside I could see a crab apple tree in the yard, its branches laden with hard green fruit. Aunt Gladys's house was completely different from our bungalow in Etah or the cottages in Landour. The rooms were smaller, with lower ceilings, and most of the house was made of wood—the floors and staircases, the clapboard walls and shingle roof. The smells were different too, the scent of clover and freshly cut grass mixed with the sour, sooty odor of the oil refineries beyond the edge of town.

We had several sets of cousins in Pennsylvania, whom I had never met before, Aunt Gladys's grandchildren. Joe and I played outdoors with them on the lawn, spraying each other with a hose and catching bees in an empty jar. Summer in Pennsylvania was warm and sultry, with none of the dust storms that we used to have in Etah. Together with our cousins we went wading in a stream called Sugar Creek, where the water was clear as cellophane. Soon after we arrived in Franklin, Aunt Gladys took us to a firemen's fair and I was lifted up into the driver's seat of a gleaming red fire engine, with hoses and ladders, something I had only seen in story books. There were Ferris wheels and sideshows, but no bullock carts full of villagers, no caged hyenas, which I remembered from the country fairs in India. My father took me into a hall of mirrors in which we saw ourselves distorted into weird grotesques with long, distended limbs and rubbery necks.

Our cousins must have found us very strange. By this time I already spoke some English, but Joe, who was three years old, knew only Hindustani. As soon as we arrived in America he refused to speak at all, for over a month, until we got to Ithaca. My accent echoed the cadences of Indian speech, and my cousins kept asking me to say words for them in Hindustani. I taught them how to count from one to ten: "Ek, do, teen . . ." and simple words for things like milk, grass, and cow. They laughed at me when I used expressions from Indian English, which they didn't understand, when I called the trunk of a car a "dickey" or referred to my shorts as "half-pants." In a way, we must have seemed as odd to them as we did to the crowds of curious children in India who gathered around us at the roadside. There were so many things we didn't understand, the difference between a dime and a nickel, the rules of baseball, or how to order ice cream at the Dairy Queen.

One of my clearest memories from that summer was a T junction on the road outside of Franklin, where I learned my left and right. As we were driving back from a visit with our cousins in Sugar Creek, my parents gave me my first lesson in directions, pointing out my right hand and my left. Since that day, whenever I need to orient myself, I still call up a mental picture of that crossing in my mind, remembering that we turned right on the road to Franklin, instead of left toward Meadville. At this junction stood a red stop sign, and down the road a ways were the rusty smokestacks of an oil refinery, which filled the air with greasy, sulfurous fumes.

. . .

My mother's hometown was a place called Utica, about twelve miles northwest of Franklin. Though she had no family living there when we went back, my parents drove us past the house in which my mother spent most of her childhood. The town was nothing more than a cluster of clapboard houses and trailer homes, nestled in a cupped hollow of the hills. There were only two streets in Utica that crossed in the center of town, with so little traffic that they didn't need a stop light. When my mother lived there as a girl the total population of Utica was 204, and the town didn't seem to have grown at all since then.

Bertha Wood, my maternal grandmother, had been a teacher in the four-room schoolhouse where my mother received her elementary and high school education. Driving through the town my father pulled up to the curb and stopped near the schoolhouse, though we didn't get out of the car. The other building which my mother pointed out to me in Utica was the Grange Hall, which had been the center of social life for the town and the surrounding rural community. The Patrons of Husbandry, a fraternal order of farmers, met in the Grange Hall once a week to conduct secret rituals and organize community affairs. My mother had told me stories about the Grange, which was headed by the "Worthy Master." There were five degrees of initiation and each member had a title—my grandmother was called the "Worthy Lecturer." Their rituals were a curious blend of Greek and Christian mythology, invocations to the goddess of fertility interspersed with revival hymns. Utica also had a Juvenile Grange, in which my mother and her classmates were members. Once or twice a week they took part in drills, a combination of exercise and dance. At certain times of the year members of the Grange presented classical tableaux, dressing up in Greek costumes and posing for scenes from Homer's epics or the tragedies of Aeschylus and Sophocles.

Bertha Wood died in 1945, when my mother was eighteen, and my grandfather remarried a few years later. On my first visit to Pennsylvania I was too confused by all of the different relationships to really understand what had taken place. Later on, when I was older, my mother occasionally spoke of her "real mother," memories which I pieced together in my subconscious. Her albums contained several photographs of Bertha Wood and I had an image in my mind of a dark-haired, pensive woman in a white blouse and a long black skirt. But I preferred to picture her in one of the Grange Hall tableaux, the "Worthy Lecturer" draped in flowing robes, playing the role of Electra or Penelope.

My mother's uncle, Braden Wood, and his wife, Aunt Alice, lived in the nearby town of Polk. Both of them worked at the State School for the Handicapped, where Uncle Braden taught carpentry and industrial arts. He was a short, vigorous man who didn't speak too much. I can remember their house because Uncle Braden was a hunter and there were deer heads on the walls, ten- and twelve-point bucks. He also had a leopard skin that my father had given him as a present on an earlier visit in 1951. The leopard had been shot near Mussoorie by one of the villagers from Kimoin and a taxidermist had mounted its head with the jaws wide open in a savage snarl, a look of ferocity in its dull glass eyes. While my father and Uncle Braden traded hunting stories, I cautiously reached out to touch the tawny fur, running my hands over the complex pattern of rosettes and fingering the sharp claws and yellowed teeth. Seeing the leopard skin in Uncle Braden and Aunt Alice's living room, I struggled to understand the connection between their house in Polk and the jungles surrounding Mussoorie, where this predator once roamed.

Our visit to Pennsylvania was the first time I heard anyone use my mother's full name, Mary Ellen Stewart. My father and everybody else in India called her Ellen, but hearing Uncle Braden and other relatives addressing her as Mary Ellen made me realize, more than anything else, that this place was once her home. Before we came to America she had told me stories about growing up in Utica, swimming in French Creek with her father and the first trip she took with her mother to Pittsburgh, where a shroud of smoke and soot lay over the city from the steel mills at the confluence of the Allegheny and Monongahela Rivers, how she bought a new pair of shoes at Kauffman's department store. I had seen photographs of her childhood, faded sepia prints, very different from the pictures of my father's youth in India. There were formal portraits of my mother in ruffled frocks, with her hair done up in ribbons, and casual snapshots of her standing in the backyards of farm houses, surrounded by people I didn't recognize. This was the world that my mother had left behind when she traveled to India, a world where she was still called Mary Ellen, a world where she had been a child no older than myself.

That same summer we also made a pilgrimage to New Wilmington, Pennsylvania, and visited Westminster College, where my parents first met. The campus was spacious, with spreading lawns and Gothic brownstone buildings, most of them deserted for the summer holidays. My parents led us past the chapel and the dormitories where they had lived as students. Taking us into the theater they showed me where the two of them performed in plays as part of a drama class. Standing on the empty stage our voices sounded loud and hollow, even though we spoke in whispers. After that we went to Isaly's soda fountain, on the corner of the campus, and I drank my first strawberry milk shake, so thick that I could barely suck it through the straw. Across the street was a five-and-dime, where I spent my pocket money on a set of plastic Civil War soldiers, Confederates and Yankees, molded into battle positions, with miniature rifles and cannons.

One of my mother's closest childhood friends from Utica was Lillian Carnahan, who had also gone to college with her at Westminster. Whenever we went back to visit Pennsylvania, our family would spend a day or two with the Carnahans, who lived on a farm about four miles outside of Utica. They had an old gray house with a front porch and a kitchen garden at the back, full of tomato vines and cabbages, sweet corn and lettuce. The country road in front of the farm was unpaved and the driveway circled up from the mailbox in a lazy curve. Farther down the hill was a trickle of a stream where we collected wild raspberries and mint. Most of the fields on the farm lay fallow, though they cut the hay a couple times each year and we would go out and search for groundhog holes in the stubble. There were a number of Amish farmers in the area and we saw them riding about in their black horse-drawn buggies, the women in bonnets and aprons, the men with beards and broad-brimmed hats. For me it was an idyllic part of America that seemed to remain unchanged from my mother's youth, what Lillian's husband, Charles, would call "God's country."

Most of our time at the Carnahans' farm was spent in the kitchen, and I remember noticing how my mother's way of talking changed whenever we were with them. As they reminisced about their friends from school, a boy named Pud and other classmates, my mother sounded more and more like Lillian, the measured drawl of western Pennsylvania creeping into her speech, the vowels and consonants melting on her tongue.

Not far from the Carnahans' house, just down the road about a mile, lay the Millcreek cemetery, where my grandmother was buried. It was a small, rural graveyard, with modest headstones. My mother took us there to see the grave and Joe and I stood around for a while, restless, fidgeting in the silence. Andy was asleep on my father's shoulder. It was a warm, bright morning and a couple of gray squirrels were watching us from the branches of a tree nearby. They looked so much larger than the striped palm squirrels we had in India. I was still too young to be able to read the inscription: BERTHA WOOD 1901–1945. There were other relatives buried in the cemetery, gravestones dating back to the 1700s, when the first settlers came to these hills.

While we were in Pennsylvania that summer, a former neighbor of my mother's died, a man named Mr. White. My parents took us to pay our respects at the funeral home and I was frightened by the dim lighting and the pale, gaunt-looking corpse in the open casket. I had no idea who this old man was or why we were there, but I remember feeling anxious as my parents wrote our names in the condolence book, as if by putting their signatures on the page we had become a part of his death. Stepping outside the funeral parlor, through the dappled shade of maple trees, into the humid green air, I felt a morbid, unsettling sense of mortality, and was aware of the intricate web of shadows beneath the blades of grass, lying close upon the ground.

I already had a vague idea about death, from the cemetery in Landour and the charred remains of cremations which I had seen on the banks of the Ganga. The winter before we came to America, one of the men on the Etah compound had died of old age. As I watched a cluster of mourners carrying his coffin to the graveyard, I felt the first tug of fear. Until that summer in Pennsylvania, death had seemed to be something far removed from my family and me, but suddenly, it seemed close at hand.

My grandfather was dying of emphysema. He had been a heavy smoker for many years and two packs of Lucky Strikes a day had finally caught up with him. Grandpa Stewart had been a history teacher most of his life, at different high schools in western Pennsylvania. Later he joined the faculty of Thiel College in the town of Greenville, where he and Grandma Stewart, his second wife, were living when we visited them in 1961. My grandfather had retired the year before, because of his health.

I recognized Grandpa and Grandma Stewart from a pair of photographs I had seen in a frame on top of my mother's dressing table back in India. Grandpa Stewart had a long, somber face with a receding hairline and gold-rimmed spectacles. I got my middle name from him, Leslie, which I didn't like very much because it sounded effeminate. Even though my grandfather's first name was Frank he was always known as Leck or Lecky. While we were staying at their house in Greenville my mother would take my brothers and me up to Grandpa Stewart's room for brief visits. I remember that he had a television on a table at the foot of his bed and he enjoyed watching baseball games, the Pittsburgh Pirates. This was probably the first TV I ever saw and I was fascinated by the indistinct gray figures moving about on the screen.

Grandma Stewart was manager of the trust department at a local bank in Greenville. My mother and father called her by her first name, Lillian, and for a while I was confused between her and Lillian Carnahan. She was a forceful woman, with firm opinions, who drove the largest car I'd ever seen. At that age I was a little afraid of her, though she had a wry sense of humor that I grew to appreciate when I was older. I remember one day in Greenville, Grandma Stewart sat me down at the kitchen table while she was making dinner and taught me the names of all fifty states.

.   .   .

Soon after our arrival in Pennsylvania, my father bought a second-hand Rambler station wagon. This car was a bright red color and much bigger than the Hindustan Landmaster we had in India. After spending a month in Franklin and Greenville, we headed west through Ohio, Indiana, and Missouri to Kansas, where Grandma Alter was living. This was the first of several road trips which our family made across the United States. When my father was a young boy, on furlough with his parents, they had driven across the country several times, from Boston to San Francisco and back. These journeys had become something of a family ritual, as if we were traveling in search of a home that no longer existed, someplace in America to call our own.

After working in India for more than thirty years, Martha and Emmet Alter had retired to a town in Kansas called Pretty Prairie. I never met my paternal grandfather, who died a few years after returning to America. He was pastor of the Presbyterian church in Pretty Prairie and suffered a fatal heart attack while presenting a slide show about India, photographs that he had taken of Kashmir and Mogul monuments, the snow mountains behind Landour. After his death, my grandmother stayed on in Pretty Prairie, taking over the pastoral duties at the church. Later she moved to a retirement home in California, where we visited her on subsequent furloughs.

It took us several days of driving to reach Kansas. Joe and I rode in the backseat of the Rambler while my parents sat up front. Andy, who was not yet one year old, was put in a cardboard box at the back of the station wagon, along with our suitcases and bags. He had his toys and stuffed animals to keep him entertained and as we drove along he could stand up and look around. Andy was teething at the time and the edges of the cardboard got torn and soggy from his chewing. By the time we reached Kansas, Andy's box had fallen apart.

For most of our journey across country I remember driving through endless miles of wheat fields and watching giant combines harvesting and baling hay. Unlike the smaller, hilly farms of Pennsylvania, the fields in Missouri and Kansas seemed to stretch from one horizon to the next. Joe and I got bored with all this driving, hot and uncomfortable in the summer heat, our skin sticking like flypaper to the plastic upholstery on the seats. We would fight and squabble until my father had to pull over onto the side of the highway and roar at us. In many ways, I suppose, we looked like any other American family setting out on their summer vacation, but for us it was entirely different from traveling on the roads in India, where we could see buffaloes or camels, bullock carts and village fairs, the lines of mango trees along the canal banks where we would stop and picnic. The highways in America seemed dull and colorless, with scattered billboards and occasionally a Howard Johnson or Dairy Queen where we would stop to buy a meal and stretch our legs.

When we finally got to Pretty Prairie the town had a dry, open feeling which reminded me of Etah, the smell of dust and straw in the air. This was the first time I met Grandma Alter. She was in her early seventies, born just before the turn of the century, a stooped but active woman with steel gray hair. Unlike our relatives in Pennsylvania, she had lived in India and knew where we were coming from. Grandma Alter could talk to me about Landour and didn't need to ask me questions. She knew the names of all the houses where we lived, the trails and landmarks on the hillside. At the same time I had difficulty picturing her in India, and I never heard her speak a word of Hindustani. It was only years later, when I began to read her letters, that I was able to place her in the context of Mussoorie and the mission stations in the Punjab where she and my grandfather had worked.

One of the things that I remember from her house in Kansas was a set of stereoscope pictures of the Civil War. Holding the twin lenses up to my eyes I looked at the photographs, which gave an illusion of three dimensions. There were soldiers on horseback, standing beside cannons, lines of tents, and sharpshooters resting their rifles on a low stone wall. My grandmother told me that my great-grandfather was wounded at the Battle of Gettysburg. He had been fighting on the side of the Union and while he was being carried off the battlefield a second bullet struck him in the head. Though he survived for a number of years, my ancestor finally died of lead poisoning from the slug that remained lodged in his skull. This story made a strong impression on me, and after that, whenever I played with my plastic soldiers, I tried to imagine myself as a Yankee sharpshooter firing on the rebel trenches.

We didn't stay in Kansas for very long and drove back east with Grandma Alter, who spent the rest of the year with us in Ithaca. As I try to reconstruct the sequence of this journey, it comes back to me in flashes, images of highways, motels, the homes of friends and family where we stopped along the way. I can remember a house in which there was a huge birdcage full of canaries, and riding on a tractor, as well as stopping somewhere in Ohio where we visited a retired missionary couple who cooked an Indian meal for us, dal and rice, which Joe and I ate with our fingers.

. . .

After weeks of traveling we finally arrived in Ithaca. I don't know exactly what I was expecting but I was disappointed when we got there. Ithaca looked like so many other towns that we had driven through, except for the steep hills, the streets and sidewalks tilting up in front of us. The sound of the Rambler's engine, straining against the gradient, reminded me of driving up Mullingar Hill though Ithaca didn't look anything like Mussoorie. There weren't any mountains and the houses stood close together in neatly ordered ranks, with crew-cut lawns and clippered hedges.

The apartment building where we lived was maintained by the Presbyterian Church for missionaries on furlough. It was situated near the Cornell campus, where my father began studying for a master's degree in rural sociology. I started kindergarten a few weeks after we got to Ithaca, and each morning my mother or grandmother would walk me down to school at the foot of the hill. Once again, my memories telescope together and are inexact. There are a few faces which remain fixed in my mind, classmates and teachers, but I can remember none of their names. In kindergarten I made a plaster of paris plaque with the imprint of my right hand, the fingers splayed apart, as if I were reaching out to grasp something. I remember the cool, moist feeling as I pressed my palm into the wet plaster, holding it there for several seconds. When I removed my hand from the white mold I could see a clear impression of my fingerprints and the intersecting lines and creases on my palm, like the trails and footpaths in Landour.

Our apartment was compact and fully furnished. Unlike in India, my mother had to do all of the cooking and cleaning, as well as the laundry. There were no servants to do the housework, no ayahs to help take care of us. My father was attending classes at the university and he would come and go from the house, on his way to lectures or doing research in the library. Though she lived in a separate apartment, Grandma Alter came over almost every day and helped look after us. Six or eight other children lived in the same building and most of them were mish-kids like ourselves. One family had been working in Mexico, another in Korea. My closest friend was Danny Martin, whose family lived in the apartment next to us. His parents were Methodist missionaries, and our fathers were both in the same program at Cornell. The Martins and my parents knew each other from Landour and they had traveled together on the same ship to India in 1956, the year that I was born. Even though he was a couple years older, Danny and I got along immediately. Whenever we didn't want the other kids to understand what we were saying the two of us would speak in Hindustani. Danny was the first African American I ever met, though I don't think I was conscious of his skin color at the time. One day, while the two of us were watching *Gunsmoke* or *Wagon Train* on TV, Danny told me in a confidential whisper that some of his ancestors had been Cherokee.

In Ithaca, we did not have the same freedom that I enjoyed on the Etah compound or on the hillside in Landour. I was not allowed to cross the street alone, and the yard at the back of the apartment building was a patch of grass without much space to run around. I missed the jungle of thorn bushes at the edge of our yard in Etah, where we would play hide-and-seek in the dusty leaves, the hedges and vegetable gardens that separated different areas of the compound, the agricultural college, the poultry farm and pig-pens. There were none of the same animals or birds in Ithaca, no mongoose scurrying into its burrow, no hornbills or bandicoots, no wildcats prowling the perimeter of the chicken coops, no para-keets in the gulmohar trees.

Former colleagues of my parents from India, Henri and Kathryn Ferger, had recently retired in Ithaca. They had been posted in Far-rukhabad, not far from Etah. Henri Ferger was a photographer and his pictures were often used in mission publications such as year-books and newsletters. Prints of his photographs were sold at the Woodstock Sale each year, black-and-white shots of famous mon-uments, the Taj Mahal or Qutab Minar, and rural landscapes from different parts of India. My parents had two or three of his pictures framed and hanging on our walls. The photograph that I liked best was a portrait of a bearded man in a turban, seated on a bullock cart. It was a simple picture but there was something about the man's face that I liked, a composed and dignified expression. The two white oxen, yoked to the cart, had their heads raised up proudly with sharp, symmetrical horns.

When my parents told Henri Ferger that I liked the picture, he offered to tint it for me by hand, coloring in the man's turban, the green line of mango trees in the background, and the brass bells around the oxen's necks. Seeing this black-and-white photograph transformed into color was magical for me, and after that I always kept the picture hanging above my bed.

Winter came early in upstate New York and for most of the time that we lived there the trees were bare of leaves. The days were short and the weather was cold and gray, keeping us indoors. I saw my first snowfall in Ithaca, waking up one morning to find the yard behind our apartment building covered in white, the powdery flakes sifting through the air and settling on the skeletal branches of the trees. Icicles hung from the drains and window ledges like crystal canines in a sabertooth's jaw. Dressed in bulky snowsuits purchased from a thrift shop at our church, Joe and I went sledding with Danny Martin on the many hills near the Cornell campus. We built a fort in the backyard and had snowball fights with other kids along our street. My father showed us how to make a snowman and we went ice-skating once, though I kept falling down.

Andy was still too young to play with us in the snow and spent most of his time indoors, sitting in a high chair eating M&M's and watching Mr. Magoo on the television. Soon after we arrived in Ithaca we bought a secondhand TV, and I watched as much as my parents would allow. Besides cartoons like *Quick Draw McGraw*, *Popeye*, and *Deputy Dog*, there were *Captain Kangaroo*, *Romper Room*, and my favorite program, *Tarzan*, which Danny and I would wait to watch each day. It came on in the evening at five o'clock, just as it was getting dark. Along with the older children in our building, we would gather on the living-room carpet and wait to hear the yodeling call of the ape man as he swung through the vine-draped trees.

Toward the end of our stay in Ithaca, my parents took us to see Walt Disney's *Pinocchio* at a drive-in theater. Propped up on cushions in the front seat of the Rambler, with the windows open, I sat and watched the giant figures of Geppetto and Jiminy Cricket projected on the outdoor screen. Unlike the cartoons on our black-and-white TV, the colors in the movie were bright and vivid, the animation much more lifelike. My brothers fell asleep, but as I watched the puppet turn into a boy, I couldn't help but feel that something would go wrong. And when it did, when the bad boys were turned into donkeys—which was almost as terrifying as having your head used as a cobblestone—I began to cry. For the rest of the movie, as the whale swallowed Geppetto and later when Pinocchio drowned, I wept and wept, unable to stop myself, tears soaking into the bag of popcorn in my lap.

• • ▪

One of the things that I hated during our year in Ithaca, and on later furloughs, was visiting the churches that supported my parents' work in India. These were congregations which contributed money to the Presbyterian Board of Foreign Missions and each missionary, or "fraternal worker" as they were called, was assigned to certain churches, with whom they corresponded three or four times a year. While we were living in Ithaca, my father was invited to preach or give a talk to each of these congregations and the whole family had to go along.

As soon as we arrived at the church, I was shepherded off to a Sunday school class in the basement and introduced to the other children. These were awkward moments, standing there beside the teacher, who tried to be reassuring but made me uncomfortable with her constant smile. I was the mish-kid from India, exhibited like a freak of nature. My clothes never felt as if they fit me right, the woolen trousers catching at the back of my knees, the collared shirt choking at my throat. The Sunday school teacher would ask me to tell the other children about India and I never knew what to say. I stood there tongue-tied, turning red in the face and trying to think of what I could describe, maybe something about the sliding rock on the Chukkar, or the time a swarm of locusts came through Mussoorie and there were so many on the ground that we couldn't help but step on them. I thought of telling them about the rogue boar my father shot in Etah or Henri Ferger's picture of the man on the oxcart. But looking at the circle of smirking faces I knew that whatever I said would sound ridiculous, so I stayed mute and motionless.

After a while the class started asking questions. Had I ever ridden on an elephant? Were there tigers in my yard? Did cobras really dance? I would nod or shake my head, unwilling to speak. The other kids stared at me as if they didn't really believe I came from India. "Do you speak Hindu?" the teacher asked, and I would nod, too embarrassed to correct her. "Can you say a word or two for us?" One of the boys would snicker and all I wanted to do was run away from that room and out to the red Rambler that stood in the parking lot behind the church, ready to take us home. But there was no escaping this ordeal, and finally, prompted by the teacher, I mumbled a word or two of Hindustani, as if I were a talking mynah: "khargosh" (rabbit), "chiriya" (bird), "tota" (parrot), the first things that came into my mind.

After the church service there was often a potluck lunch or dinner, and as the guests of honor we were invited to the head of the line. My mother would help me fill my paper plate, with spoonfuls of macaroni casserole, baked beans, and Jell-O salad that melted into bright green puddles, with bits of pineapple floating in the middle. I was reminded of potluck suppers at the community center in Landour, missionary gatherings on the hillside, the Fourth of July. My brothers and I would cling to our parents, hating every minute of those church visits, the way the other children watched us, the raucous laughter of adults, repeated jokes about "the altar boys," and those interminable prayers in which the minister of the church would ask God's blessings on our family as we spread the message of Christ's gospel to the farthest corners of the world.

The Presbyterian headquarters were in Manhattan, at 475 Riverside Drive, in a concrete office tower which was sometimes called "the God Box." Many of the other missions had their offices in the same building, a huge, characterless structure overlooking Grant's Tomb and the Hudson River. While we were living in Ithaca we had to go down to New York City several times so that my parents could meet with administrative staff and members of the mission board. Just down the street from the God Box was an apartment house where we stayed whenever we came to Manhattan. It was an old building, grim and poorly lit, with linoleum floors and steaming radiators. Visiting New York, I would stare out of my bedroom window at the drab mosaic of brick walls and fire escapes, wondering why anyone would choose to live in a place like this. One time, when we drove down from Ithaca and parked our Rambler on the street outside the mission offices, someone broke into the car and went through our suitcases in the back. Afterward, when my parents explained to me what had happened, they said that a thief had "rifled" through our car, an expression which made the robbery seem much more dangerous and threatening than it really was. Though nothing of value was stolen it made me feel uncomfortable in the city, a feeling which I never quite outgrew.

*   *   *

Toward the end of our stay in Ithaca, during June of 1962, we drove back to Pennsylvania for a final visit with my mother's family. It was summer once again and the snow had disappeared. The oaks and maples formed a leafy wall of green along the turnpike and I felt a restless sense of setting out for an unknown destination. Every few minutes I asked my parents how much longer until we got there, wishing that we were on our way to India instead. Kindergarten was finished for the year and our sea freight had already been packed and shipped. I was looking forward to going back to India and pestered my mother and father with questions about Hindustani words that I'd forgotten, the names of my friends in Etah—Saroj, Eddu, Kushan, and Nagma—or stories that I remembered from Landour.

On this visit we stayed for only a couple of weeks in Pennsylvania and spent most of our time in Greenville. Grandpa Stewart's condition was getting worse and my brothers and I were told to be quiet inside the house so that he wouldn't be disturbed. Whenever Joe and I started roughhousing we were chased into the garden, where we wrestled in the grass and hunted for bugs in the flower beds. There was a depressing feeling about that visit, a hushed sense of loss and separation. My mother knew that her father was dying and that she would never see him again once we returned to India. Though she kept her feelings hidden from us, it must have been a difficult time, and I could sense her grief.

The thing that I remember most clearly from our last visit to Greenville was learning how to read. My parents had got several books for me, including *Dick and Jane*, a textbook that I would be using in first grade. While sitting in the living room of Grandma and Grandpa Stewart's house, my mother pointed to the letters and syllables until I could recognize the sounds phonetically: "Look, Jane, Look. See Spot Run. . . ." Moving my finger slowly across the page I read each word in a cautious, deliberate voice. It was an exciting moment and I can recall my mother's delight, and my own sense of accomplishment, as well as those pictures of scrubbed white children playing on a sidewalk, the words and images connecting like the shapes of a puzzle. Soon afterward, my mother took me upstairs to Grandpa Stewart's room, where he lay in bed, propped up against a mound of pillows. His skin looked pale and his features were drawn, though he smiled at me as I came through the door. By the yellow light of my grandfather's bedside lamp, I read aloud to him.

MONSOON

I started first grade during the monsoon. Returning to Mussoorie in July of 1962, we moved into a house called Hearthstone, near the top of Landour Hill. Each morning I would walk down the Zig Zag path with Bagh Chand, a Garhwali man whom my mother hired to help run errands and take me back and forth from school. Bagh Chand wore a khaki coat, torn and patched in places, over a pair of baggy pajamas, with rubber chappals on his feet. Setting out in my Duckback raincoat and gum boots, I carried an umbrella and a green canvas book bag on my shoulders. As we made our way down to Woodstock School, Bagh Chand and I would talk in Hindustani, the language coming back to me after a year away in America. During the monsoon it rained almost every day, the trail turning into a muddy torrent and water streaming off the points of my umbrella like strings of beaded glass.

About halfway down to school we passed the largest tree in Landour, a giant ban oak that grew at the side of the Zig Zag path, its spreading branches stretching out over the valley. Through the wet leaves and mossy limbs of this tree I could see the red tin roofs of Woodstock several hundred feet below. Here I began to feel my first misgivings, slowing down and making excuses to stop. Bagh Chand would urge me on with warnings that I was getting late for school, but there were plenty of distractions along the way—a reindeer orchid on the khud above me, just out of reach, or a skink disappearing into the cracks of a pushta wall. Every few feet I would stop to check my legs for leeches or to pluck a sprig of wild balsam, the seedpods bursting at my touch. All this while, as I tried to slow our progress, an uneasy feeling was knotting up inside my chest. Instead of going down to school, I wanted to climb that massive oak, its arms draped with ferns and polypods. It looked so easy, the broad trunk growing at right angles to the hillside like a detour along the path; I imagined walking straight out onto the branches, using my umbrella to balance, as if I were an acrobat.

As my footsteps slowly came to a halt, Bagh Chand would take my book bag and grab my hand to keep me moving. He was responsible for getting me to school on time and told me stories as he led me down the Zig Zag path, Garhwali fairy tales about bhoots and devtas. I complained that I was too tired to walk any farther and Bagh Chand promised to carry me up the hill when he came to fetch me in the afternoon. No matter what he said I hated the thought of going to school; an anguished, unhappy feeling remained inside of me, a curdled, sour taste at the back of my throat. Every stride took me closer to Woodstock; each turn on the path was like a spiral leading downward, closer and closer to those corrugated tin roofs. We passed Woodside and Redwood cottages, taking a shortcut that led to Tehri View. The roof of the gym and the gravel playground were right below us now and we could hear the shouts and laughter of other children. I told Bagh Chand that I was feeling sick and tried to turn around, though he kept dragging me along with his strong, rough hands that smelled of bidi tobacco and woodsmoke. My book bag looked ridiculously small slung across his shoulder.

"Chalo, Chalo, Stevie Baba, your teacher will be angry if you are late."

At that moment I hated Bagh Chand for taking me to school, despite his patient, coaxing voice. I hated my mother for sending me off each morning and remaining behind at Hearthstone to look after my brothers, both of whom were still too young for school. I hated my father for being far away on the plains in Etah, out there beyond the farthest branches of the giant oak. I hated the rain and mist. I hated the clammy feeling of my gum boots and the thought of sitting in a classroom all day long, struggling with arithmetic and spelling.

Some years later my father would tell me that he had cried so much when he first went to Woodstock that Miss McGee, his teacher, sent him home to his mother and he didn't go back to school until the following year. There was no such reprieve for me, and by the time we reached the steps below Tehri View, the tears were running down my face as steadily as the rain dripping from the leaves. In desperation, Bagh Chand would pick me up and carry me, losing patience and knowing that I was already late. We could hear the ringing of the school bell in the quadrangle, an insistent, melancholy sound that carried up and down the hillside, like a death knell, tolling out my grief.

I can't say exactly what it was that made me cry. The year before I had gone to kindergarten in Ithaca without any complaints, but first grade was different. My teacher, Miss Schroeder, was a gentle, soft-spoken woman and I was not afraid of her. Perhaps I was jealous of my brothers, who got to stay at home. Perhaps it was the distance down the hill, that sinking feeling of descending into the valley. It could also have been the monsoon, the relentless rain and mist, the dank, wet feeling of being surrounded by clouds and moisture all day long. I don't really know what troubled me but every morning I would weep and wail as Bagh Chand carried me down the last few turns of the path, behind the school kitchens, through a narrow passageway, and up the dark staircase to the first-grade classroom on the second floor. The other students were already seated at their desks, watching in amusement as Bagh Chand put me down outside the door, took off my raincoat, and gave me the book bag, wiping my tears with his callused hands. Miss Schroeder smiled and called my name but I didn't move, snuffling into the damp sleeve of my shirt.

When I turned to look behind me Bagh Chand was gone, disappearing down the stairs as fast as he could go. Once or twice I chased after him, but he was too quick for me and I knew that I had been abandoned. I stood there and howled in the stairwell, feeling the sadness twisting inside my bones, the tops of my gum boots chafing at my calves, the raincoat and book bag lying at my feet and my umbrella leaving a wet puddle on the cement floor. After a few minutes Miss Schroeder came and got me, leading me back to my desk and giving me a wad of tissue paper with which to blow my nose.

This ordeal must have continued for a couple weeks, though it felt like months, before I was reconciled to school. I have very few other memories of first grade and spent most of my day waiting for the final ringing of the school bell which signaled my release. When I got out of class, Bagh Chand would be waiting for me at the bottom of the stairs, and without saying anything he took my book bag and held out his hand for me to hold. I would remind him that he had promised to carry me up the hill but Bagh Chand complained that his back was hurting and persuaded me to put off my ride for another day.

"Chalo, Chalo, Stevie Baba, let's go home."

Even though the climb to Hearthstone was steep and tiring, I didn't mind walking up the hill and I would often race ahead. There were no distractions now and I ran up the steps to Tehri View without pausing or looking back. Bagh Chand did not need to tell me stories or cajole me and he would light a bidi, the sweet acrid smoke following me up the hill. If it was raining, I would spin my umbrella around and send a spray of droplets shooting in all directions or I would splash through the channels of rushing water that flowed across the path. I passed the giant oak without even breaking stride, its spreading branches no longer beckoning to me, for I was headed home to Hearthstone, seven or eight bends farther on. In my eagerness, I scrambled up the shortcuts, leaving Bagh Chand far behind.

*　*　*

Each year, before the monsoon broke in June, we could see the rain clouds in the distance, a dark blue smear on the horizon, as if the sky were bruised. Gradually the clouds would build up over the plains until their shapes became distinct, muscular formations of indigo and black. Fired by the heat of summer, the monsoon sky became alive and volatile, dark thunderheads expanding and contracting like monstrous bellows. We could see the lightning spitting out of the clouds, bright metallic sparks, and the thunder pounded in the distance, with the irregular beat of hammers in a foundry.

For weeks the hills had been dry, the spring rains tapering off in April, grasses turning a brittle yellow, oak leaves listless in the summer air, pine needles crackling underfoot and forest fires burning across the Tehri hills. Most of the streams and springs were dry and the air smelled of smoke and flint. Each day we waited for the monsoon to arrive, waiting for the restless phalanx of clouds to breach the Siwalik hills. As they approached, we could see the first showers slanting down upon the plains, and the sunlight changed from brassy yellow to copper and then to bronze. The force of the storm could be felt several hours before it reached us, the deodars bristling at the first hint of rain, the oaks agitated by the breeze, flocks of crows suddenly taking to the air in panic, tossed about on the wind like flying cinders. You could smell the monsoon as it approached, the earth releasing a scent of fertility from deep within its glands, a moist, fecund odor. As we watched from our veranda at Hearthstone, the mountains seemed to lean forward, bracing themselves to receive the impact of the storm. When the monsoon finally arrived, not as scattered drops of rain, but as a sudden deluge, an avalanche of water, it battered the trees and rooftops with such intensity that I held my breath, afraid that I might drown.

Within minutes the gutters along the edges of the roof were overflowing, water spewing out of every crack and hole, turning staircases into waterfalls, filling the slate drains with swirling, brown currents, dry leaves washing down the paths, forming fragile dams until the water broke through, carrying with it sticks and debris. All of the gullies and ravines on the hillside became rivers and in the first rush of the monsoon whole sections of the ridge were washed away in landslides, trees uprooted, boulders breaking loose and crashing down onto the Tehri Road below. The first few rains of the monsoon were always the heaviest and caused the most damage, as the mountains struggled to absorb all of that water and the trees steadied themselves against the onslaught, which would continue for the next twelve weeks.

Even when the rain stopped, for a few brief hours, the air was saturated with moisture and dense mists swept in over the hillside. The dampness penetrated everything. Cupboards stank of mildew. Metal hinges and barrel bolts began to rust. Doors and windows swelled until they were too tight to open or shut. Clothes and shoes never dried completely and everything was covered with a powdery dusting of yellow mold.

During the monsoon, hundreds of different species of shrubs and plants erupted in a profusion of greenery, vines snaking their way up the trunks of trees, jack-in-the-pulpits bursting out of the soil, their hooded flowers like swaying cobras with long green tongues. Ferns uncoiled out of the moss, maidenhair and red-bearded Christmas ferns, edible fiddlesticks and Bible ferns, with delicate lacelike fronds that we pressed between the pages of the Scriptures. The rarest variety of all was the mouse-eared ferns, with furry round leaves. Mushrooms and toadstools popped up between the rocks, and banks of stinging nettle grew along the edges of the paths, leaving red welts on our legs if we brushed against them. The only cure for stinging nettle was "doc leaves," a common weed which we crumpled into a wad and rubbed on our skin. The green juice from these leaves helped soothe the itching.

All kinds of insects and reptiles appeared during the monsoon, as if by spontaneous generation—toads, leeches, snakes, beetles, snails, and skinks. In every cottage on the hillside there were giant house spiders, three or four inches across, which lived in our bathrooms and cupboards. The female spiders carried white egg sacks that looked exactly like the bundles of laundry which the washermen carried up from Dhobighat. If we popped these sacks, dozens of tiny spiders came scurrying out in all directions. The house spiders were harmless, unlike the poisonous scorpions which we killed without mercy, crushing them under our heels. Getting dressed for school during the monsoon, I always shook out my clothes and shoes before putting them on, afraid of finding a scorpion inside.

One of the first signals of the monsoon was the calling of cicadas in the oak trees. With the coming of the rains they started their rasping cry, like schoolboys humming through the teeth of a comb. This sound became an incessant chorus, one cicada answering the next until the entire hillside was astir with the rubbing of their wings. Often it got so loud it seemed to make all the leaves and ferns vibrate, loud enough to drive a person mad. The cicadas were perfectly camouflaged, their bodies a mottled green and their transparent wings veined with dark lines that made them blend into the moss and bark. Whenever I tried to locate a cicada by sound it was impossible with so many of them calling at once. As soon as one fell silent another started up, like the revving of tiny engines buzzing from one tree to the next. Their monotonous cries sounded mechanical to my ear, like the grinding of gears and bearings. Sometimes the noise reminded me of sand and pebbles grating against the bottom of a metal basin. At other times the sound was almost musical, a reedy lament that used to make me feel depressed, a steady drone like the sympathetic strings on a sitar.

Each cicada was no more than a couple inches in length but in concert they were capable of raising a crescendo equal to any orchestra. To my ear it was a rustling, primal sound, as if the mountains themselves had begun to sing.

The only thing that silenced the cicadas was the rain. As it rattled against the tin roofs, the two sounds would blend together, until the crying of the cicadas was finally obliterated by the thunder of the storm. Lying in bed I would listen to the rain, and when it stopped I waited in the hushed quiet until somewhere down the hill, the first cicada began to call again, winding up like a clockwork toy, answered by another and another, until the forest echoed with the shrill vibration of their wings.

*   *   *

To entertain ourselves on rainy days, my brothers and I invented games and hobbies. One of our favorite monsoon activities was making moss gardens. We would go out with our umbrellas and gum boots to gather different kinds of moss from the pushta walls and oak trees in the yard. Returning indoors we arranged the pieces carefully on a kitchen tray to create a miniature landscape. Using rocks and clay to form mountains and valleys we constructed tiny Edens out of our imagination. To make a lake or pond, we used a pocket mirror, covering the edges with moss so that it looked like water. For trees and shrubs we planted small ferns and lichens. Sometimes we added animals to our moss gardens, snails and beetles, which crawled about like prehistoric creatures in a virgin world. My father, who had made moss gardens when he was young, showed us how to fashion peacocks out of the purple orchids which bloomed during the monsoon. Picking the flowers and turning them upside down, we broke off the two small petals that enclosed the stamen and stuck one of these in the hollow stem to make the peacock's head. The exposed stamen looked just like the feet of a bird, and the larger petals, which were different shades of purple and blue, spread out to form the peacock's tail. These orchids provided the final touch for our moss gardens, birds of delicate plumage, captured in a dream.

I remember one time, trying to re-create the blue willow pattern from a set of crockery my mother had, making a Chinese bridge out of toothpicks and carving a fishing boat from the soft bark of a pine tree. It was intricate work and I sat for hours piecing together the layers of moss, the different textures and shades of green. Trapped indoors by the incessant rain, we created our own idyllic worlds, lush green hillsides and exotic trees, a peaceable kingdom on a kitchen tray.

Another favorite monsoon hobby in Landour was beetle hunting. The electric bulbs on the lampposts along the Chukkar and the Tehri Road attracted hundreds of flying insects during the rains. As soon as dusk began to fall, my brothers and I took bamboo poles or fishing rods and set out to hunt for beetles. They often perched on the brackets of the lampposts, atop the metal shades, or sometimes on the nearby trees. We listened for the steady hum of their wings as they circled overhead like miniature buzz bombs homing in on the lights.

The mist was draped around us and the naked bulbs cast a faint halo of light through the drizzle and rain. We approached the lampposts like stealthy burglars, carrying our unwieldy poles, eyes alert for the gleam of a cherry rhino or the dull black silhouette of a stag. After knocking down our prey we searched the ground with Eveready torches until we found the beetle lying on its back, six legs clawing at the air. We had to be careful when we picked them up, catching the beetles just behind their heads, so they couldn't bite our fingers. Once captured, these insects were kept in old Bournvita tins, with holes punched in the lid and a layer of moss at the bottom. In each tin we put a mango seed on which the beetles fed, sucking at the sweet yellow pulp. After a day or two the mangoes began to ferment and a sickly sweet odor escaped from the beetle tin every time we opened the lid.

More than a dozen different species of beetles were found in

Mussoorie. I never learned their Latin names but they were carefully identified according to our own system of classification. There were "common stags" with long pincers, which looked like antlers. These beetles were larger than the "cherry stags," which had glossy shells and wingplates. The females of both species, called "cows," were smaller in size, with tiny pincers that were sharp as razor blades. The "rhino" beetles had horns instead, and the females of this species were called "swear beetles" because of the angry chirring sound they made. Most prized of all were the "five-horned rhinos," which were very rare, about three inches long, orange and black in color, with the luster of a precious stone, a tiger's eye. Two other species that we collected were the "saw-tooths," which had serrated pincers, and the "stone carriers," with long antennae that curved back over their bodies like the straps that coolies used to carry heavy loads. The most common species were june bugs, with iridescent green shells, and "bamboo beetles," which were a reddish color and looked something like a cockroach.

In elementary school our day began with show-and-tell. After settling into our desks, each of us was given a chance to present the rest of the class with something we had made, collected, or discovered. For some it was a coin or stamp from another country, for others it was a new toy, a Matchbox car or a miniature crane made from an Erector set. But for many of us show-and-tell became a chance to exhibit the strangest, most unusual bugs or beetles, reptiles, and other crawling creatures that we could find. I remember Scotty Bunce bringing a skink to class and demonstrating how, if you grabbed it by the tail, the body would break off and run away. Another time Craig Wertz caught a grass snake on his way to school. He held it up for all of us to see, its writhing body coiled around his wrist. The teacher made him go outside immediately and release it down the khud.

When I was in second and third grade I used to bring my beetles to class and make them crack matchsticks between their pincers. One time a cherry stag that I had caught the night before got loose in the classroom and flew about, buzzing over our heads and crashing into the windowpanes as all of us, including my teacher, ducked for cover. After show-and-tell was over I would let the beetles crawl about inside my desk, waiting to see how long it took for them to find their way out of the inkwell, creeping into the light, like miniature dragons emerging from their lair. As we got older Scotty Bunce and I scared the girls with our beetles, quietly putting a cherry cow on Patricia Howard's red pigtails or letting a stag climb up the sleeve of Amy Burkhalter's sweater. As we waited for their shrieks and cries the two of us chewed on our shirtsleeves to keep from laughing.

The beetles also served as gladiators. During recess one of the school desks was emptied of books and John Wysham placed his stag inside, a five- or six-inch goliath that had never been defeated. Reluctantly I released my challenger from its tin, a rare sawtooth that I had captured near Sisters' bazaar. The two beetles were then pushed together, goaded into fighting, prodded with pencils and rulers. The stag reared up like a centaur as my sawtooth moved in to grapple with the champion. Their legs thrashing together, both beetles made an angry, buzzing sound. For several minutes neither of the insects seemed to gain the upper hand. Finally John Wysham's stag pivoted around and caught my sawtooth in his pincers, squeezing until a thick brown juice flowed out of the beetle's abdomen. Humiliated and on the edge of tears I put my dead warrior back in its tin, the sickening smell of rotting mangoes like the stench of defeat. After school I took my sawtooth home and with a pin I stuck it to my cupboard door.

John Wysham's stag remained invincible for weeks until one day Shunil Borpujari placed a bamboo beetle in the ring. Its tiny jaws opened and closed with the quickness of a nail clipper. This challenger was too agile for the stag and needed no encouragement to attack, moving in swiftly from the rear and snipping off one of the champion's legs before he could turn around. With relentless ferocity the bamboo beetle darted in and out, clipping off all six legs, until the stag was crippled and couldn't move. We watched in horror and fascination as the champion lay helpless in the center of the empty desk. In desperation he opened his wingplates, attempting to fly away, at which point the bamboo beetle made its final lunge, cutting through the stag's papery wings and burying its savage jaws in the soft tissues beneath. The champion's pincers opened and closed helplessly in one last, vain attempt to grab his attacker before he died.

· · ·

The Fourth of July fell within the first few weeks of the monsoon, and each of the different missions on the hillside held separate celebrations. The Methodists got together on the flat behind South Hill or down at Eastwood Estate; the Mennonites gathered at Ellangowan along with some of the smaller, more conservative denominations; and the Presbyterians congregated at the community center. In the evening there would be a potluck supper with baked beans and potato salad, hot dogs with mustard and pickle relish, corn on the cob, and apple pie.

Families arrived in a flurry of umbrellas, cooking pots and casseroles wrapped up in dishcloths, raincoats and ponchos dripping on the veranda of the community center, and a jumble of gum boots near the door. Woodstock had a two-week holiday at this time of year and many of the fathers would try to come up to Landour for the Fourth of July. There were usually more men around than earlier in the season, a bustle of activity, jovial greetings and conversations; one of the memsahibs complaining that her bread rolls hadn't risen the way they should have, or that there was a landslide on the Chukkar and she had to walk down the Zig Zag path instead of taking the shortcut past Hamilton House. Children rushed in and out, skidding over the slick cement floors, while the fathers stood in solemn groups, watching this melee with bored expressions, wishing they were down on the plains again. The community center was filled with the sound of forced laughter and

the constant chatter of rain on the tin roof. Sooner or later someone would shout, "Leech!" and everything would stop. The crea-
ture had been spotted, sliding across the floor, like a bloated
exclamation mark, engorged with blood and leaving a bright red
smear. Everybody would pause in the middle of whatever they
were doing and check their feet, the men and boys drawing up
their pant legs, the women and girls raising the hems of their skirts
and dresses, looking for blood.

"It's me. It's me. It's come off me," one of the memsahibs
would cry, her skirt hitched up to the knee, exposing a smooth
white calf on which the leech had left its mark, a thin trickle of
red, staining her sock.

"Get some salt. Get some salt," someone else would shout, and
into the kitchen we rushed, grabbing one of the saltcellars and racing to kill the leech, which was still inching its way across the floor,
swollen with the memsahib's blood. The saltcellars never poured
easily during the monsoon and in our eagerness we pried open the
lid and emptied the entire contents on top of the bloodsucker,
watching it squirm beneath the pile of salt. Within seconds the
leech would burst, the white salt turning a bright raspberry red,
while the memsahib dabbed at her wound with a tissue and someone went to get a Band-Aid. Leech bites took forever to heal and
often got infected, swelling up into dark red welts that itched for
weeks.

Before supper was served there would be a few remarks by the
president of the community center committee, welcoming a new
family to the hillside, announcing the next Reading Club or the
deadlines for a revised edition of the cookbook. Then one of the
men would say grace, usually the senior Presbyterian on the hillside, whoever that happened to be, a long-winded prayer in which
God's blessing was invoked on our gathering, on the collections of
degchis and casseroles that filled the buffet, and this celebration of
our nation's independence, the United States of America, our
president and Congress, our astronauts orbiting overhead, and our

courageous troops stationed around the world, in Germany, Korea, and Vietnam. At the beginning I bowed my head and closed my eyes, but within a minute or two I would look up to see everyone standing in an attitude of reverence as the prayer droned on like a cicada, monotonous and interminable, while I could only think of the leech attaching itself to the memsahib's calf, sucking open her pores and drawing the red blood from her veins.

An American flag hung above us on the wall, and after the prayer was finally over and everybody said amen we sang "The Star-Spangled Banner." I never learned the words completely and the only phrase I knew by heart was "the rockets' red glare, the bombs bursting in air." That was my favorite part of the Fourth of July—rockets and bombs. But the fireworks were the last event of the evening and I had to wait until after the second and third helpings had been eaten and the fathers, fattened like sacrificial bulls, lounged on the folding chairs with coffee cups in hand, buttons straining, passing wind discreetly as they shifted in their seats, exhausted from their journeys up the hill. As we ate our soggy wedges of apple pie, I listened for the rain to stop, knowing that this was the signal to go outside onto the tennis court of the community center and set off fireworks. Reluctantly the fathers rose from their chairs and, deputizing several of the high school boys, shuffled outdoors, grimacing as drops of rain continued falling from the leaves. Warnings were shouted as we raced outdoors and the younger children were herded by their mothers into the safest corner of the tennis court to watch the pyrotechnic display.

With the dampness of the monsoon it was difficult to get the fireworks to light. Matches failed to strike and fuses sputtered out. The mist blew in so that we could only see the men as ghostly shadows, crouching near the fence, a brief tongue of light, silence, someone stepping backward quickly, a few sparks and then the sudden rush of fire as a bottle rocket ignited and shot up through the mist, bright as a comet, ricocheting off the oak branches overhead and spiraling out across the valley, where it exploded in a muted ball of light. This was followed by more rockets and clay fountains, their plumes of sparks rising ten or fifteen feet into the air and lighting up the faces of everyone around, our eyes dazzled by the colors. There were spinners too, which danced like whirligigs across the tennis court, skittering over the cracks and coming closer and closer to where we stood until one of the older boys stepped out and bravely kicked it away. I remember one Fourth of July, when someone left the boxes of fireworks too close to the rockets and they all went off at once, the men leaping out of the way and everyone screaming as rockets and crackers blew up together in a wild, uncontrollable blast of flares and explosions.

My favorites were the atom bombs, though the memsahibs complained, "No loud ones please!" I clapped my hands over my ears, hair damp from the mist and shivering with cold and excitement, waiting for the deafening explosions which made the ground shake. Far off down the hill I could hear the Methodists firing their arsenal of bombs and above us the streaks of light from Ellangowan, where the Mennonites and the Assemblies of God were setting off volleys of rockets. Sometimes it felt as if there was a battle going on, a sectarian war between the different missions on the hillside. After the fireworks were over, the younger children would be given sparklers and we ran about the tennis court waving our dazzling wands and challenging each other to fiery duels. The air was thick with the sulfurous smell of gunpowder and the tennis court was littered with charred bits of paper.

•   •   •

India's Independence Day was also celebrated during the monsoon, on the fifteenth of August, which was a school holiday. In the morning we had a flag raising at Woodstock and, if it wasn't raining, all of the students and staff gathered at the flagpole in front of Parker Hall. Each of us dressed in Indian costumes, kurta pajama for the boys and sari or salwar kameez for the girls. On our heads we wore white Gandhi caps and stood together on the terraces near the flagpole, listening to a speech in Hindi, delivered by a visiting dignitary. One of the teachers, usually Brij Lal, would run the Indian flag up the pole, where it opened in a shower of rose petals, the saffron, white, and green tricolor with a blue chakra in the middle. All of us shouted, "Jai Hind!" three times in unison and the whole school sang the national anthem, "Jana Gana Mana." Once again I did not know all of the words and hummed along until I came to those few lines that I remembered, ". . . Vindhya, Himachal, Yumuna, Ganga . . ." If it was raining, as it often did, we gathered inside of Parker Hall, the flag pinned to the velvet curtains above the stage and the lights flickering as the voltage dipped during the storm, our voices singing as loudly as we could, competing with the drumbeats of the rain.

On Independence Day the students at Woodstock hosted a lunch for all of the Indian employees, or karamcharis. At noon the cooks and bearers, chokidars and sweepers gathered in the elementary auditorium while volunteers from the high school served the meal, as a gesture of respect and gratitude. The karamcharis looked after us all year long, with generosity and good humor, though they seldom got the acknowledgment they deserved. Most of them had worked at Woodstock for many years and watched us growing up.

Later in the evening there was an Independence Day banquet for the staff and students, followed by a Hindustani music concert and a talent show. Each year the school sweepers, most of whom came from villages on the plains near Bijnor, performed a folk dance to the accompaniment of a dholak drum. A ring of men danced wildly on the stage in Parker Hall, striking at each other with bamboo canes in a mock swordfight. Some of these canes had firecrackers attached which went off with a bang whenever they were hit. Later in the program, Bhulan played the harmonium and sang ghazels and film songs, his voice as plaintive and full of emotion as that of Muhammad Rafi, the famous playback singer. The other regular performer was Nathu, who sang classical ragas, his voice somewhat ragged with age but no less fervent.

Many of the students at Woodstock also played Indian instruments and performed Bharat Natyam and Kathak dances. Master Mubarak Masih, the Hindustani music teacher, was an imposing man who sat on the stage throughout the performance, his hair combed straight back from his wrinkled brow, a shawl wrapped around his shoulders, directing his students as they played sitars and bamboo flutes, vinas and tablas. My brother Joe took lessons on the tabla, a pair of drums played with the fingers, the sound of which reminded me of monsoon rain on the tin roofs. Often during the Hindustani music concerts a storm would break and the crescendo of rain beat an accompaniment to the tabla or the tempo of a Kathak dancer's feet on the wooden stage, so that it seemed as if the musicians and dancers were competing with the monsoon, each one trying to drown the other into silence.

•　•　•

By the middle of August we were ready for a break in the weather and Woodstock had a tradition of one "fair-weather holiday" each year. After two months of endless rain, we would wake one morning to a cloudless sky, the sun rising bright and warm, the first hint of dryness in the air. My brothers and I ate breakfast hurriedly, glancing out of the windows in disbelief at the sunlight on the oak leaves, the blue expanse of the sky. After weeks of overcast mornings, of dripping branches, thunderstorms, and mist, it was like a miracle. As I walked to school, I kept looking up for clouds, expecting that any moment a shadow would cross in front of me as the sun was hidden from view. If no clouds were visible by the first bell that morning, by eight o'clock precisely on the principal's watch, a fair weather holiday was declared. In anticipation, I could feel the dampness lifting off the classroom floors and out of the joints in the wooden desks, the swollen window frames contracting, the trees soaking in the sunlight and giving off a musty fragrance, the sweet scent of deodar and oak, the resinous odor of the pines. We stared expectantly out the window as our homeroom teacher paused a moment, perhaps waiting for an errant cloud to creep up over the ridge. Shouts could be heard from other classrooms as a fair-weather holiday was announced, cries of celebration. Without waiting any longer we burst into the halls and stampeded through the quadrangle, saluting Miss Wait, the headmistress, as she stood scowling in front of her office. The chokidars grinned at us as we escaped from school, out into the first clear day in weeks, set free from the depressing monotony of the monsoon. It didn't matter where we ran, out along the Tehri Road as far as Jabberkhet or into the bazaar, down to the dormitories or up to the top of the hill.

By afternoon the clouds usually rolled in again and the early brightness of the morning was obscured by the returning mist, a heavy shower of rain that would catch us unprepared, without our umbrellas or ponchos, and return the hillside to its opaque contours, the shifting layers of mist.

Around the middle of September the monsoon finally came to an end. The ferns began to turn brown, the beetles disappeared, and the mist burned off before dawn. The nights turned clear and brilliant and the temperatures grew cold enough to make us realize that winter was only a month or two away. The cicadas fell silent and shed their skins, crisp dry husks clinging to the twigs of oak trees, emptied of life. The scorpions and spiders vanished, our leech bites healed, and the peacock orchids withered away. The moss lost its luster, turning darker shades of green or brown. And when it rained there was none of the force and fury of the monsoon. The sustained battering of earlier storms became a softer, gentle patter on the corrugated tin roofs.

DOWN ON THE PLAINS

From the Landour hillside we looked southward over the plains of North India, across an area known as the Doab, the land of two rivers. To the east was the Ganga, flowing out of the mountains at Rishikesh, a broad seam of water, stretching in a straight line as far as I could see. The Jumna lay to the west, a smaller, more sinuous river, curving like a python as it cut through the low escarpment of the Siwalik hills. Much older than the Himalayas, this parallel range of mountains enclosed the Dehra Dun Valley, a fertile strip of sal forests and rice fields, no more than fifteen miles across. The Siwaliks had been worn down by centuries of erosion, the ridges carved into strange, surrealistic shapes and overgrown with dense jungles. Looking down from the elevation of Landour the horizon lay far beyond the Siwaliks, where the two rivers disappeared into the dusty haze of the Gangetic Plain.

The sources of the Ganga and Jumna were only forty miles apart, in the snow peaks and glaciers to the north, but they flowed over four hundred miles before finally converging at their confluence in Allahabad. On a clear day the sunlight reflected off both rivers with a metallic sheen and they looked like two veins of ore running through the land. For me the Ganga and Jumna seemed to be borders, lines drawn upon a map, the boundaries of my boyhood world.

A few weeks after I was born my parents moved from Landour to Allahabad, where they spent the winter months continuing their language study. Ewing Christian College and the Agricultural Institute were located in Allahabad, the largest Presbyterian mission station in Uttar Pradesh. According to my uncle Jim, who wrote a history of Christianity in North India, the mission at Allahabad was established by accident. In the middle of the nineteenth century a printing press, which had been donated by church groups in America for publishing evangelical literature and Bibles, was being shipped upriver from Calcutta to the Punjab. The riverboat in which the press was being transported hit a sandbar at Allahabad and sank. The cargo was salvaged and the missionaries decided that this was as good a place as any to set up their printing operations. Eventually Allahabad became an important center for publishing and a government press was established as well as several newspapers and A. H. Wheeler & Company, the first publishers to print Kipling's books.

Though I don't remember living in Allahabad, my parents would later tell me about sailing excursions we took in wooden country boats, tacking across the breeze between the bridges. For anyone who has lived in North India, the Sangam, or confluence of the Ganga and Jumna, had a spiritual significance, the union of two sacred rivers that enclosed the verdant plains of the Doab. It was also a place where religions converged. The literal translation of Allahabad is "the city of God," and this name was given by Muslim rulers several centuries ago, but Allahabad was also an important pilgrimage center for Hindus. Every twelve years, during the Kumbh Mela, hundreds of thousands of worshipers descended on the city to bathe at the temple ghats, near the confluence. As a child, I also heard stories of a third river which flowed into the Ganga at Allahabad, a mythical, subterranean stream that joined the waters of the Sangam, forming a sacred triad. I remember hearing my parents and my aunt and uncle talking about these rivers and how they represented the three major Hindu deities—Siva, Vishnu, and Bhrama. In a juxtaposition of symbols, I understood that the confluence of these three rivers could just as easily serve as a metaphor of the Christian trinity—Father, Son, and Holy Ghost.

.   .   .

Until 1966, when we moved permanently to Mussoorie, our lives were divided between the mountains and the plains of Uttar Pradesh, the largest and most populous state of India. In summer we would come up to Landour with my mother and live in one of the houses on the hillside, but as soon as it got cooler on the plains we would return to the mission compounds, where my father worked. I have no recollection of Allahabad, where we lived when I was very young, though I can place myself in Fategarh, when I would have been three or four years old. Our home was a mud-brick bungalow with deep verandas and high, vaulted ceilings. The walls were whitewashed and the windows were covered with dusty screens upon which chipkalis, or geckos, stalked mosquitoes and moths. There were termites in the woodwork and lying in bed I could hear them chewing at the beams and lintels of the house. In the garden was a frog pond near the poinsettia bushes and a hand pump where every morning the bhishti would come to fill his goatskin water bag. He would circle our bungalow, spraying a jet of water between his fingers to lay the red dust in the driveway. The smell of wet earth filled the air, a fresh, clean scent. In front of our bungalow stood a giant banyan tree in which there lived a cobra that we never saw. While our ayah watched over us, Joe and I would swing on the vines of the banyan tree, those twisted, snakelike tendrils hanging down from the spreading branches.

Fategarh was situated on the banks of the Ganga, about fifty miles upstream from Allahabad. There was a mission hospital across the road from the compound and several Christian schools nearby. I remember going for picnics on the banks of the Ganga with Ted and Jeannette Moore, who were public health workers at the hospital in Fategarh. The Moores had a red jeep station wagon and we would drive out onto the broad, sandy banks of the Ganga, not far from the burning ghats, where Hindus cremated their dead. While we sat and ate our sandwiches and carrot sticks, Uncle Ted and Aunt Jeannette would walk along the riverbank and collect the remains of human skeletons in gunnysacks. These bones were sometimes sent to Christian medical schools for students to study anatomy. One time, while Joe and I were digging in the sand, we discovered part of a skull which was charred and blackened, the grisly relic of a recent cremation.

In winter most of the water from the Ganga was diverted into a network of canals that irrigated the Doab. We often went for picnics on the canal banks near Fategarh, which were lined with groves of mango trees. Joe and I would climb the lower branches or dig holes in the termite castles that grew at their roots. The water in the canals was full of silt, with flecks of mica reflecting the sunlight. Though I hadn't yet learned how to swim, I would wade in up to my knees and splash about in the cold water. The canals flowed steadily past, their chalky currents cutting into the grassy embankment. My parents told me that this water came from the Himalayas and I imagined that if we got in a boat and sailed upstream we would eventually reach Mussoorie.

While we lived in Fategarh we had a pet black buck, an antelope which my parents bought from a group of tribal hunters. The black buck was a young male and had long spiral horns. He was taller than I, with black and white markings and thin, tapered legs. We named him Hira, which means diamond, and kept him in our angan, the walled enclosure at the back of the bungalow. Hira was very shy and I would stand at the edge of the angan and hold out a Britannia biscuit for him to eat. He approached me cautiously, one step at a time, his delicate hooves leaving heart-shaped prints in the dust, and took the biscuit from my hand. There was a custard apple tree growing in one corner of the angan and Hira used to eat the leaves and the green fruit off the lower branches.

Black buck were once plentiful all over India and my father used to tell me that he remembered riding by train from Bombay to Delhi when he was a boy and watching them racing alongside the tracks. The herds of antelope kept pace with the steam engine, like porpoises leaping in front of the bow of a ship. By the late fifties and early sixties the number of black buck had declined significantly, killed off by hunters, their habitat destroyed. While Hira lived with us, he remained wild and uncontrollable, jumping about the tiny enclosure as if someday he might spring over the brick walls and run away. When we moved from Fategarh to Etah, my parents gave Hira to Lois Visscher, one of the doctors at the mission hospital in Fategarh. Aunt Lois was a spinster, a missahib, very tall and thin, with a brusque, no-nonsense manner. Later, when we went back to Fategarh for a visit, my parents took me to see Hira. He had become more tame and Aunt Lois would wrestle with him, grabbing both of his sharp horns in her hands as he tried to butt and shake free from her grip.

* * *

Of all the mission compounds where we lived on the plains, I remember Etah most clearly. It was a dusty roadside town in the heart of the Doab region. There was a small agricultural college in Etah and the Slater Poultry Farm, named after a former Presbyterian missionary who had introduced American breeds of chickens to the area, White Leghorns and Rhode Island Reds. My father's work was mostly with the village churches, which were scattered throughout the district. He also started several development projects with rural Christian communities. One of these was a weaving center for women, and he designed and built the looms himself, as well as a machine for beating moonj grass, which was woven into place mats. This machine worked by pedal power and had a series of large wooden mallets that came crashing down like a medieval battering ram. At the back of our bungalow in Etah was a workshop where my father built all kinds of things, including the prototype of a prefabricated shop for bicycle repairs and a plywood boat for duck hunting that leaked so badly it was never used. The workshop was piled high with discarded pieces of my father's inventions and had a sweet, astringent smell of sawdust and turpentine.

By the mid-sixties many of the Presbyterian missionaries had started to leave India, and my parents were among the last to remain. For years the churches in America had supported hundreds of village congregations all across North India, but this paternalistic relationship eventually had to end. One of my father's duties in Etah was to retire and pay off the village pastors, or padris, who received a monthly salary from the Presbyterians. It was a difficult job, for many of these padris were men whom my father had worked with closely. Most of them came from tiny, impoverished congregations which the Indian church was unable to support. I remember very clearly when the village padris gathered on the lawns in front of our bungalow to receive their severance pay. Cotton dhurries were spread on the grass for the pastors to sit upon and altogether there must have been forty or fifty of them. My father was seated at a table, with a cashbox and ledger in front of him. As he called out each of their names the padris came forward and signed the documents that ended their employment and took the envelopes of money. My brothers and I watched all of this from inside the house, not fully understanding what was taking place but sensing the solemnity of this occasion. Some years later, my father was also given the job of transferring most of the Presbyterian properties to the Church of North India, including the mission compounds where we had lived. In this way he oversaw the dismantling of the Presbyterian mission in India, an empire of sorts.

During the seven years we lived in Etah, my brothers and I had free run of the compound, where we played with our friends, the children of Indian Christian families. Unlike Fategarh, where we lived near the main bazaar, our compound in Etah was located on the outskirts of town. Etah district had one of the highest crime rates in all of India and the area was famous for dacoits or bandits. We were often warned not to wander beyond the compound walls for fear of being kidnapped. Not far from our house was the district jail, which looked like a feudal fortress, with high brick walls and watchtowers on either side of a heavy iron gate. Almost every day we would see parties of policemen walking by on the road, leading prisoners in chains and leg irons. Though we were never attacked by dacoits, the threat was always there and I was told a story about a young boy who had been held for ransom. When his parents failed to pay the money for his release, the dacoits cut him into pieces and shipped his dismembered body home in a tin trunk. We also heard stories about traps which the dacoits set for travelers along the Grand Trunk Road. One of the bandits would lie at the side of the highway, pretending that he had been hit by a car or truck. If anyone stopped to offer help the rest of the dacoits would ambush him from the sugarcane fields nearby. My father preached a sermon about that story once, in which he used the parable of the good samaritan as his text, helping an injured man at the side of the road.

Everything that lay beyond the perimeter of the compound was dangerous and threatening. We heard stories about Teli wallahs, who would kidnap children and drill holes in their skulls, hang them over a fire, and drain the precious oil from their bodies. There were also stories about hyenas, wolves, and wildcats that lived in the ravines around the compound. My brothers and I were particularly frightened of the wildcats that came to raid the poultry farm at night, and my father would sit up for them with his shotgun. We had a chokidar, or night watchman, on the compound and he would do his rounds each evening, tapping a bamboo lathi against the steps of our bungalow and blowing a whistle to chase off intruders. Whenever I woke up at night I would listen for that sound, the reassuring tap tap of the chokidar's staff and the shrill, insistent whistle.

There was one other American family living on the Etah compound, Walter and Margaret Griffiths, who left after we had been there for a year. Once they moved away, we were the only foreigners in Etah. Whenever we went outside the compound with my parents, into town for shopping trips or visiting village churches, crowds would collect around our car. This was something that I got used to, for there was no escaping the fact that we were objects of curiosity, with our sunburned faces and blond hair. The crowds stared at us with puzzlement and wonder, whispering among themselves and pointing at our clothes. Mostly there were children who gathered around, watching us as if we were some kind of traveling circus. Inevitably someone would ask where we were from and I would say, "Etah" or "Mussoorie."

"Yes, but from where else? Which country?"

"Am'rika," I'd reply reluctantly, as if the secret had to be told. The children would try out English words that they had learned in school. "Hello. Hello. How are you? Good afternoon. Good afternoon." As soon as one of them started there would be a chorus of eager voices calling out to us in clipped copybook phrases. My brothers and I would answer them in Hindustani and this only added to their amusement. Most of the time we tried to ignore the staring crowds but their constant gaze could get irritating and I would tell them to go away and leave us alone. This never worked and if we got angry one or two of the children would start calling us names: "Bhurrey" (Blondie), "Gorey" (Whitey), and "Lal Bandar" (Red Monkey). I would reply with my own insults in Hindustani, getting angrier and more frustrated all the time. As we got back into our car and drove away a pebble or stone might hit the rear windshield or the crowd of children would race after us and climb onto the bumper, shouting and jeering, chasing us out of town.

My own mother tongue was a mixture of Hindustani and English. For the first five years of my life I used both languages interchangeably, even with my parents. Our ayah and our cook, as well as the other servants who worked in our home, spoke to me in Hindustani. As I grew older and made friends with children on the mission compounds, I absorbed the dialect of eastern Uttar Pradesh without learning the formal rules of grammar. My brothers also grew up speaking Hindustani and that is what we spoke among ourselves when we were small, throwing in an English word or phrase whenever necessary. I don't think, when I was very young, that I was conscious of the distinctions between one language and the other. Hindustani and English seemed to flow together naturally without dissonance or contradictions. It was only when I started school that I had to separate the two, discovering that I had learned each language imperfectly and spoke a pidgin dialect all my own.

In Etah and Landour, my brothers and I grew up as sahibs—"Stevie sahib," "Joey sahib," and "Andy sahib." That's what we were called by our cooks, bearers, ayahs, gardeners, and sweepers. There were people in Mussoorie who remembered my father from the days when he was a boy and sometimes he was still called "Bobby Alter sahib." As children we took these titles for granted, as if they were simply part of our names. When we spoke with the servants we referred to our parents, not as "Dad" and "Mom," but as sahib and memsahib. Though we never referred to ourselves as sahibs, we accepted this title from others and played the role. There was a comfortable security about being sahibs, even "chotta sahibs"—little big shots. On the Etah compound and the Landour hillside, a hierarchy existed, from the "Burra sahib" right down to the dhobis who washed our clothes and the jamedars who swept our homes. Whether we realized it or not—and I'm sure we did—

there was a rigid caste system surrounding us and we were at the top. Looking back, I realize the injustices and exploitation, the racism and prejudice inherent in our relationships, though at the time it seemed to be the way things worked.

My closest friends in Etah were some of the servants' children, and even though there was an acknowledged difference between us, for most of the day we played and fought and argued as if there were no distinctions. At dusk, however, my brothers and I would be called indoors and my mother threw us into the tin bathtub to wash the dust and grime from our limbs. The bungalow in which we lived was a large brick building with cavernous ceilings and doorways opening in all directions. Our friends would retreat to the line of quarters at the back of the compound, where their families lived in one or two small rooms. After supper my parents put us to bed, under the white mosquito nets, which looked like giant cobwebs. As moonlight filtered through the roshandans, we listened to my mother read us books in English, Kipling's *Rikki Tikki Tavi* or *The Just So Stories* and C. S. Lewis's *Narnia* series. Falling asleep to those bedtime stories, I would dream of running beyond the limits of the compound, out into the ravines where the hyenas and jackals waited, where the mongoose danced around the cobra, where the dacoits cut children into pieces and the Teli wallahs squatted in front of their campfires, where black buck raced beside the railway tracks with graceful, bounding strides. In the safety of my charpoy bed, under the rustling tent of mosquito netting, I would move between one imaginary world and the next, where Mowgli the wolf-child encountered *The Lion, the Witch and the Wardrobe*.

The following morning, as soon as the sunlight came streaming through the roshandans, I leaped from my bed onto the cold brick floors, pulled on my clothes, and raced outdoors to find my friends waiting for me: Saroj and Eddu (whose real name was Edward), Kushan and Nagma, Charaunji's children, and a boy named Moon, whose face I can't remember. Together we would go hunting with our gullails, slingshots which we made out of the forks of shesham branches and strips of rubber cut from bicycle tubes. Each day we hunted for birds and rabbits in the palm groves and channa fields on the far side of the Agricultural College. We would lie in wait for the gray hornbills, which nested in the tamarind trees near the poultry farm, watching for their slow, uneven flight and firing all of our gullails at once, a volley of pebbles arching into the sky and missing the bird by an inch or two. Most of the time we hunted for doves, pigeons, and edible swifts which nested in the dry wells and ruined buildings at the back of the compound. Sometimes we even hunted for rats and bandicoots that lived in a network of burrows beneath our bungalow.

During the winter months, my father and Mr. Watford, the principal of the Agricultural College, would go hunting for nilgai, a large antelope, as big as a horse. Nilgai were common in the scrub jungles and sugarcane fields around Etah and they often destroyed the crops. The name, nilgai, literally means "blue cow," and the males had horns very similar to a bull's. For this reason the Hindu villagers would not kill or eat nilgai, though as Christians we were free to hunt them. Whenever my father and Mr. Watford were successful the whole compound would have meat.

Within a few miles of Etah there were a number of jheels or seasonal ponds. From November to March, migratory ducks and geese settled on the jheels and my father went duck hunting early in the mornings or just at dusk, when the birds circled overhead in wheeling rings. He would come back with mallards and pintails, teal and bar-headed geese. Our cook, Ram Dayal, roasted the ducks or made a curry out of them, though I never liked their gamy taste or picking the pellets of lead from between my teeth.

One of the projects that my father started in Etah was raising pigs. Many of the Christian villagers in the area came from lower caste backgrounds and ate pork, unlike the Muslims or higher-caste Hindus, for whom it was taboo. In one section of the Etah compound my father established a pig farm where he raised White

Yorkshire sows to distribute among the villagers. These pigs, which were a fleshy pink color, originally came from England and weighed twice as much as the local breeds, which were small and had a ridge of coarse black bristles on their backs, like wild boars. My friends and I often played near the pig farm, a walled enclosure with breeding pens and feeding troughs. I remember watching the pigs mating, the boars' penises like pink sticks of peppermint candy, and the newborn piglets suckling at their mother's teats, the shrill squeals and the smell of mud and filth.

The caretaker of the pig farm was a man named Budh Singh, though everyone called him Buddhoo, which means simpleton. When the pigs were eight or ten months old the sows were herded off to the nearby villages and the boars were shipped away to a government slaughterhouse in Aligarh. Only two or three of the larger males were kept for breeding purposes. One of them was an enormous, mean-tempered boar who finally gored Buddhoo in the leg. Ordinarily, when the pigs had to be rounded up, half a dozen of the young men on the compound would go into the enclosure and wrestle them to the ground. We enjoyed watching this frantic chase through the mud, the boars grunting and screaming as all of us cheered them on. But after Buddhoo was gored nobody had the courage to enter the enclosure and my father was forced to shoot the boar.

Most of the compound came out to watch and there must have been more than a hundred people standing along the wall as my father entered the enclosure with his rifle. The boar was about thirty yards away, rooting in the mud with his snout and ignoring the crowd. My father pulled back the bolt action on his .30-06 and eased a shell into the chamber. Raising the rifle to his shoulder he took aim. The boar was standing broadside, offering an easy target. He seemed quite harmless, his coiled tail flicking away the flies. I had my ears plugged and the loud blast of the rifle made me blink my eyes. When I opened them the boar was lying on his side, all four legs kicking furiously. The other pigs had scattered at the sound of the shot and there was a frantic chorus of squealing and grunting.

The boar kept kicking for a while before it died, dark ribbons of blood seeping out of its shoulder and flowing into the gray mud. My father worked the bolt on the rifle and picked up the brass casing from the ground as the crowd of people who were watching leaped into the enclosure and surrounded the dying animal. Soon afterward, a fire was lit in the center of the compound and the dead boar was lifted up by its four legs and lowered into the flames to singe away its bristles. The smoke had a sharp, pungent smell of charred skin and hair. After fifteen or twenty minutes the carcass was removed and placed on a sheet of corrugated tin, where it was butchered and the meat divided among the residents on the compound. One of the first things to be cut off were the boar's ears, which were given to my friends and me. We stuck them on two sticks, roasting the ears over the remains of the fire and eating them as soon as they were crisp.

It is surprising that my brothers and I did not get sick more often. Ram Dayal would boil our drinking water and wash our vegetables and fruit in potassium permanganate but with our friends we would eat almost anything we gathered on the compound, whether it was the mulberries which we picked from the trees in the poultry farm and sprinkled with salt and red chili powder, or the green tamarind pods that we shot down with our slingshots. The raw tamarind was so sour it made my ears ring. Just beyond the compound was a brick kiln, with two large chimneys which sent out columns of black smoke when the fires were lit. The men who worked there used to let us bury sweet potatoes in the mounds of dirt that covered the kiln. After an hour or so, we dug them out of the ground and the sweet potatoes would be completely cooked. We also raided the sugarcane carts that passed by on the road in front of our house. When the cart drivers weren't looking we would grab a stalk and yank it free. Breaking the sugar-cane and peeling strips away with our teeth, we chewed the sweet pulp, sticky streams of juice trickling down our chins.

A procession of vendors passed by on the road each day and we would wait at the gate of the compound to buy peanut toffee and gol guppas, a hollow pastry filled with pepper water. If we didn't have any pocket money left, the chaat wallahs took bits of brass or copper as payment instead of coins. I would search through my father's workshop for any scraps of metal left over from his projects, strands of copper wire or steel washers. Once I stole a brass faucet from the tapstand in the garden, exchanging it for a kilo of gajak, a kind of candy made from sesame seeds and raw sugar. Several times a week the churan wallah would come by on his bicycle. He sold a sour-salty potion made of different minerals and herbs, which was supposed to be good for the digestion. As we held out our hands, he dipped his spoon into the jars of churan and sprinkled a little onto our palms for us to lick. The churan had a sharp, sour taste that made our eyes water, but we always asked for more.

There were only two times that I remember really getting sick in Etah. Once was when I jabbed my leg on a thorn from a babool tree and my knee swelled up to the size of a cantaloupe. I had to be rushed to Fategarh, where Dr. Robinson removed three syringefuls of pus and gave me a shot of penicillin. The other time I climbed into a pile of straw which had been used as litter in the chicken coops, after which I developed an allergic reaction and broke out in hives. Every day for a week my mother painted me with a solution of Gentian Violet, which turned my skin dark purple, the color of an eggplant.

*　　*　　*

There was a cyclical rhythm to our lives in Etah, the winter months that we spent on the plains and the summers in Landour, as we migrated with the seasons. Once I started school at Woodstock we stayed up in the mountains for longer periods of time and I kept wishing that we could return to Etah, where my days were spent playing endless games within the boundaries of the compound. But once we moved down to the plains for the winter holidays, I longed to be in the hills again, with a separate set of friends, missing the winding trails and the oak and rhododendron forests.

One winter, when I was nine years old, I got a pair of homing pigeons, which I kept in an empty chicken coop behind our bungalow in Etah. I fed them millet from my hands until they were so tame they let me pick them up and stroke their feathers. I used to release my pigeons from our roof and watch them wheeling overhead, circling beyond the edges of the compound, diving and tumbling in the wind. These birds were mottled white and black, unlike the wild pigeons, which were a sooty gray. Sometimes they flew so far away that they disappeared, but in an hour or two they would return, spiraling down through the air and landing with a flutter of wings at the door of their cage.

By the next year my pigeons had multiplied. Several of their young had hatched while we were away in Mussoorie, and I bought two or three more birds from the Etah bazaar. Altogether I must have had more than a dozen pigeons and each of them had a name. One day, after they returned from flying, I discovered that there was an extra pigeon which I didn't recognize. It had light brown feathers and a ring around its foot. This bird must have belonged to someone else but it was lost and had joined my flock. The new pigeon was timid though eventually it came and ate from my hand. Catching it, I trimmed the feathers on the inside of its wings so it couldn't fly for several weeks. By the time these feathers grew out again the pigeon recognized my cage as home, and when I set it free it always returned with the rest of the birds.

The following spring, when we went back up to Mussoorie, I took two of my pigeons with me. I wanted to see if they would fly all the way back to Etah on their own. Two or three days after we arrived in the hills I released the pair. They took off from the porch of our house at Pine Rock, flying out across the valley toward

Dehra Dun. It was a clear day and I could see their white wings flapping as they flew south over Witch's Hill, heading in the direction of the plains. I watched until they were tiny specks that disappeared into the clouds. That evening I waited to see if the pigeons would come back, listening for the drumming of their wings or the cooing sound they made, but the birds did not return.

My father was still in Etah, and I sent him a postcard telling him that I had released the pigeons and asking him to let me know as soon as they arrived. Each day I waited for word that they had reached Etah safely, but when my father's letter finally came, he said the pigeons had not appeared. My disappointment hung over me for several weeks and I tried to imagine what had happened to the birds. They could have been killed by hawks or crows but it was more likely that they had joined another flock, unable to find their own way home.

·   ·   ·

The closest city to Etah was Agra, about two hours away by car. We would go there once or twice a year, usually when my parents had visitors who wanted to see the Taj Mahal. As we approached the city each of us would try to be the first to spot the white marble dome in the distance. There was a railway crossing before we entered Agra and a bridge across the Jumna. On the banks of the river stood a line of Hindu temples and shrines with brightly painted idols of Hanuman, the monkey god, and the goddess Kali with her scarlet tongue and eight arms flailing wildly as she danced over the body of the buffalo demon. I remember being frightened and fascinated by those images when I was very young. There was something grotesquely appealing about these idols, and their bright colors and dramatic postures reminded me of cartoon characters in a comic book.

Whenever we visited the Taj Mahal my parents took a picnic lunch with us and we would sit in the shade of the neem trees at the edges of the garden, eating hard-boiled eggs and sandwiches.

Dozens of brahminy kites and crows perched in the trees around the garden, and the birds swooped down and snatched things from our hands. Rhesus monkeys also lived in the garden and they would come up boldly, a few feet away from where we sat, and beg for food.

The Taj itself never really impressed me as a boy and I didn't like going inside the tomb. We had to take off our shoes or wear cloth slippers before entering the mausoleum. On the walls of the central chamber were inlaid flowers made of semiprecious stones, irises with petals of lapis lazuli, and carnelian poppies with leaves of agate and jade. The tomb was dark inside and smelled of incense, stuffy and full of tourists shuffling about. The only part I enjoyed was climbing the minarets, going up the spiral staircase that made me dizzy. Stepping out onto the circular balcony I could see the garden spread below with fountains and reflecting pools. In the opposite direction was the river Jumna, beyond which lay the rooftops of Agra and the red walls of the sandstone fort, where the emperor Shāh Jāhan was imprisoned by his son, Aurangzeb.

Once or twice we went to see the Taj Mahal by moonlight. The tall minarets and the marble dome seemed to glow with an eerie luminescence as the full moon rose above the shadowy branches of the neem trees. While my parents and their friends sat and admired the scene, my brothers and I took off our clothes and swam in the reflecting pools. Splashing about in the shallow water, our pale skin white as moonlit marble, we must have looked like playful ghosts.

After visiting Agra we often drove on to Fatehpur Sikri, a Mogul city built by Akbar. Wandering about the empty sandstone structures, I tried to imagine what it must have been like when the emperor was in residence. There was a giant ludo board where dancing girls were used as gaming pieces, and the guides showed us iron rings in the ground, where the royal elephants were tethered. Condemned prisoners were said to have been crushed to death under the elephants' feet.

Inside the walls of Fatehpur Sikri was an abandoned mosque which faced west, toward Mecca. On one of our visits I remember seeing a lone Muslim praying there, bowing down until his forehead touched the floor. Unlike the Hindu shrines with their painted idols, there were no images in the mosque. The walls were bare except for a few geometric patterns carved into the stone, abstract symbols of a faceless God. A short distance from the mosque lay the tomb of Sheikh Salim Chishti, who inspired Akbar to start his own religion, Din Illahi, a combination of Islam, Christianity, and Hinduism. Pilgrims visiting Sheikh Chishti's grave would tie colored threads to the marble screens in the hope that their prayers might be answered. The tourist guides who showed us around always made a point of telling us that one of Akbar's wives was Christian. Her name was Miriam and the guides showed us the rooms in the harem where she once lived.

The city of Fatehpur Sikri was abandoned soon after it was built because there was not enough water to supply the population. The emperor moved back to Agra, leaving his palaces deserted. Near the Buland Darwaza, the massive gateway to the city, was a tank of stagnant green water, and whenever we visited Fatehpur Sikri I would watch young boys from the nearby village diving for coins from the ruined sandstone walls.

.   .   .

Outside the compound gate in Etah, about a furlong down the road, was a small mud hut, the home of the fireworks man, who made rockets and firecrackers. My friends and I would sit and watch him rolling the gunpowder into paper cylinders and inserting the fuses with his fingers, which were stained black as charcoal. The old man made different kinds of fireworks, clay fountains shaped like pomegranates that spewed out jets of colored sparks, flaming hoops the size of bicycle wheels which spun around on bamboo frames, and bombs as big as sticks of dynamite. Diwali, the Hindu festival of lights, was the most popular time of year for setting off fireworks, and the sky over Etah would be lit up with rockets and flares. My friends and I bought bombs and firecrackers from the old man, who sold them for much less than fireworks cost in the bazaar. We set them off all over the compound, like a band of anarchists, bursting tin cans and flowerpots, terrorizing the pigs and chickens.

The Dasehra festival preceded Diwali in late October or early November, depending on the Hindu calendar. The Ram Lila, a reenactment of episodes from the Ramayana epic, was performed each year during Dasehra. The festivities would begin with a procession in which the actors, dressed as gods, were paraded through the chowk at the center of Etah's main bazaar. Riding in an open truck decorated like a chariot, Rama and his wife, Sita, sat on thrones, with gilded crowns and sequined costumes. Hanuman stood beside them, carrying a heavy mace, his wire tail swinging back and forth. Each night at dusk, as villagers arrived to watch the epic unfold, bullock carts and horse-drawn tongas would line the roads near the Ram Lila ground, an open field on the far side of the bazaar. We never went to see the Ram Lila performances, for they usually started late at night, and the Christian community kept their distance from these events. The only part of Dasehra that we watched was the final night, when Ravanna and his brothers were set on fire. This was the climax of the epic, when Rama rescues Sita and, with the help of Hanuman, sets the city of Lanka ablaze. At the far end of the Ram Lila ground stood three statues of the demon Ravanna and his two brothers. Brightly colored heads and arms made of paper and bamboo were attached to the huge masonry figures and these were filled with fireworks. At sunset the three demons were set on fire, their heads exploding in a barrage of bombs and rockets. I remember watching this from my father's shoulders, looking out over the heads of a multitude of spectators. The dusty twilight was ripped apart by a staccato rattle of firecrackers going off, the flames bursting from Ravanna's mouth, his eyes becoming pinwheels of fire and jets of colored sparks shooting from his ears. Within a few minutes the whole thing was over, as the flames consumed the painted paper, tinsel, and bamboo, which burned to nothing and left only the headless figures standing in the gathering darkness.

At other times of the year the Ram Lila ground was used for country fairs and circuses. Once again, villagers from miles around would come to Etah in their bullock carts, lined up along both sides of the road. The oxen chewed patiently at their feed bags while the owners wandered through the sideshow stalls and the vendors sold cheap toys, hollow rubber parakeets and dolls, cheap lozenges and sweets, bottled drinks of every color from bright green to dazzling magenta. There were Ferris wheels and merry-go-rounds at the fair, and dancing monkeys that performed pirouettes in time to the rattle of tiny handheld drums.

Every winter the Apollo circus came to Etah and huge tents were set up on the Ram Lila ground. My parents would take us to see the circus along with all of our friends from the compound. In one of the sideshows I saw a caged hyena that paced back and forth, as if waiting for a chance to leap out at me. The fetid, feline stench of the tigers and lions filled the tent and we watched them snarl at the trainers, who wore pith helmets and carried whips. One time we sat in the front row and a tiger's tail was sticking through the bars in front of us, twitching only a few feet away. Crowds of villagers were packed into their seats and Hindi film songs played over the loudspeakers. There were acrobats and clowns, as well as elephants that kicked soccer balls and acted as if they were drunk, dancing bears, and horses which raced around the ring with women on their backs. These acts were followed by the globe of death in which daredevils on motorcycles circled around and around like human gyroscopes. There were other miraculous feats like the strong man who lay down in the middle of the ring while an elephant stood on his chest. But for me the high point of the circus was when the clowns set up two wooden ramps on either side of the ring and we could hear the revving of an engine outside, throttled to a menacing roar. Everyone fell silent and then, at a signal from the clowns, a white jeep came racing through the flaps of the tent and up the ramp. For a second or two the vehicle was airborne, flying over our heads, then disappearing through the other side of the tent. My brothers and I were so impressed with the jumping jeep that we built ramps of our own in the driveway of the compound and rode our bicycles across, defying gravity.

．　．　．

When we celebrated Christmas in Etah we used a potted cypress and hung our stockings above the brick fireplace in the living room of the bungalow. It got cold during December and January and in the mornings there was frost on the ground. It never snowed in Etah, though the floodplains near the compound were covered in a crust of white saltpeter which I tried to imagine as snow. Christmas was the most important holiday in our family and we often got together with Uncle Jim and Aunt Barry and our cousins Marty, John, and Tom. My brothers and I waited eagerly for our presents, soccer balls and cricket bats, badminton sets and new clothes my mother had tailored for us in Mussoorie, cotton bush shirts and khaki shorts.

Each year my father made special presents for us in his workshop. One Christmas I got a miniature loom, just like the ones he made for the women's weaving project. The same year Joe got a go-cart, which we took up to Landour and rode down the hills. The brakes didn't work very well and we nearly killed ourselves before the go-cart finally fell apart. Another time my father made a slingshot gun for me, something like a crossbow, with rubber thongs and a bamboo trigger. It was much more powerful than my gullail but impossible to aim. The only thing I ever shot with the slingshot gun was a parakeet in the eucalyptus trees behind our house.

What I remember most about Christmas in Etah were the bands that used to come to the compound early in the morning.

These were wedding bands from the town and they would arrive at three or four o'clock and begin to play outside our bungalow. At least three different bands came around each Christmas morning, refusing to leave until my father gave them money. They played a couple of Christmas carols but most of their repertoire was Hindi film tunes and one song which sounded like "The Bear Climbed Over the Mountain." These tunes were played at top volume on trumpets and trombones, with a few shrill clarinets and a thundering bass drum.

On Christmas morning we would go to a special service in the brick church near the Christian girls school in town. The sanctuary was decorated with crepe paper streamers, colored balloons, and a tiny Christmas tree weighed down by strands of tinsel and bits of cotton. My father and the pastor of the church stood at the front, near the altar, dressed in their white cassocks and stoles. The women all sat on one side of the aisle and the men on the other and we sang Christmas hymns in Urdu, "Sunno Falki Fauj Sharif," which didn't quite translate as "Hark the Herald Angels Sing." After the service we would go for tea and dinner at the homes of Christian families, the Watfords' and the Saunders' as well as Mr. Timothy Lall's, where we would be given special sweets, ladoos and barfi, and always a wedge of Christmas cake, a dense compost of candied fruit and nuts, iced with brittle marzipan, so sweet that it made my gums itch.

*   *   *

After we left Etah and moved permanently to Mussoorie in 1966, I missed those winter months that we spent on the plains. The landscape of the Doab always had nostalgic associations for me, the brilliant yellow of mustard fields, the tawny mud walls of thatch-roofed huts, a village tank in which purple water hyacinths bloomed above a floating carpet of leaves, the prehistoric shapes of buffaloes wallowing in the black ooze. There were distinctive sounds on the plains, the calls of lapwings, the "Did you do it?"

birds, the creaking of an unoiled oxcart wheel and the rhythmic pulse of tube wells in the distance, the dry whisper of sugarcane stalks. Each time of day had a different quality, the pale dawn seeping through the dark foliage of a mango grove, the midmorning sun warming the bricks on the roof of our bungalow, pendulous weaverbird nests hanging from the branches of thorn trees in the afternoon, and with the approach of evening, the most magical hour of all, "cow dust time," when the cattle were herded back to the villages, the ringing of bells and the shouting of children walking home along the rutted country roads, through a lingering twilight of dust and woodsmoke.

By the end of February it began to get warm again and during March the first andhi, or dust storm, would arrive in Etah, the sky turning the color of cured tobacco as yellow waves of sand blew in from the deserts of Rajasthan. We would close all of the doors and windows of the bungalow, breathing in the tiny particles of dust, a choked, uncomfortable feeling in my throat. The hot, dry wind of the andhi blew the castor trees about, their broad leaves flapping like broken wings. The chickens in the poultry farm huddled on their roosts and the pigs burrowed into the mud. Everyone would run for cover, cyclists pedaling frantically along the road, trying to get home before the storm. From the roof of our house we could see the clouds of dust approaching, dark formations billowing above the horizon, palm fronds scraping in the wind and flocks of pigeons sailing overhead, flecks of white and gray against the ominous sky. As the andhi drew closer, we could hear the shutters banging and the sand clawing at the screens. Miniature dunes and drifts appeared along the crevices of the doors and windowsills. The air became unbreathable and I felt as if I would suffocate, drowning in a sea of sand.

Soon after the dust storms started and the temperatures began to climb, we would pack our trunks and duffel bags to leave for the hills, driving through the oppressive heat toward Mussoorie. The Doab was transformed into a dry and lifeless wasteland, the canals reduced to narrow channels choked with mud, and the mustard fields plowed under, barren furrows and clods of gray earth. The ducks and geese had already flown north, beyond the high Himalayas, and the jheels dried up into cracked mudflats. Even the leaves on the mango trees lost their luster, and the only flowers that bloomed were the limp purple blossoms on the besharam booti, a hardy shrub that needed very little water; its name meant "shameless plant." Heading north from Etah we would drive through the towns of Aligarh and Bulandshahr, which were once important Mogul cities. In the relentless midday heat, they seemed bereft of life, drained of history and almost colorless under a shroud of dust. At the sides of the road we saw flocks of vultures huddled around the carcass of a dead horse or buffalo, squabbling over the entrails and tearing the rotting flesh from the bones. We drove and drove, until eventually we came to the Siwalik hills and Dehra Dun, the higher mountains still obscured behind a khaki haze. Only as we began to climb the winding motor road to Mussoorie did I feel the first hint of coolness in the air, leaving the plains behind, escaping the dust storms and the dry, unending heat.

RIDGEWOOD

Soon after I started third grade my parents put me into boarding and returned to Etah. On the afternoon before they left Mussoorie, my father and mother walked me down the winding cement path to Ridgewood, a dormitory for younger boys, grades one through eight. A coolie followed behind us, carrying my trunk and bedding roll. It was the middle of September and I had just celebrated my eighth birthday. The monsoon was almost over and the rain had stopped, though the mist lingered on for a few more weeks. My parents must have expected me to cry and carry on, the way I'd done when I started first grade, but this time I had prepared myself. Though I felt the same hollow, plunging sensation in my chest as we made our way down the hill, there was also a feeling of excitement and anticipation, as if I was setting out on a new adventure. When we arrived at Ridgewood, Shunil Borpujari and two or three other classmates were playing in the gravel yard in front of the dormitory. I quickly said good-bye to my parents and ran to join my friends. In the confusion of whatever game we played, I completely forgot that I would not be seeing my family again for the next three months. By the time the supper bell rang, my parents had already left and I began to feel the first pangs of uncertainty, knowing that they were driving down to Etah the following day. Later that evening, after lights-out, I was overcome with panic and despair as I lay awake in the strange bunk bed. Curled up on a lumpy cotton mattress, I wept into my pillow. Despite the snuffles and snoring of the other boys in the dorm, I felt abandoned and alone.

Though I soon got used to being in boarding and enjoyed the companionship of my friends, there were recurring bouts of unhappiness at Ridgewood—the night I spilled my dinner tray and Mr. Edwards, the kitchen supervisor, shouted at me, or the time I was teased for admitting that I thought Amy Burkhalter was the prettiest girl in our class. At these moments a feeling of homesickness overwhelmed me, the sadness so deep it made my stomach ache.

The dormitories at Ridgewood were constructed by my grandfather, during the early forties, when he was principal of Woodstock. Looked at from above, the three sections of the building reminded me of giant boxcars derailed at the foot of the hill, their red tin roofs following the crooked alignment of the ridge. The dorms were long, rectangular halls with two parallel rows of bunk beds and wooden cupboards at either end. Between each dorm were apartments for houseparents as well as a dining room and study hall. On the east side of Ridgewood, just below the gravel yard, was a line of quarters where the chokidars and bearers lived.

Bo Singh and Mangal were the bearers responsible for our dorm and they looked after us with a patient and protective manner. The two of them were very different from each other. Bo Singh was overweight and jovial, ready to put up with any of our mischief and tease us back. Mangal was thin and angular, a much more sober man, who spoke to us in a restrained and quiet voice.

Every morning at seven o'clock, after the first bell rang, Bo Singh or Mangal would wake us up and make sure that we got to breakfast on time. They helped us sort our laundry and one of them walked to the bazaar each day to purchase supplies, a tin of Cherry Blossom boot polish or a new tube of Colgate toothpaste, whatever we needed. While we were away at school the bearers tidied up the dormitory for our return, tucking in the sheets and blankets that we had left hanging out in the daily rush to make our beds.

Three times a week Bo Singh and Mangal supervised our baths, lining us up in the shower room downstairs and moving us along as quickly as possible before the hot water ran out. We would queue up at the bottom of the steps, towels wrapped around our waists, clutching soap dishes and shampoo, clouds of steam rising out of the line of open showers. When our turn came, each of us stripped hurriedly and dived under spitting shower heads, soaping quickly as others shouted encouragement and insults, dirty jokes and limericks. Inevitably someone's towel would get pulled off and a goosing fight began, two or three boys circling each other like feisty bantams, protecting themselves with one hand, the other reaching out to grab their opponent's genitals. Bo Singh and Mangal would shout and throw up their hands in disapproval but by this time there was so much noise nobody paid any attention until the dorm supervisor arrived, blushing with anger, and threatened to give us all a cold shower if we didn't behave. As it was, the hot water often ran out and Bo Singh or Mangal would have to drag the last few boys in line under the shower and force them to bathe in the icy spray.

We had a number of different houseparents at Ridgewood. Some were strict and demanding like Mr. Edwards and Mr. Skelton, who paddled us with a cricket bat that had holes drilled in it to increase the pain. Others were gentle and motherly, like Mrs. Fitzroy, who was in charge of the first- and second-grade dorm, and Miss Fluff, the third-grade dorm mistress, who would go from bunk to bunk each night before lights-out and give us each a good-night kiss. By the end of the semester most of us were in love with Miss Fluff and we were jealous of her fiancé, one of the high school teachers, who came to visit every evening. Scotty Bunce claimed that he had seen them kissing through the window while he was sneaking around after lights-out.

• • •

One of the many things that I was required to bring with me to Ridgewood was a Bible, so a few weeks before I entered boarding my mother took me to buy one at the Christian bookstore on Mullingar Hill. Against her wishes, I chose a Bible with a zipper so that I could close it up like a purse or wallet. The cover was made of fake crocodile skin and the zipper ran around three sides. The pages were as thin as airmail paper, compressed together and dyed red along the edges, so that when I unzipped my Bible it looked like the crocodile was smiling, showing a scarlet mouth and serrated teeth.

Every night at Ridgewood, after study hall, we had devotions before we went to bed. Dressed in our pajamas and bathrobes we sat on the edge of our bunks while one of the houseparents read Scripture verses and prayed with us. All of my friends in Ridgewood had Bibles but very few of them had zippers, which made me feel superior. There were also pictures at the back, maps of the Holy Land and illustrations of Jesus performing miracles, healing the sick and hanging from the cross. In third grade I had difficulty reading my Bible because it was a King James version and the print was very small. Whenever I tried to focus on the dense columns of words, numbered like a railway schedule, chapter and verse, my eyes began to circle the page, confused and bored by the archaic language of the text. For devotions we were often required to memorize Scripture passages, and I would recite the words in a singsong voice, unaware of what they meant. At that age I was still too young to appreciate the poetry of the King James version and most of the stories I'd already heard in Sunday school—Moses in the bulrushes, Samson and Delilah, Jonah and the whale, David and Goliath, the Christmas tale, the parable of loaves and fishes, the prodigal son. I saw no point in reading these stories when I already knew what was going to happen in the end.

At home my parents had several different translations of the Bible, including one in Roman Urdu, which my father used when he preached in the village churches near Etah. The Urdu text was transcribed into the English alphabet, and if I stared hard at the page I could recognize a few of the words. Though the Urdu was flowery and difficult to understand, it was no less accessible to me than the verses in my King James edition. I loved the sound of Urdu as it was spoken in Etah, the congregation reciting the Lord's Prayer:

Ai hamare bap
Tu Jo Asman par hai;
Tera Nam Pak Mana jae;
Teri marzi jaise Asman
Par puri hoti hai
Zamin par bhi ho . . .

(Our father, who art in heaven,
Hallowed be thy name . . .)

As soon as I got my new Bible I went out and picked a handful of ferns to press between its pages. Growing in dense banks along the pushta walls, the Bible ferns were like a fringe of green filigree. Unzipping my book, I let the pages open at random, then gently laid each fern in place, pinching off the stems where they protruded. Every time I opened and closed the zipper on my Bible it gave me a feeling of satisfaction, the tautness of the cover and the compact weight of the Scriptures in my hand. After a week or so the pressed ferns lost their color, turning dry and brittle. I had to open the pages cautiously for fear of breaking them, and over time the Bible ferns began to disintegrate like scraps of rotted lace until there was nothing left but a powdery dust which I finally blew away.

For many years afterward, whenever I opened my Bible to one of those pages, I could see the residual impression of the ferns. A faint, indelible stain remained upon each page, the ornate silhouette of their delicate fronds. Superimposed on the printed verses, the outline of the ferns looked like a phantom script, a secret language which would never be deciphered. Trying to read my Bible I found my eyes tracing these intricate lines and shapes instead of following the text itself.

.   .   .

Our days at Ridgewood were marked by the ringing of bells. Hanging from an oak tree outside the dining room was a rusty length of iron I beam. To wake us up every morning one of the bearers would hammer on it with a metal rod, a steady beat that roused us from our beds. Later the bell was rung to signal breakfast and to tell us when to go to school. There were different beats for different times of the day, three short strokes and then a pause followed by three more, or a rapid banging that ended with a trilling flourish to call us in for supper. The ringing of the Ridgewood bell carried all over the hillside and we could hear it from as far away as the bazaar. At times it was a depressing sound, a reminder of the dull routines and loneliness of boarding.

Every weekday morning after breakfast we would have to walk up the hill from Ridgewood to the school. It was a steep climb, two-thirds of a mile, and I was often late, hurrying up the path with my shoelaces untied and shirttails flying. The high school dormitories were situated near Ridgewood, and between eight and eight-thirty swarms of students and teachers were headed in the same direction so that it almost felt as if we were racing each other up the hill.

The elementary classrooms were part of the original buildings at Woodstock, which dated back to the 1850s. Most of the rooms were dark and cold, heated only by kerosene stoves that emitted oily fumes which made our eyes sting. The walls of the school were plastered with limewash, a jaundiced yellow color. The roofs were a standard postbox red and most of the woodwork was painted green. At the center of the school lay the quadrangle, which was actually an L-shaped courtyard, paved with slate flagstones. The surrounding buildings had open verandas facing inward, with flower boxes full of pink geraniums along the upper levels. On the ground floor were the kindergarten room, a small library, and the dining hall, where everybody ate lunch. Dormitories for the younger girls were located on the upper floors, overlooking the quadrangle, a forbidden zone where boys were not allowed.

Our school days revolved around the quad, and until we entered fifth grade we seldom went up the ramp to the high school buildings or Parker Hall, except for assemblies and church services. Before school or during lunch and recess, we stayed within the confines of the quad, an unruly, shouting swarm of kids. The games we played were suited to the enclosed space, pom pom polloway and red rover, with boys and girls darting back and forth between the yellow walls, pirouetting around the pillars on the verandas and dodging outstretched hands that tried to catch them. A version of tag, pom pom polloway seemed to have been invented for the Woodstock quadrangle, and whenever I played the game anywhere else, it was never quite the same.

A brass school bell sat in one corner of the quad, near the entrance to the classrooms. It was so heavy that I had to use both hands to pick it up, the kind of bell that was made to hang around an elephant's neck. At eight o'clock each morning, one of the chaprassis, Bhawan Singh or Sattar Singh, would ring the bell to signal the start of school. A loud clanging reverberated within the courtyard walls and the chaos and shouting which had filled the quad ceased abruptly. Each class lined up in sequence, facing our teachers, from kindergarten to fifth grade. With the ringing of the school bell, Hazel Wait, our elementary headmistress, emerged from her office and patrolled the perimeter of the quad, making sure that nobody lagged behind. She inspected our lines with Napoleonic scrutiny, frowning at our red, perspiring faces, the buttons which had been torn off our shirts during the frenzied games, the cuts and bruises on our knees. At a curt nod from Miss Wait, each grade would file away to their classroom, like prisoners marching to their cells.

I don't remember much of what I was taught in elementary school. The textbooks which we used were mostly from America, even though the world of Dick, Jane, and Sally was something I had almost forgotten, along with the sidewalks and fire hydrants of Ithaca. Our teachers read us chapters from *Tom Sawyer* and taught us how to spell Mississippi, despite the fact that there weren't any picket fences in Landour and the Ganga was a more familiar river (and easier to spell). Our math books contained pages of exercises in which we were taught to add pennies, nickels, dimes, and quarters, while our pocket money consisted of five– and ten–naya paisa coins, annas and rupees instead of dollars. In many ways Woodstock and the hillside community attempted to re-create the essential elements of small-town America, that imaginary point of origin, to which we would all return. There was an underlying assumption that eventually every mish-kid would go back to the States one day, and for that reason the curriculum we studied was intended to prepare us for repatriation, that inevitable moment when we migrated back to our promised homeland across the seas.

The music we learned to sing at school was either hymns or American folk ballads, "Onward Christian Soldiers," "Way Down Upon the Swannee River," or "John Henry," songs of the pioneers. We had Scripture classes every day and some of the Bible stories which we read were accompanied by pictures of a world that was even more dislocated than our own. One image that stuck in my mind was a poster of Christ seated on a park bench with an elm tree in the background and a group of Sunday school children gathered around him, the boys in bow ties and jackets, the girls in flowered dresses. Underneath was the caption "Suffer the Little Children to Come Unto Me . . ." I never understood what this picture had to do with suffering but I assumed that Jesus lived in America and someday we would all be taken there to meet him.

In elementary school we were also required to study Hindi. Though I had grown up speaking the language I did not know how to read or write. My teachers, Saroj Kapadia and Ruth Sanwalia, had to correct my grammar and pronunciation because the dialect I spoke was peculiar to the villages around Etah, a very different language from the "purer" Hindi that we were taught in school. For the first time I learned the Devnagri alphabet—क ख ग घ (ka, kha, ga, gha)—and simple words: घर (ghar), which means "home," and किताब (kitab), the word for "book." The texts we used in Hindi class were different from our other books at school. They were usually thinner and printed on cheap paper, and the illustrations were not as finely drawn, though the images were more familiar and appealing. There were drawings of peacocks and pipal trees, oxcarts and mangoes.

.   .   .

As soon as school let out in the afternoon we raced back down to Ridgewood, descending the staircase from the quad to Tehri Road, taking two or three steps at a time, then sprinting around the corners on the path and plunging headlong down the shortcuts, trying to be the first to reach our dorm. At three-thirty we drank our tea in the dining hall, a steaming, sugary brew with plenty of milk that was served in plastic tumblers, along with a couple of soda biscuits to keep us going until dinner.

About two hundred yards beyond Ridgewood was Midlands dormitory, the residence for high school girls. Approximately the same distance in the opposite direction was the boys' hostel, and the only route between the two passed in front of our dormitory. After tea Scotty Bunce and I would wait and watch the high school couples walking by, sometimes hand in hand or with their arms around each other. If it happened to be one of my cousins, John or Tom, or Scotty's brother or sister, we would hoot and whistle at them. Girls were something we kept away from at that age and the idea of being in love was still repulsive. We teased each other about being "plussies" and wrote S.B. + P.H. on the bathroom walls and sang the usual schoolyard songs, "Scotty and Patricia sitting in a tree, K-I-S-S-I-N-G . . ." Occasionally there were secret love notes passed back and forth, and once, on a dare, I tried unsuccessfully to give Amy Burkhalter a kiss.

From Ridgewood there were two paths to Midlands. One was called "Royalty," which went straight up the hill, a shorter route which the faculty and dorm supervisors always took. The other path circled around the hill and was called "Frivolity." The couples preferred to take this path because it was longer and gave them more privacy. Curious to see what was going on, Scotty Bunce and I would spy on them. Crouched near the water tanks below Midlands, we waited in ambush until one of the high school girls and her boyfriend came along. When they stopped to kiss, as they always did, we would snicker into our fists, voyeurs hidden in the barberry bushes. Holding our breath to keep from laughing, we saw the lovers clasp each other in their arms and put their mouths together. Certain couples were better to watch than others, those that kissed the longest and those who went a little further while making out, their hands exploring forbidden places.

Within a few minutes one of us would burst out laughing or throw a pinecone at the couple. Realizing that they were being watched, the boy would break out of his embrace and turn on us, embarrassed and enraged. This was the moment that we waited for with almost as much anticipation as the spying itself. Bunce and I knew every path and secret getaway on Midlands Hill. As the two of us scattered in opposite directions the angry high school boy wouldn't know which one to chase, blundering through the bushes and cursing as we scurried to safety, racing back to Ridgewood or escaping into the valley near the Dhobighat stream. Once or twice we were caught and threatened with sadistic tortures, but there was always the girlfriend waiting on the path, and after his initial fury died away, the boy would leave us alone and go back to her.

Our favorite playground at Ridgewood was "the Mount," a nearby hill covered with scrub oaks and thorn bushes where we played cowboys and Indians or king of the mountain, mock battles that raged for weeks. There were no fixed rules and some of us moved back and forth between the two armies, traitors shifting our allegiance from one team to the other. We dug foxholes and trenches in the Mount, the red clay caked beneath our fingernails. With penknives we cut spears from the viburnum bushes, stripping the bark and sharpening the ends. Attacking our enemies, we waved our spears and shouted like barbarian hordes. For ammunition we collected buckets of acorns that we hurled at each other, and pinecones served as grenades. With all the savagery of the lost boys in *Lord of the Flies*, we fought pitched battles on the Mount, dueling with bamboo rapiers.

Another popular Ridgewood game was "chessies" or "conkers," played with horse chestnuts, which we collected from the trees that grew on the hillside. In October, when the chestnuts were ready to pick, we often had to compete with the langur monkeys who feasted on the nuts. Peeling away the green fruit to reveal the seed, we carefully selected our chestnut warriors. Once the chessies had dried and hardened we drilled a hole through the middle and strung them on an old shoelace. The object of the game was to break the other person's warrior by hitting it with your own. Each player got three tries and victories were tallied up in a complicated points system of "kills" and "warrior years." The larger, black chessies were never as good as the smaller ones with wrinkled red skins. To strengthen our warriors we soaked them in linseed oil and lined them up on the windowsills of the dormitory to dry in the sun. The chessie fights were usually short and decisive, though some went on for several rounds. A direct hit often shattered one of the nuts and by the end of the day the playground in front of Ridgewood was littered with the cracked hulls and broken kernels of defeated warriors.

The dinner bell signaled the close of battle and, beating a quick retreat, we pocketed our hundred-year warriors and ran to wash our hands. Most of the food at Ridgewood was inedible but we were forced to eat whatever was spooned onto our trays. My least favorite meal was shepherd's pie, a gelatinous mutton gravy concealed beneath a layer of cold mashed potatoes. This delicacy always seemed to have been made several days in advance and every time I ate it the roof of my mouth was coated with grease. Once or twice a week we got Indian food but it was bland and flavorless, watery curries with bits of gristle and bone served over a mound of sticky rice. The only vegetable they seemed to cook at Ridgewood was lauki, a phlegmy white marrow that slid down my throat and made me gag. Even the desserts were awful, bread pudding full of raisins that looked like swollen ticks and clotted bits of custard that wobbled on my fork as if it were alive.

If we were lucky one of the mothers on the hillside would invite us out of boarding for the weekend, a brief respite from dorm routines and a chance to eat a home-cooked meal. Each grade in elementary school had a "class mother," who would organize parties for us once a month. Sometimes we got Kool-Aid, packets hoarded from a recent furlough or sent from America in food parcels. One of our class mothers used to make raised doughnuts and angel food cake which we devoured like starving refugees who hadn't eaten for several weeks. There were a few other sources of food to supplement our diet. Near the quadrangle was a tuckshop, where we could buy bull's-eyes and mango papad, a sticky candy made of dried mango pulp that we ate with salt and red chili powder. At Ridgewood we also had "candy cupboard," a weekly rationing of sweets that our parents sent with us to boarding. Many of the mish-kids had American candy, Milky Way bars and Sweet Tarts, but the classmate I envied most was Bablu Kapoor, who had tins of Cadbury's chocolates that he would sometimes share with me.

*   *   *

On Saturdays almost everybody at Woodstock went to the bazaar, which we called "the buzz." As Ridgewood boys, we were allowed to go into town in groups of three or more. Signing out in the morning, after breakfast, we had to be back in time for tea at four o'clock. The shopkeepers in Mussoorie knew that we were Woodstock students and they kept a protective eye on us. Most of the teachers and parents from the hillside also spent their Saturdays in the bazaar, so we were never really alone. Mussoorie had only one main street, which ran the length of the town, and it was impossible to get lost. The shops in the bazaar opened onto the street and it was like walking through an arcade, with brass merchants, jewelers, chemists, vegetable sellers, tailor shops, and tea stalls on either side. Accompanied by my friends, I would wander from shop to shop, looking at the firecrackers in Khalsa store, admiring the khukri knives and switchblades at Rastogis, or eyeing the pyramids of candy at Omi's sweet shop, barfi and milk cake, jalebis and gulab jamuns which the halwai made fresh each day in huge iron skillets over an open fire.

Near the Landour post office there was an old man who used to sit at the side of the street selling peanuts, which he roasted in hot sand. The peanut vendor looked as though he was at least a hundred years old, knotted with age and his eyes filmed over with cataracts. I would often buy five or ten naya paisa worth of peanuts from him, which he weighed out on a tiny scale, as carefully as if they were pieces of gold. The roasted peanuts were then wrapped up in a paper cone made of pages torn out of old notebooks salvaged from the school, which were often covered with math problems and spelling tests.

In the same section of the bazaar where the peanut vendor sat lived a troop of rhesus monkeys who perched on the balconies and rooftops overlooking the street. Sometimes we would throw them peanuts, which the monkeys caught deftly in their hands. Unlike the langurs, which were much bigger creatures with aloof black faces and silver coats, the rhesus monkeys were bold and scruffy, with bright red buttocks and stubby tails. If we teased them they showed their teeth, and they were known to bite. The males strutted about as if they owned the bazaar and the females often had babies clinging to their stomachs. Sometimes the rhesus monkeys stole fruit and vegetables from the subzi wallahs, like a gang of miscreants loitering about in the bazaar.

My favorite store was Vinod's Top Shop, which was located directly under the clock tower. Most of the space was filled with antiques, broken furniture salvaged from the homes of maharajas, old books and pictures, lamps and bric-a-brac. At the back of the store Vinod had a small workshop with an ancient lathe, which he used to make our tops. Every boy at Ridgewood owned one of these and they came in all sizes, ranging from enormous "lunkers" that you could hardly hold in one hand to the tiny, streamlined "lattoos" that we used for "ups and downs." A soft-spoken man with a slow, deliberate manner, Vinod listened patiently as I explained the kind of top I wanted him to make. Brushing away the sawdust which covered his lathe, he poked two bare wires into a socket on the wall and the electric motor rattled to life. I loved to watch as Vinod turned the wood into tapered shapes, the sweet, sharp smell of pine and the sound of sandpaper smoothing the rounded surface. As if by magic his chisel etched spiral grooves to hold the string, and he painted our tops with colored stripes by touching a crayon to the spinning wood. When he was done Vinod would hammer a spike into the narrow end of the top and hand it to me, the wood still warm from his lathe. Wrapping a string tightly around my top I tested it on the floor of the shop, watching it spin amid the scrolls of wood chips and piles of sawdust.

Next to the Top Shop was an Ayurvedic clinic, which had a sign, SEX SPECIALIST, printed in bright red letters on the door. We often joked about the sign and whenever my friends and I passed the clinic I couldn't help but glance inside, expecting to catch sight of unknown, erotic secrets, which tempted my imagination. In fact, there wasn't much to see at all, except for a small, dark room with shelves of bottles on the wall. The Vaid, or herbalist, who owned the clinic prescribed traditional medicines and tonics for impotence and infertility. He also treated more mundane ailments, such as gas and constipation.

The clock tower stood at the end of Landour bazaar, rising forty feet above the street, four dials facing north, south, east, and west. Most towns in India had similar towers, a temporal legacy of the British Raj, monuments to punctuality. Every hour and half hour the clock tower would chime, though the hands on each of the four faces were seldom synchronized. Beyond the clock tower the street widened and became the Mall Road, a promenade for tourists, continuing on toward Kulri, which was as far as Ridge-wood boys were allowed to go.

In Kulri bazaar there were a couple of newsagents and station-ers who sold American comic books and magazines. Though we couldn't afford to buy them very often, my friends and I would flip through the comics, reading *Yogi Bear* and *The Jetsons,* or *Batman* and *Superman,* until the shopkeeper chased us away. In third grade my pocket money was three rupees a week. One rupee was spent on lunch at the Sindhi Sweet Shop, where puris were twenty-five paisa apiece and served with as much pumpkin subzi and pota-toes as I could eat. Another rupee went for a movie at the Picture Palace or Rialto Cinema, where they showed English films on the weekends, Jerry Lewis comedies or Westerns with John Wayne. My last rupee bought a Coca-Cola at Ram Chander's store, or one of the small Cadbury's chocolate bars, wrapped in blue-and-silver foil. It was always a difficult choice between one of those or a plate of potato tikkis drenched in tamarind chutney, from the chaat wallah near the cinema hall.

. . .

Despite the many distractions of Ridgewood life, I often felt the pangs of homesickness while I was in boarding. My mother would write to me from Etah once a week, describing things that were happening on the mission compound, adventures that Joe and Andy were enjoying in my absence, stories about wildcats in the chicken coops, news of more pigeons having hatched, a pair of pet geese that chased my brothers around the yard outside our bungalow, snapping at their heels. Every Sunday, with the dorm mistress looking over my shoulder, I would have to write a letter to my parents, recounting trips to the bazaar and games we played on the Mount. I also complained that I was lonely and begged my parents to come up and take me out of Ridgewood, trying to sound more miserable than I really was.

My first semester in boarding, I fractured my arm playing pom pom polloway in the quad, when Leroy Redding knocked me into the rain gutter. Howling with pain, I was helped up the stairs to the dispensary on the third floor above the quadrangle. The school nurse examined me, asking if I could move my fingers, and sat me down while she called for a dandie to take me to the hospital. Even though the nurse gave me a toffee and wiped my tears with a wet washcloth, I couldn't stop myself from crying. More than the pain itself, it was a feeling of being far away from home that made me weep, snuffling into the collar of my shirt, as the nurse wrapped a splint around my forearm and tried to comfort me.

At the hospital, Dr. Wertz showed me the X ray of my greenstick fracture, a thin fissure where my bone had been split, like a piece of bamboo. The sight of it made me feel light-headed, though most of the pain had stopped by then. Mrs. Charles, one of the nurses who had assisted at my birth eight years earlier, put my arm in a cast, dipping the strips of gauze in wet plaster and wrapping them around my wrist and forearm, a cold, clammy sensation as each layer began to harden.

Around teatime, I was carried back to Ridgewood in a dandie, like a casualty of war. The coolies set me down in front of the dorm and my classmates gathered around to look at my cast, touching it and writing their names in the damp plaster. For those few minutes I was almost glad that I had broken my arm, but later that evening, after lights-out, after Miss Fluff had kissed me on both cheeks, I lay in bed and wept, the unfamiliar weight of my cast beside me on the pillow, the cracked bone beginning to throb as the painkillers wore off, and once again that sense of unrelenting sadness, of being separated from my family on the plains.

The cast remained on my arm until after Going Down Day, when Woodstock closed for two and a half months' winter break and all of the students were shipped off down the hill. We were divided into separate parties, depending on where we were traveling. There was a Calcutta party and one for Delhi, another for those who were going to Bombay, the Orissa and the Punjab parties, each of them setting out in different directions. I was assigned to the Lucknow party, and two days before we left our boxes were packed and bedding rolls made up, labels pasted onto all the luggage. My trunk was locked and banded with metal strips, then hoisted onto the back of a coolie and carried to the Railway Out-agency in Kulri bazaar. In a small attaché case I kept a change of clothes with me, my comb and toothbrush, as well as a few toys, tops and chessies, a dead beetle, and half a dozen marbles that I had won. Along with all of the other students in the Lucknow party I rode down the hill in a bus and boarded the train at Dehra Dun, piling into a special third-class carriage which had been reserved for us.

Going Down Day was an occasion for celebration and mischief. The week before was spent making bum wads and water bombs. These were carefully hidden inside our attaché cases, and as soon as the train began to pull out of the station at Dehra Dun we

fired bum wads at the people on the platform. Hurriedly the water
bombs were filled and tossed from the moving train at anyone who
was unfortunate enough to be standing at the side of the tracks.
Each party was accompanied by two or three teachers or parents
who traveled with us as chaperons. They tried their best to keep us
out of trouble but in the exuberance of leaving school and going
home, we stayed awake for most of the night, chasing each other
around the carriage and buying candy and soft drinks from the
vendors at each of the stations along our route.

The following morning, just before daybreak, our train arrived
at Bareilly station, where my parents had come to meet me. This
was the closest stop to Etah, along the Lucknow line. One of the
chaperons woke me up when we were still a few miles outside
Bareilly, passing through a station called Clutterbuckganj. Still half
asleep I rolled up my bistar bag as tightly as I could and wrestled
with the long leather straps. The freezing winter air and cinders
from the steam engine were blowing through the cracks in the
window. The carriages creaked against their couplings and the slow
rattle of the wheels added to my impatience as we approached the
station. Before the train had even come to a stop two railway
coolies in red uniforms piled into the compartment to collect my
baggage. Through the barred windows of the carriage I could see
my mother and father standing on the platform. Struggling out the
door and into their embrace, I held up my cast, as if to prove that
I had survived my first three months in Ridgewood.

. . .

Fortunately I did not have to remain in boarding for very long. The
year I started fifth grade, in 1966, my parents left Etah and moved
to Landour, where my father took over as director of accounts at
Woodstock. Even though I was no longer living in the dormitory,
our house was less than two hundred yards from Ridgewood, in
the faculty duplex below Midlands. After school and on the weekends I continued to play with my classmates, taking part in war

games on the Mount or spinning tops in the gravel yard. The only difference was that when the dinner bell rang, I retreated home, while the others had to line up in front of the dining hall.

In fifth grade I had a teacher named Mr. Goodwin, who also worked as a houseparent at Ridgewood. A tall, gaunt man with thinning hair and wire-rimmed spectacles, he belonged to one of the smaller, evangelical missions. Mr. Goodwin was married and had two children at the school. As a fifth-grade class, we were viciously cruel to him. He was a maimed and helpless adult surrounded by a pack of savage ten-year-olds intent on pulling him down. Ultimately, our baiting and disorderly behavior caused Mr. Goodwin to have a nervous breakdown and he went from Woodstock to Nurmanzil, the psychiatric hospital in Lucknow.

Before we started fifth grade, I had already heard stories about our teacher. There was a rumor that one of the eighth-grade boys had misbehaved at Ridgewood and Mr. Goodwin took him into his room, locked the door, and prayed over him. I don't remember what the boy had done wrong, but it must have been something serious. After he finished praying, Mr. Goodwin rolled up his sleeves and told the boy that he was taking his sins upon himself. Then he slit his wrists with a razor blade.

That was the story I was told. It made Mr. Goodwin seem weird and unpredictable and I was never quite sure how he survived the bleeding and why he remained at the school. During class I remember looking for the scars on his arms but he kept his shirtsleeves carefully buttoned at the wrists. Because of his nearsightedness, Mr. Goodwin was barely able to see to the back of our classroom, and we took advantage of his blindness, crawling about on our stomachs, throwing paper airplanes, and firing spitballs at each other. The few times he caught us, we were sent straight off to Miss Wait's office to be punished. During Scripture class, which was the longest period of the day, Mr. Goodwin led us in prayer and delivered homilies on the need to be washed clean of sin. Once, while reading to us from the Bible, he came to a verse about the children of Israel dancing for joy. Eric Blickenstaff, one of the wilder boys in our class, got up on his desk and began to do the twist, gyrating his hips and swinging his arms from side to side.

Mr. Goodwin exploded. He slammed the Bible down and his face changed from its usual pallid color to a furious red. Grabbing Eric by the neck, he flung him off the desk and turned on the rest of us, enraged. He told us that Eric was possessed by the devil and that people who danced like this were doomed to eternal hell. It was a frightening moment for all of us. This quiet, fumbling man was suddenly talking like a prophet out of the Old Testament. Still holding Eric by the arm Mr. Goodwin hauled him out of the room and slammed the door. I was sure that our teacher was going to cut his wrists again, though he returned a few minutes later, after sending Eric to see Miss Wait. In those days there was a rule against dancing at Woodstock, though some of the high school students held parties in their homes. Conservative missionaries like Mr. Goodwin were strongly opposed to dancing of any kind and considered it sinful and depraved.

Around the end of fifth grade, Mr. Goodwin took all of the boys in my class on a hike to Bhatta Falls. None of us had been there before and it was about five or six miles from Ridgewood, near the Galogi power station on the road to Dehra Dun. Setting off on a Saturday morning, it took us about two hours to reach the Bhatta stream, where we found a large pool of water, deep enough for swimming. Most of us had brought our bathing suits and it was a hot day, so we quickly changed and jumped into the water. There must have been about fifteen boys altogether, splashing about and doing cannonballs off the rocks. For half an hour or more, Mr. Goodwin sat on the shore and took a few pictures with his camera, watching us with a distracted expression on his face.

Most of us were so caught up in our games that we didn't even notice when our teacher began to remove his clothes. Before we knew it, Mr. Goodwin was completely naked, wading into the pool. Laughing nervously, he explained that he had forgotten his swimming trunks at home. His skin was a translucent white and he looked emaciated and misshapen. Mr. Goodwin had also taken off his glasses and couldn't see that we were gawking at him. He was almost hairless except for the dark ruff of fur around his penis. For us the pool was deep enough to swim in but the water only came up to Mr. Goodwin's knees. He splashed himself and floated on his back, kicking his legs listlessly. To me, his exposed body looked as if it had been stretched like plasticine.

All of us got out of the water as soon as Mr. Goodwin lowered himself into the stream. Squatting on the shore, we watched him paddle around while he tried to coax us back into the pool. None of us said anything at all, silenced by his nakedness and sensing that something mysterious was going on. Fifteen minutes later a group of village women arrived, carrying brass water vessels on their heads which they were coming to fill at the stream. As the women approached, we shouted a warning to Mr. Goodwin and he quickly waded out of the pool, toweled himself dry, and put on his clothes.

By this time it was nearly one o'clock in the afternoon and we took out our packed lunches and began to eat the dry tuna fish buns, hard-boiled eggs, and limp carrot sticks which had been prepared for us in the Ridgewood kitchens. As soon as we finished lunch, Mr. Goodwin called us together and made us sit around him in a circle. I thought he was going to lead us in prayer but instead he began to talk in a quiet, earnest voice, explaining that each of us would soon be entering puberty. Realizing what was coming, I listened in embarrassment, staring at the ground between my feet, as Mr. Goodwin gave us our first lecture in sex education. He told us that he had gone swimming without any clothes because he wanted all of us to see what our bodies would look like when we grew up.

As I remember, Mr. Goodwin presented us with a fairly complete and balanced lesson about the facts of life. He wasn't shy or crude and on the other hand he wasn't sanctimonious. Even after spying on high school couples along the Midlands path, there were a lot of questions in my mind that Mr. Goodwin answered. I would have expected a much stranger view of sex from a man like him, but the description he gave us was simple and straightforward. At one point he told us that the first time he made love to his wife was "the most wonderful experience on earth." He didn't bring Christianity into the discussion and described in some detail the physical process of sexual intercourse. Of course, to us the whole thing seemed terribly dirty and perverse, hearing him use words like "erection" and "ejaculation." For years afterward I was so ashamed of what had taken place on our hike to Bhatta Falls that I didn't even tell my parents. Mr. Goodwin was probably a very different man from what we imagined him to be. I can remember that as he stood there naked in the pool, a myopic smile wrinkling up his face, I stared very carefully at his wrists and I could see no scars.

FURLOUGH, 1967~68

Returning to the United States in 1967, we flew by way of the Pacific and stopped in Hong Kong, Tokyo, and Honolulu before we reached Los Angeles. I remember looking forward to this furlough, eager to leave India and get back to the world of television and supermarkets. My fragmented memories of Ithaca had been reinforced by secondhand impressions of the States, seductive images from movies, magazines and comic books, Sears catalogs, and stories that I'd been told by friends and cousins about toy stores and paper routes, ice-cream sundaes and TV shows. In my mind America was a place where everything was available, a promised land of milk and honey, where you could buy the contents of a food parcel right off the shelf. Now that I was almost eleven years old the material pleasures of that country seemed all the more enticing.

From Delhi we took a Pan Am jet to Hong Kong and stayed overnight at the Imperial Hotel in Kowloon. Our rooms were on the fifteenth floor and this was the first time that I remember riding in an elevator, my stomach dropping as we were sucked upward at rocket speed. In the evening, after supper, we went out and walked along Nathan Road, which was lined with department stores and rows of tiny shops selling transistor radios and cameras, all kinds of duty-free gadgets, tape recorders, stereo systems, and wristwatches that looked like decorations on a Christmas tree. The street was lit up with neon lights and the shop windows were full of glittering displays, revolving mirrors and brand names written in English and Chinese. My father needed to buy a camera and we visited several shops before he found what he was looking for, an inexpensive Minolta with a built-in light meter, which was used to take our family pictures for the next ten years. At one of the many toy stores on Nathan Road I persuaded my parents to let me buy a miniature machine gun. It was made of molded plastic with four batteries loaded into the clip, like rounds of ammunition. Lights flashed when I pulled the trigger and the gun made a chattering sound followed by the electronic whine of bullets ricocheting.

In Hong Kong we saw large numbers of American soldiers and sailors, most of whom must have been on leave from duty in Vietnam. On our way back to the hotel, a group of marines walked past us in their uniforms, talking loudly among themselves. They seemed so much bigger than everyone else on the street, their rowdy voices rising above the din of Kowloon traffic. Though I knew that there was a war going on, I had no clear idea of what was taking place in Vietnam.

The next day we flew on to Tokyo, where we stayed at an even fancier hotel, called the New Otani, which had a Japanese garden on the grounds, with stunted evergreen trees and wooden bridges overlooking mossy pools full of golden carp. We didn't get a chance to see much of the city but there was a television set in our room and my brothers and I watched Deputy Dog dubbed in Japanese, frustrated because we couldn't understand the words. That evening Joe and Andy fell asleep before supper and my parents took me downstairs to one of the restaurants, which had a live band and a singer crooning, "I'm leaving on a jet plane, don't know when I'll be back again. . . ." She was an attractive Asian woman with long slits on either side of her sequined dress. As my parents and I ate dinner I remember feeling embarrassed by her husky voice and the sensual way she moved to the soft, suggestive pulse of the double bass.

The Presbyterians must have arranged a special deal with the airline, which put us up at each of the hotels. In Honolulu we were taken to the Ilikai on Waikiki Beach and given a top floor suite, from where we had a view of Diamond Head. Before we left India, I had heard my parents using the phrase "culture shock," and now that we were in America I kept waiting to experience this strange phenomenon. It sounded like a procedure that was carried out with electrodes when travelers passed through customs and immigration. I imagined that culture shock was a physical affliction, like getting carsick or being affected by a change in altitude. As soon as we got to Hawaii I kept expecting to feel a shortness of breath and weakness in my limbs. The only thing I experienced was jet lag from our journey and we spent most of our time inside the hotel, watching television and sleeping. The morning before we flew on to Los Angeles my father took us swimming on Waikiki Beach and we played in the surf and dug tunnels in the dark volcanic sand. I had never been swimming in the sea before and the salt water burned my eyes and nose. Flying over the Pacific I had looked down at the curved expanse of blue, imagining that this ocean went on forever.

Being in the airplane itself was a form of culture shock—the Pan Am stewardesses in their blue polyester uniforms, the constant roar of the Boeing 707 which carried us across the international date line, the junior captain's badges we were given and my first trip up the aisle to see the cockpit, the pilot and copilot in white shirtsleeves staring at a console covered with dials and levers. Everything seemed so streamlined and organized after India, our meals arranged on plastic trays with little wedges of cheese and sugar in paper packets. Even the milk which the stewardesses served us in cardboard cartons tasted better than the buffalo milk that we were used to drinking in Landour. Sitting in the airplane I imagined America to be a country where things fitted together as neatly as the stainless steel buckle on my seat belt or the plastic latch which held the tray table in place. Even though I was nervous about flying and closed my eyes and clutched the armrests whenever we took off, there was also a secure and comforting feeling of enclosure inside the cabin, the reassuring lipstick smiles of the stewardesses, their smooth, efficient hands, and the captain's gruff voice of authority crackling over the intercom.

. . .

Since our last visit to America, Grandma Alter had moved to a retirement home for Presbyterian missionaries in Duarte, California. Westminster Gardens was like an oasis in the dry, smog-laden suburbs of Los Angeles, twenty or thirty acres of lush vegetation and tiny cottages interspersed with goldfish ponds and flower beds. On one side of the retirement home was the San Bernardino Freeway, an endless stream of cars roaring past on elevated ramps. I could smell the exhaust fumes in the air, a sharp chemical odor that made my eyes water. Duarte itself was a dusty, colorless town of strip malls and car dealerships. In a peculiar way it reminded me of Dehra Dun, for there was a line of mountains to the north, obscured for most of the day behind a poisonous yellow haze. Once or twice, when the air cleared, we could see Mount Baldy in the distance, with a patch of white at the summit, an unimpressive mole hill compared to the snow peaks beyond Mussoorie.

Westminster Gardens had been established and endowed by a wealthy Chinese convert who donated part of his fortune to the Presbyterian Church. There were more than fifty retired missionaries living in Duarte, many of them from India or Pakistan and others who had served in Lebanon, Iran, and China. We stayed with my grandmother for several weeks, in an empty apartment next door to hers. Though Westminster Gardens was a pleasant and attractive place, I felt restless and uncomfortable living among a community of elderly people who had returned to America after spending most of their lives abroad. As I listened to their conversations, there was a depressing hint of exile and nostalgia in their voices, as they reminisced about the past, sharing memories of faraway lands.

My grandmother's apartment was filled with a collection of objects which she had brought back with her from India—Kashmiri carpets on the floors and a carved Saharanpur screen, brass and copper trays, ornate lamps and bookends made of papier-mâché, embroidered tablecloths and a procession of rosewood elephants lined up along a shelf in the living room. On her bedroom walls Grandma Alter had a series of watercolors which she had painted years ago, pictures of Himalayan wildflowers, yellow primulas and red anemones. Her apartment had only two small rooms and every inch of space was filled with memorabilia, pictures of her children and grandchildren, knickknacks and mementos from her life in India.

My brothers and I were much more interested in Grandma Alter's TV set, a large-screen Zenith that had a remote control. During our stay in Duarte we watched everything there was to see on television—cartoons and sitcoms, *Green Acres* and *The Beverly Hillbillies*, game shows like *Jeopardy* and *Hollywood Squares*, as well as our favorite program, *Let's Make a Deal*. Each night Grandma Alter and my parents would watch the *CBS Evening News* with Walter Cronkite which carried daily reports from Vietnam, reminding me of the American soldiers we had seen in Hong Kong. During the day Joe, Andy, and I sat for hours on the floor in front of the television like hypnotized supplicants at the shrine of an oracle.

There wasn't much else for us to do. We did go shopping at the supermarket with my grandmother, eyeing the shelves of American food that we had dreamed of eating, boxed cereals and tins of Campbell's soup and Spaghetti Os, Hershey's chocolate bars and packets of M&M's. My grandmother and her friends took us out for meals at nearby restaurants, smorgasbords where we could eat as much as we wanted, filling our plates again and again with Swedish meatballs and potato salad. My brothers and I had such ravenous appetites that my mother got worried and made an appointment with the doctor to check if we had worms.

The first Sunday we were in Duarte my grandmother took us to her church in the nearby town of Arcadia. It was an enormous modern structure, with a white concrete spire and countless rows of pews. The pulpit seemed so far away and the stained-glass windows had stylized figures of the apostles and Christian symbols, a fish, a cross, an abstract dove, through which the sunlight entered in bright crayon colors. Instead of the dreary interior of Kellogg Church there was an electric brightness and a surrounding sense of wealth and opulence. At the beginning of the service the minister, whose name was Reverend Hamburger, announced to the congregation that Martha Alter's son and his family were visiting from India, where they worked as missionaries. He asked us to stand up so that everyone could see who we were, and I felt self-conscious and exposed with all those eyes staring at us. It reminded me of the game show we had been watching on TV, *Let's Make a Deal*, when members of the audience would be asked to stand up and they were given a chance to win a million dollars.

It hadn't taken me very long to realize that in comparison to most Americans, my parents didn't earn a lot of money. This was something that troubled me; in India I was used to living a privileged and comfortable life, not lavish, but certainly more secure and wealthy than most of the people around us. As soon as we arrived in America my parents had to keep reminding me that we couldn't afford many of the things I wanted, all of the merchandise that I had dreamed of buying off the shelf, toys and candy, shoes and clothes. When my mother took me shopping, I couldn't understand why we only went to clearance sales. In India my pocket money had been three rupees a week, which had seemed more than adequate, but when my parents calculated the exchange rate and gave me fifty cents, I realized how little I could buy. For the first time in my life it seemed that we were poor and I felt cheated and deprived.

My grandmother and one of her friends from Westminster Gardens took my brothers and me to Disneyland, which was something we had been promised. Joe and I rode the roller coaster up and down the Matterhorn, while Grandma Alter and Andy watched from below. We saw the "Pirates of the Caribbean" and rode on the "Jungle Cruise," in which fiberglass hippos surfaced near our boat and a mechanical rhino chased a white hunter and his black gun bearers up a tree. I also remember the submarine ride, where we had to stand in line for almost an hour to see plastic fish and artificial coral through the tiny portholes. Later in the afternoon, my grandmother insisted on taking us to see the robot of Abraham Lincoln deliver the Gettysburg Address. Coming from India, Disneyland seemed all the more bizarre, a world of strange juxtapositions and skewed realities. A futuristic Skyrail soared past the turrets of Snow White's castle and costumed figures of Mickey Mouse and Goofy wandered amid the crowds of sunburned tourists. On later visits to California we went to Disneyland two more times, but this first encounter was the most surreal of all, giving me a distorted sense of America, an artificial, automated world of make-believe.

        •   •   •

At one of the many used-car lots that lined the streets of Duarte my father bought an old Dodge Dart to take us across the country. After visiting with my grandmother for three weeks we left California, heading east for Princeton, New Jersey, where we would spend the rest of our furlough. The second day of our journey the car broke down in Carson City, Nevada, and we had to spend two nights in a motel, where they gave us complimentary gambling coupons. My brothers and I wanted to play the slot machines but my parents refused, and we spent most of our time swimming in the motel pool while the car's transmission was replaced. From there we headed on to Idaho and Wyoming, driving through the Grand Tetons and Yellowstone National Park, where we saw the geysers and boiling mud pits. It was early July and the park was overcrowded. Every time we saw an elk or a bear there were several dozen cars lined up with people taking pictures. The mountain landscapes of Wyoming were dramatic but I missed the wildness of the Indian forests.

Driving across the country seemed to take forever and we stopped with friends along the way, retired missionaries and Woodstock alumni. Once again I felt a sense of rootlessness, wandering the highways of America in search of a forgotten home. My father's brother, Uncle Joe, and Aunt Marion lived in Cincinnati, and we stayed with them for about a week. Their daughter Janet was the same age as I and her brother Rob a few years older. They had a pool table in their basement and we played countless games with our cousins and drank gallons of Hawaiian Punch. After that we drove on to western Pennsylvania, where we visited my mother's relatives and stayed at the Carnahans' farm, which I remembered from our first furlough. We also spent a couple nights with Grandma Stewart in Greenville and went to see my grandfather's grave. From there we circled down to Washington, D.C., and visited Uncle Dave and Aunt Cleo. My cousin Davey, their youngest son, had been badly injured in a car accident while they were living in Zambia a few years before. He was confined to a wheelchair and unable to speak or take care of himself. My aunt and uncle were still hoping that Davey would recover but his progress was very slow and I was disturbed to see my sixteen-year-old cousin reduced to a child of three or four.

After what seemed like weeks of driving we finally arrived in Princeton and moved into an apartment building for missionaries, similar to the one in Ithaca. In preparation for his new job, as principal of Woodstock, my father would be taking courses at Columbia Teachers College in New York. He commuted into the city several days a week by train. Instead of living in New York, my parents had decided that we would stay in Princeton, where the public schools were good and the neighborhood was safer. I attended sixth grade at Community Park Junior High, a modern single-story structure about three quarters of a mile from our home. Joe and Andy took a school bus to their elementary school but I was given a bicycle to ride, a yellow Schwinn with rusted chrome. I already knew how to ride a bike, but I was used to having brakes on the handlebars instead of pedaling backward, and I nearly killed myself until I got the hang of it.

Most of my classmates had grown up in Princeton and there were only a couple of new kids in my class. I made friends slowly and others treated me with curiosity because of the way I spoke. They asked me questions about India, though I noticed how quickly they lost interest in the subject once I began to explain myself. I realized that fitting in to junior high required more than just boasting about my experiences in Landour. There was a whole new culture that I had to assimilate and comprehend as quickly as I could. If I wanted to become an American I had to act and sound like one of them. Most of sixth grade was a struggle to be accepted, to blend into the tumult of an American adolescence. I did not want to be seen as different from my classmates even though I knew that their upbringing was opposite to mine.

In India, one of the things that I had very little exposure to was rock and roll. The Beach Boys and the Beatles were groups that I had only heard about in passing, the sound of drumbeats and guitars that emanated from my cousins' rooms at Tehri View and Rajpur. There was a magazine published out of Calcutta, called *The Junior Statesman*, which I used to read sometimes and it had articles about Elvis Presley and Jimi Hendrix though I had never heard their music. The only record player my parents owned was broken, its motor burned out by a voltage fluctuation. We seldom listened to the radio in India, but this absence of music in our home was never something that bothered me until we moved to Princeton. Most of my classmates were listening to rock and roll and knew the lyrics of all the latest hits. The only song that I could sing was "Louie, Louie" because it didn't matter if I knew the words or not. There was a radio in our Dodge Dart and I would turn it on whenever we were driving in the car. Some of the rock groups appeared on television and one night I saw the Doors performing on *The Ed Sullivan Show*. For several weeks afterward I went around humming "Come On Baby Light My Fire," though I was too embarrassed to sing the words themselves. During our year in Princeton, the Beatles brought out their *Sgt. Pepper's* album and my music teacher at school let us listen to their songs in class. Some of these contained sequences of sitar music, played by George Harrison and Ravi Shankar.

In March of 1968, the Beatles made their celebrated pilgrimage to India with the Maharishi Mahesh Yogi. American newspapers and magazines were full of articles about John and Ringo, Paul and George traveling to an ashram in Rishikesh, which was only forty miles east of Mussoorie. Suddenly, India was seen as a place of mysticism and peace, transcendental meditation and enlightenment. Everyone was going there from Mia Farrow to the Beach Boys. I found it hard to understand, for the India that I knew was very different from this psychedelic wonderland. While my classmates were tuning in to the exotic rhythms of Indian music, I was unsuccessfully trying to tap my toes to the unfamiliar tempo of the States.

More than music, though, it was television which provided me with a peephole on American culture. One of the first purchases my parents made, as soon as we got to Princeton, was a small black-and-white TV with rabbit-ear antennae. We positioned the television on a side table in the living room, as if it were a household shrine. For the next ten months, my brothers and I spent a good part of our free time staring at the flickering gray impulses on the screen, as if they were part of an encrypted code. Trying to decipher these images I felt like a secret agent, a *Man From Uncle* or one of the characters in *I Spy*, working undercover in a foreign land.

Cartoons remained our favorite shows, and there were still a few that I could remember from five years before—*Tom and Jerry*, *Tweetie and Sylvester*, and *Yogi Bear*. I was also familiar with many of these characters from reading comic books in Mussoorie but seeing them on television was very different. The most intriguing part was the sound effects and music, as well as the voices of the characters, the curious blend of accents and speech mannerisms, from Fred Flintstone's midwestern banter to Top Cat's sassy New York twang. More than these, however, a whole new genre of superheroes and action cartoons caught our interest, *Spiderman*, *Speed Racer*, and *Roger Ramjet*. Every Saturday morning we would turn on the TV to watch exaggerated human figures in skintight outfits, capes, and masks fighting ruthless villains who seemed intent on destroying the world. In each episode our planet seemed to be perpetually on the brink of annihilation and it was only the vigilance of those animated superheroes that kept us from subservience to evil.

Though my mother and father restricted how much television we could watch, I couldn't help being taken in by the seductive imagery on the screen. It was as if all of the answers to my questions about America lay within those cathode tubes, the stereotypes which I absorbed as easily as the paper towels which soaked up kitchen stains in the advertisements that I watched. American housewives were always blond, and they were either benevolent witches or subservient genies, depending on the channel or the time of day. I loved Lucy as much as anyone but when it came to being one of the boys, I dreamed of riding with the Cartwrights through the gate of their Ponderosa ranch. Between the ads for Shake 'n Bake chicken or Frito-Lay potato chips, I watched Hogan's

Heroes tunneling beneath the German lines and fantasized about being a castaway on Gilligan's Island, with the glamorous movie star and Mary Ann.

· · ·

Even after our fifth-grade hike to Bhatta Falls, sex remained a mystery for me and I was still puzzled by the specific details of a woman's body. For a while I was even tempted to send away for a pair of X-ray glasses, one of those novelty items advertised on the back pages of comic books, with a picture of a lecherous man leering at a skeleton in a dress. If I'd had a sister the situation might have been different but being in a family of three boys, female anatomy wasn't something that we discussed. My parents never explained very much to me about sex, but they must have sensed my curiosity and one day they brought home a surprise, an unexpected present for my brothers and me. When we first opened the large paper bag I thought that they had given us a doll, but looking more carefully at the gift I realized it was a Visible Woman, a clear plastic model that we could take apart.

Peeling the cellophane away from the box I felt embarrassed and disappointed. A Visible Woman was hardly the sort of toy I wanted. A battery-operated racing car or truck would have been more interesting. Though she was completely nude, the woman's skin was transparent and her internal organs were exposed. I could see right through the impassive contours of her face, into her eyes and skull, the muscles on her neck and jaw. Snapping her open at the hips, I removed the color-coded viscera, her mammary glands, her lungs, her heart and spleen, even her uterus. By this time my curiosity had diminished, and after a few timid vivisections my brothers and I packed the Visible Woman away and left her to languish inside her box.

A few weeks later, I saw my first *Playboy* magazine, shown to me by one of the boys in the neighborhood. Together we unfolded the glossy centerfold, Miss January 1968, with airbrushed thighs and breasts that looked like freshly risen dough. Until then, the only erotica I'd seen were the lingerie pages in the Sears Roebuck catalogs. Secretly, I had studied those pictures of smiling, wholesome models wearing lace bras and panties. The photographs exposed so little, yet there was a sensual quality about the women in the catalogs which underlined my own desire for all of the other things that were available at Sears. Throughout my early adolescence I was a mail-order voyeur, and even when I was looking through the catalogs for camping equipment, fishing gear or toys, I couldn't help flipping back to the pages of intimate apparel.

Studying the *Playboy* centerfold, I felt a guilty fascination, as if the lingerie had been removed at last. Though I sensed that I was doing something wrong, staring at dirty pictures, in fact, Miss January revealed even less than I had seen through the Visible Woman's transparent skin. For half an hour or so I pored over the photographs, trying to memorize each line and curve before my neighbor slipped the magazine inside the sleeve of his jacket and hurried home to put it back in its hiding place, under a pile of shirts in his father's closet.

．　．　．

My sixth-grade homeroom teacher was Bob Parsons, whom I liked, even though he taught me math. He was a stocky, amiable man who kept us in line with a combination of jocularity and discipline. Mr. Parsons was a Yankees fan and during the World Series he brought a portable television set into class so that we could watch the final game. I had never played baseball before and did not understand the rules, though the following spring I signed up for Little League. The stiff leather glove on my hand felt awkward and I struck out whenever I was up to bat, except one time when I got walked. Still, I made an effort to learn the game, as if it were a necessary part of my initiation in America. My father and I played catch together on the lawns of the Princeton Seminary, across the street from our apartment building. Toward the end of the season he threw a ball at me that broke the webbing on my glove and hit me in the face by accident. I ended up with a black eye, which put an end to my baseball career and made my classmates think that I'd been punched.

There were a lot of fights at Community Park Junior High. During recess I would often hear a shout from somewhere on the playground and see two boys scuffling in the grass or circling each other with their fists clenched. I'm not sure what caused these fights but for the most part it was little things, an insult or a dare. We were getting interested in girls but not enough to fight over them. The same four or five boys, troublemakers and bullies, were the ones that usually got into fights and tried to beat each other up before the teachers intervened. I used to keep my distance from them, though I remember being intrigued and fascinated by the sudden fury of those conflicts, the flushed red faces and torn shirts, swear words and bloody noses.

Toward the end of sixth grade one of my friends, Jay Panzer, told me that a boy named John Woodhouse wanted to fight with me. John was in my homeroom but I didn't know him very well. Even though he was smaller than I, he must have thought that he could beat me up. I had no interest in fighting but it was clear that I was being forced to prove myself and reluctantly accepted the challenge, claiming that I could whip him any day. Jay Panzer egged the two of us on, like a ringside promoter, telling us lies about each other to make us angry. Both John and I were too afraid to fight at school but Jay arranged for us to meet one afternoon behind the chapel at the university. The time and place were carefully planned but when we got there one of the custodians came out and chased us off. The following weekend, Jay set up the fight again, this time at a park on the other side of town. Saturday morning I showed up on my bicycle, feeling sick with fear. John Woodhouse was already waiting there with Jay and two or three other boys. I don't think either of us wanted to go through with the fight but we started feinting and dancing around, the way I imagined Cassius Clay and Floyd Patterson circled each other in the ring. A group of neighborhood children gathered around, younger kids. For several minutes nothing happened and our audience began to get impatient, taunting us and saying we fought like girls. Finally, more out of embarrassment than anger, I took a swing, a wild roundhouse punch that caught John accidentally in the throat. It was luck and I'm sure I had my eyes shut but John Woodhouse went down, clutching his Adam's apple and making gargling noises in the grass.

I was so surprised that I didn't move for several seconds, looking down at him and trying to figure out what had happened. His eyes were bulging and he was rolling around, unable to breathe. My instinct was to turn and run. Jay Panzer followed me, both of us afraid that I had inflicted a serious injury. Getting onto our bikes we pedaled frantically home, glancing back to see if anyone was in pursuit. The next day I was afraid to go to school but when I got there John was in his seat. He did not look at me; I did not look at him, and that was the end of it.

* * *

Soon after my fight, our sixth-grade science class went on a field trip to the Museum of Natural History in Manhattan. From Princeton it was about a two-hour ride by bus and we joked and teased each other on the way, flirting with the girls. By this time there were several couples in the class who sat together, but most of us kept to ourselves, watching the swamp grass and factories slide past along the margins of the New Jersey Turnpike. I was interested in a girl named Andrea Corelli, who sat next to me in class, though I was too shy to speak with her. She had straight black hair with bangs and sometimes painted her nails, red and pink.

When we got to the museum our teachers divided us into groups and took us through the exhibits, past the dinosaur skeletons, the tusks of mastodons and fossils of trilobites. We saw the exhibits of North American animals, white-tailed deer and elk which had been shot by Teddy Roosevelt. After that we moved on to Africa, where stuffed lions prowled their glassed-in savannas and Masai herdsmen stood in the distance holding spears.

After an hour or so we arrived at the Indian exhibits. As my classmates and I crowded around the diorama of two Bengal tigers I was asked if I had ever seen a tiger in the wild. I lied and said that I had, describing a trip my family had taken to a game sanctuary called Corbett Park. As I spoke I stared at the stuffed predators crouched by an artificial pool, the fake bamboo and painted foliage on the concave wall, which gave an illusion of the Indian jungle. It reminded me of the moss gardens my brothers and I made during the monsoon, except on a larger scale.

For those few minutes, with my sixth-grade class, I was the acknowledged authority on everything we saw. Next to the tigers was a diorama with two leopards in a tree, the lights dimmed to suggest a moonlit scene. I explained that the spots on a leopard's coat were called rosettes and that black panthers were really the same species as leopards and the only difference was the color of their fur. I also told my class how the leopards would come and lie on our veranda in Landour and the time my dog, Penny, was almost eaten by a leopard while chasing langur monkeys. Warming to my audience, I recounted the story of a leopard which my father shot, on the south side of Midlands Hill, at a place called Lookout Point.

I recognized other Indian animals as well, barking deer and chital, sambar and a Himalayan black bear with the white V on his chest, like a crescent moon. Even my teacher fell silent as he listened to me explain which animals were found in the mountains and which ones lived on the plains. One of the displays included a black buck with spiral horns, like Hira, our pet antelope in Fategarh. Later, after we left the museum and boarded the bus, Andrea Corelli slid into the seat beside me and asked questions about India.

Passing through the Lincoln Tunnel, as we left Manhattan, the bus darkened for a few minutes and Andrea reached across and held my hand.

. . .

Two or three times during the year we had emergency drills at school in case of a nuclear attack. When the alarm went off we had to leave our desks and march into the gymnasium, which was designated as a fallout shelter, with black-and-yellow signs. Instructed by our teachers, we practiced how to crouch down and cover our heads to protect ourselves, though I kept thinking that if the Russians actually dropped a bomb on us, these precautions weren't going to do much good. Living in India, I had been mostly unaware of the cold war paranoia that followed the Cuban missile crisis. Of course, I had heard about atom bombs and nuclear warheads, but in a naive way I felt protected in Mussoorie, as if we were far away from the dangers of an apocalyptic war. In America, however, the threat seemed very real and present, as if our school itself had been identified as a specific target. I was soon convinced that the Communists were intent on destroying the world, like villains in the superhero cartoons that we watched every Saturday morning. The whole time we were in Princeton, I kept hoping that the Russians would wait until we got safely back to India before they launched a nuclear attack.

Though I was too young to understand much of the upheaval that was taking place during 1967 and 1968, I can remember certain events that happened during our furlough. The war in Vietnam had reached its most brutal and senseless phase. The Tet offensive occurred during the winter we were in Princeton and on the nightly news I watched G.I. Joes crawling through rice paddies, Phantom jets catapulted from the decks of aircraft carriers, helicopters ferrying wounded marines and body bags. I kept thinking of the American soldiers that I'd passed on the street in Hong

Kong, their clean pressed uniforms and the way they swaggered through Kowloon, as if they had already won the war. The names of places in Vietnam stuck in my mind—Da Nang, Hue, and Khe Sanh—the chopped syllables like acronyms for a sequence of tragedies. A few years earlier, I had seen several articles about Vietnam in *National Geographic* magazine, including one on the Montagnard tribes. Accompanying the article were color pictures of U.S. military advisers taking part in tribal rituals, exchanging their camouflage fatigues and M16 rifles for loincloths and bamboo spears. This was my preconceived idea of what was going on in Vietnam, white men playing war games in the jungle, Green Berets disguising themselves as natives and painting shadowy patterns on their skin. As far as I can remember, *National Geographic* carried no pictures of wounded Americans or napalm spilling from the sky. That was something which I saw on television, along with each day's tally of the dead, the anchormen keeping score of casualties as if it were a baseball game, the World Series.

Another clear memory from our furlough was Martin Luther King Jr.'s assassination on April 14, 1968. Our television showed us the motel balcony in Memphis with the civil rights leader bleeding to death as his associates pointed in the direction from which the shots had been fired. That image was repeated so many times on the screen and in the newspapers that I almost felt as if I had witnessed his death firsthand. A couple months later Bobby Kennedy was shot, and here again the television pictures were imprinted in my consciousness, the jostling crowd in a Los Angeles hotel, bright lights and the sudden popping sound of gunfire, cameras careening frantically, heads and bodies moving in shadowy confusion, and finally a picture of the candidate lying on the floor in the pulsating glare of flashbulbs. Everyone who watched those events on their television screens must carry similar images in their minds, but for me the pictures were so much stronger because I saw them as single points of reference during that one year when we were living in America. Nothing seemed to precede or follow those events and they became encapsuled in my memory, representing the escalating violence and discontent.

By the time we left Princeton I had come to think of the United States as a threatening, unsettled place. I saw pictures of the antiwar protests and the riots following Martin Luther King Jr.'s death, which disturbed me almost as much as the nuclear drills and fallout shelters. My perceptions of America had changed and I wanted to get back to India as soon as possible. This country, which I had imagined to be so modern and stable, where everything fit together in neat packages like airline trays and seat belt buckles, now seemed full of controversy, bloodshed, and danger.

*   *   *

Before leaving America, in June of 1968, my parents packed our sea freight into eight steel barrels. During our stay in Princeton we had bought a number of things to take back with us to India, all kinds of necessities which we could only get in the States. Seeing the barrels, packed and ready to be shipped, I felt as if we were setting off on an expedition to explore an unknown corner of the world, stockpiling provisions for a distant journey, carrying with us the ritual objects of our cargo cult.

An inventory of those barrels included camping gear—sleeping bags from Sears, folding cots and chairs, a blue canvas tent that was big enough to sleep eight people, air mattresses, and army surplus canteens. There were toys as well, at least a dozen games, including Avalanche and Twister, battery-operated racing cars, the plastic machine gun I had bought in Hong Kong, which no longer worked, superhero costumes for Halloween, plastic battarangs, several boxes of Tinkertoys, a baseball mitt, and the Visible Woman, still lying in her box like Sleeping Beauty. We packed our sleds, which we had bought that winter, and two pairs of wooden skis, which we never used in Mussoorie because the mountains were too steep. The barrels were full of foodstuffs, sachets of Fleischmann's yeast, tins of Hershey's cocoa, bags of chocolate chips,

bottles of vanilla and maple essence, food coloring, jars of spices—
thyme, rosemary, and oregano. My mother had bought an
assortment of kitchen utensils with green stamps that she collected
from the supermarket, a set of Oneida silverware, carving knives
and an electric mixer, measuring cups and a folding stepstool.
There were also plenty of clothes to be taken with us to India—
socks and underwear, jeans and T-shirts, winter jackets, sweatshirts
and pajamas, all of them a couple sizes too large so that we'd have
time to grow into them. In one of the barrels my father packed
boxes of rifle and shotgun shells, as well as a reloading kit and tins
of gunpowder, percussion caps, primers, and hollow-point bullets
for his .30-06. There was also a Crossman pellet gun which I had
purchased with money that I saved up over the year. All of these
objects were loaded into the barrels and wedged into place with
wadded pieces of newspaper so that nothing would rattle about.

Each of the barrels was sealed and locked and on the side my
father painted his name and address in white lettering: Robert C.
Alter, Woodstock School, Mussoorie U.P., India. When the ship-
pers came and took the barrels away, I felt as if our sea freight contained everything that we would need for the rest of our lives.
There was no reason for us to ever come back to America again.

THE LYRE TREE

A solitary chir pine stood in front of the administrative buildings at Woodstock School, its branches curving upward in the shape of a Grecian lyre. With coarse, reticulated bark and a delicate cross-stitching of needles, this tree served as an emblem for the school and appeared on Woodstock's flag and crest. The graceful symmetry of its limbs suggested the classical ideals of ancient Greece but the tree was also an enduring symbol of the natural history of Garhwal, the Himalayan forests, which provided a unique setting for the school.

Woodstock's Latin motto, "Palme Non Sine Pulvere" (No Palm of Victory Without the Dust of Struggle), suggested a philosophy of education steeped in Victorian rhetoric and hyperbole. Founded as a Protestant girls school in 1854, Woodstock was originally staffed by a group of English women who were members of the Society for Promoting Female Education in the East. Their objectives were to teach "the basics of literacy and mathematics and also included sewing, embroidery, darning, knitting, music, drawing, deportment (posture and presence), morals (catechism) and the proper address of superiors, inferiors or equals." In 1874 the school was taken over by the Presbyterian Board of Foreign Missions and became an institution for missionary children, while continuing to serve British and Anglo-Indian students. From the very beginning Christianity remained the guiding principle at Woodstock, bringing together the diverse and conflicting theologies of the hillside community. These religious tensions underscored the insularity and isolation of Landour, as well as the pettiness and dogma which so many of the missionaries inflicted upon the school.

When my grandmother arrived in Landour in 1917 and saw the mountains for the first time, she wondered how the Indians failed "to receive from them a purer spiritual inspiration." Nearly fifty years later I was forced to ask myself how it was possible that so many of the missionaries could fail in the same regard. For me the Himalayas represented the overpowering presence of nature which could never be confined within the narrow boundaries of religion. Standing at the top of the hill and looking out across the Aglar Valley, it was impossible for me to understand how anyone could limit his beliefs to a single doctrine. Set against the broad panorama of white snow peaks and the tangled green foliage of a monsoon jungle, the red tin roofs of the school and mission properties were reduced to insignificance. The incoherent babble of proselytizing voices, some of them speaking in tongues, was muffled by the silence of the trees.

As a child I had accepted Christianity without hesitation, though even at a young age it seemed a dull and uninspiring religion compared to the fireworks of Hinduism. The burning effigies of Ravanna, which I witnessed during Dasehra celebrations, and the brightly painted idols of Hanuman and Ganesh, seemed much more interesting, even if I couldn't conceive of them as gods. By the time I came back to Mussoorie after our furlough in Princeton,

I had begun to doubt that there were any deities at all. Gradually, as I grew older and entered high school, I came to accept the fact that I didn't believe in God. From time to time I tried to search within myself for some hint of faith, encouraged by friends and teachers at Woodstock, but there was nothing there, not even the slightest trace of conviction.

My nascent atheism could easily have become a crisis, except that my mother and father did not impose their religion on me. I was free to question the existence of God yet never felt that I was challenging my parents' values or beliefs. Instead, I was turning against the self-righteous, charismatic forms of Christianity that were so prevalent in Landour, the hysterical preachings of funda-mentalist missionaries who believed that India was full of satanic evil and that they and their brethren had taken it upon themselves to save the souls of eight hundred million sinners.

For me the existence of symbols in nature, such as the Lyre Tree, stood for something much larger and more profound than any rigid system of beliefs. The inescapable irony of Landour was that even though the mountains reached all the way to heaven, so many of the missionaries refused to acknowledge the potency of myth and metaphor. They believed in a literal interpretation of the Bible which dictated that the natural world was nothing more than the handiwork of a single master craftsman, the tinkerings of divine ingenuity, constructed over the space of seven fateful days. Even as they admired "the Lord's creations" these missionaries failed to realize the irrelevance of their simplistic beliefs in the face of nature's complex serenity. To my mind the shape of a tree, the arch of its branches and the invisible strength of its roots, presented the most powerful enigma of all.

. . .

In the summer of 1968, my father took over as principal of Wood-stock. Even though my parents had worked at the school before, the circumstances were entirely different now. Woodstock became the central focus of our lives, with all of the traditions, privileges, and obligations that my father's job entailed. Up until this time my parents had avoided most of the squabbles and politics of Landour, but now it was impossible for them to escape the swirling controversies that surrounded the school.

For the first year or two after we came back from furlough I was oblivious of much of what was going on in my parents' lives. Occasionally I listened in on their conversations at the dinner table or overheard discussions during one of the many meetings that were held in our living room, planning sessions and conferences, which would determine Woodstock's changing character. From behind the door of my father's office I could hear his voice, mumbling into the Dictaphone, as he wrote a steady stream of letters and reports, minutes and memorandums. My parents and others believed that Woodstock needed to become more of an international school and open up the enrollment to students from different backgrounds, particularly students from India. At the same time it was difficult for many people on the hillside to accept these changes, and there were heated debates about the future of the school.

The principal's residence, known as Woodstock Cottage, was situated just below the Tehri Road, about a hundred feet from the Lyre Tree and the main school buildings. It was a comfortable, boxy house, much more substantial than most of the other cottages in Landour but not as spacious as our bungalows on the plains. The front yard, which was covered with gravel, overlooked Landour bazaar and the Dehra Dun Valley. At the back of the house was a set of godowns, storerooms with servants' quarters on the second floor.

Canon and Mrs. Burgoyne, the former principal and his wife, had employed Prem Masih as their cook for many years. When we moved into Woodstock Cottage my parents hired him to work for us. Our old cook, Ram Dayal, had retired and gone back to his village on the plains near Etah. Prem was from Kumaon, an area of the Himalayas to the east of Mussoorie. Unlike Ram Dayal he was a Christian, having converted when he was still a teenager, while working at the British officers' mess in Ranikhet. A reserved man, slight of build and dignified, Prem always dressed in Western clothes, shirt and trousers, though he wore a Gandhi cap on his head. Perhaps because he worked at the principal's house, Prem styled himself a notch above the other servants on the hillside. As a cook, he had a wider range of menus than Ram Dayal and he was a master at preparing meals for large groups of people, which was a good thing because my parents entertained at least twice a week.

Prem and his wife, Panna, had three daughters and two sons, who lived with them in the quarters behind our house. The eldest daughter, Umma, went away to college just before we moved into Woodstock Cottage, but their younger daughters, Lila and Usha, and their sons, Pritam and Parvesh, were about our age. It didn't take my brothers and me very long to strike up a friendship with Prem's children and we played together in our yard almost every day, hard-fought games of gulli danda, pittu, and kabbadi. Several other boys from the nearby quarters at the school joined us as well, Ratan, Mukesh, and Pyare Lal.

In school, I had a different set of friends, many of whom had been with me at Woodstock since first grade. Throughout the day I spent my time with them but after school most of my classmates returned to the dormitories and I went home to play with Pritam and Parvesh. The two of them attended Rama Devi, a Hindi medium school in the bazaar, and even though they knew a little English we always talked in Hindi. Having been away from India for a year, I found myself struggling to speak the language correctly. I kept trying to construct complete, grammatical sentences and match the endings of my verbs to the masculine and feminine nouns; for that reason my Hindi sounded awkward and self-conscious. It took at least a month or two before I was able to retrieve the natural cadences of my speech, including the colloquial twists of syntax and the odd English word or phrase which I slipped in from time to time.

The correct forms of address for superiors, equals, and inferiors were no longer part of the Woodstock curriculum but the complex grammar of Hindi allowed for class distinctions with a choice of three personal pronouns—"tu," "tum," and "aap." When I was speaking with my brothers or Pritam and Parvesh, I used "tu," which would have been considered rude if I said it to anyone else. "Tum" was a slightly less familiar version of "you," which I employed when I spoke to the servants or coolies on the hillside. "Aap" was the most polite form of address, and that was how I referred to my parents and teachers, shopkeepers in the bazaar, and other adults. The significance of these pronouns I understood instinctively, the subtle gradations of politeness and courtesy which governed the hierarchy of our relationships in Landour.

Pritam and Parvesh often came indoors to play with my brothers and me, but as soon as it was time for dinner, Prem would call them out and send them home. We seldom went into their quarters, which consisted of two small rooms and a cramped veranda. As I grew older and entered high school, my relationship with Prem's children changed and I began to spend more time with my classmates at school. Though I still played gulli danda or kabaddi with them off and on, our friendships became more complicated and slowly we moved apart, as I became aware of the invisible boundaries that lay between us.

I had grown up with servants all my life and it was something that I took for granted, even though I sometimes wondered about the roles we played. To help Prem in the kitchen, my parents hired a young man named Chandu, who came from Pauri Garhwal. He was in his early twenties, but not much taller than my brother Andy, who was seven years old. Chandu served as a bearer and masalchi, helping to run errands and wash dishes in the kitchen. He also traveled with us when we went camping and became an expert at cooking meals over an open fire.

The school provided us with a part-time mali, or gardener, whose name was Akbar, a tall, soft-spoken man who tried valiantly to maintain the flower beds which we trampled in our careless games. One of the Woodstock sweepers cleaned our house, a man named Bhulan, who was an accomplished musician and performed on Independence Day and other occasions, playing the harmonium and singing ghazels. In the living room of Woodstock Cottage we had an old upright piano and sometimes, if my parents weren't at home, Bhulan could be persuaded to play a song or two for us, usually film tunes from Hindi movies like *Anarkali* and *Dev Das*. He had a mellow, romantic voice and used only one hand to pick the music from the keys.

Occasionally, when Bhulan was assigned to other duties at the school, Shiv Charan would sweep our house. He was much more talkative than the other servants, and greeted us with an exaggerated salute and a vigorous "Salaam." Shiv Charan was something of a clown and Prem and the other servants teased him mercilessly. Most of the time he put up with it in good humor, joking back at them or laughing at himself, but if any of us used the word "kaith" within his hearing, Shiv Charan lost his temper. This was something that nobody could explain. As far as I knew, kaith was nothing more than a harmless green fruit, though Shiv Charan responded to the word as if it was the worst kind of obscenity. After sweeping the house, he would drink a glass of tea outside the kitchen and just to goad him on, I would ask Shiv Charan if he wanted me to get him some kaith for breakfast. Immediately he would explode and begin to berate me in an angry voice, saying that it was a terrible thing (he never uttered the word himself) and I should be ashamed of myself for speaking to him like this. Prem and Chandu always laughed and joined in the teasing though I finally stopped because I sensed a resentment and bitterness underlying the absurdity of the joke.

. . .

By the end of the sixties Woodstock was facing a declining enrollment and there was a possibility that the school was going to have to close down. The number of missionaries in India had diminished considerably and financial support from church groups in America was tapering off. One of the possibilities was that Woodstock might merge with another mission school, at Kodaikanal, in South India. Both institutions offered an American curriculum and shared many of the same traditions, but when it came to deciding which of the schools would actually shift, nobody was prepared to make that move. I'm sure my father never had any intention of closing Woodstock down but he was open to discussing the matter, and a joint committee was set up to decide which location was most suitable. Each school felt that they had more to offer. Kodai was located in the Palni Hills of Tamil Nadu, with a beautiful campus overlooking a lake. The board members from Kodai conceded that they did not have the snow views of Landour, but jokingly offered to whitewash some of the Palni Hills to make them look like the Himalayas. One of their main complaints about Woodstock was the steepness of the ridge and the amount of climbing that was required, hiking back and forth between the dormitories. They were also worried about the dangers of students falling down the khud, though my father and others kept insisting that the hillside was perfectly safe.

One Saturday morning, as the delegation from Kodai was meeting with my father and other administrators on our front veranda, my brothers and I were playing with Pritam and Parvesh in the backyard of Woodstock Cottage. We had been told not to disturb the meeting as negotiations were reaching a critical point and recommendations had finally been made that Kodai should close down and move up to Mussoorie. Meanwhile, my brothers and I were making paper airplanes and flying them off the edge of the yard below Prem's quarters. The khud dropped away steeply beneath the pushta wall, a vertical drop of about seventy feet to the path below. Most of our paper airplanes landed in the trees and bushes just below the house but one of mine circled out and caught an updraft, sailing above the tops of the nearby oaks. A few more feet and the plane might have cleared the trees and made it all the way to Witch's Hill. I watched the airplane hover like a paper moth, trembling in the breeze. Then, just as it was about to dart across the valley, the plane banked suddenly, wheeled around, and came back toward us, landing about fifteen feet below where I was standing.

Determined to retrieve my plane, I climbed over the fence and down the pushta wall to a ledge below. From there I could see the plane stranded in the branches of a yellow jasmine bush, and I edged my way down the slope to try and reach it. The rubber chappals I was wearing offered little traction and just as I was about to reach out and pick up the plane, my foot slipped and I began to slide down the hill. I grabbed at one of the tree dahlias growing on the khud but the stalk broke off in my hand and this threw me into a tumble. There was nothing I could do to stop myself as I hurtled down the slope, crashing head over heels through the undergrowth.

The next thing that I remember is finding myself lying on the cement path below Woodstock Cottage. At first there was no pain, only a heaviness in my arms and legs, as if I could not move. My clothes were torn and I couldn't see out of my left eye, because of the blood that was collecting in the socket. Dirt and bits of grass were in my mouth and my right foot was beginning to throb.

The meeting with the Kodai delegation was continuing on the veranda, when Prem came bursting through the front door to tell my father that I had fallen over the khud. Within a few minutes all of the committee members came running down the hill to find me lying there, spread-eagled on the path. I must have looked much worse than I felt, for I could see that several of them were badly shaken, thinking I was dead or paralyzed. My father knelt beside me and told me not to move. For some reason I was laughing, embarrassed and relieved, still breathless from my fall. A dandie was brought from the school and I was loaded into it and carried off to the hospital. The X rays showed no broken bones, though I was badly bruised and had a mild concussion. A cut on my scalp had bled a lot and I needed seven stitches.

A few days later my father told me that the delegation from Kodai had almost been persuaded to merge with Woodstock, until the moment of my accident. Seeing me lying there, injured on the path, and looking at the vertical slope down which I'd fallen, they decided that it was better to remain where they were instead of moving up to Landour.

*   *   *

More than a dozen boarding schools were located in Mussoorie, almost all of which were English medium institutions. Waverly Convent, the oldest school in town, lay on the other side of Library bazaar. Beyond that was the Tibetan School in Happy Valley and Vincent Hill, which used to be run by the Seventh-Day Adventists and was later sold to a group of Sikhs who renamed it Guru Nanak Fifth Centenary School. Some of the other schools were Hampton Court, Mussoorie Modern School, Pinewood, and Bramleigh Towers, which went bankrupt. Across the valley from Woodstock was Wynberg Allen, a coeducational school, where the boys and girls were housed on different campuses. Farther down the ridge in Barlowganj was St. George's College, a Catholic boys' academy that was run by Irish brothers. Beyond that was Oak Grove School in Jharipanni, which was exclusively for children of Indian railway officials.

Most of our encounters with these schools took place on the playing field. The Mussoorie Schools Sports Association organized tournaments throughout the year and our teams competed in a variety of different games. Woodstock never did very well at field hockey, badminton, table tennis, or soccer, though we were the perennial champions in basketball and held our own in cricket, swimming, and tennis. I played hockey and soccer but my favorite sports were cross-country and track.

I started running in seventh grade, as soon as we got back from Princeton, and by the time I was a freshman I made it onto the varsity cross-country team. Our races were held along the Tehri Road, which was still unpaved, a steady climb to Ashton Court. When it rained, as it often did, the hard-packed surface of the road turned slick with mud, and the other runners disappeared behind me in the mist. I enjoyed cross-country because it was a solitary sport, escaping the cheering crowds and running against the mountain itself, the steep gradient that slowed my pace, the altitude that made my lungs ache. On weekday mornings before breakfast, my brothers and I would train together, running three or four miles out the Tehri Road and back. Though I set records at the school, I seldom timed myself, not really caring about the minutes and seconds. Much more important was that feeling of release, breaking free of the pack and being the first to reach the turning point, then hurtling down the hill, dropping my arms and lifting my knees, sprinting around the corners, a weightless feeling in my legs. Sometimes I thought that if I just kept going straight, instead of turning with the road, I would fly right out across the valley to the other side.

Sports Day, the intramural track and field competition, was held on Hanson Field, which was the only level section of the Landour hillside large enough to fit a 220-yard running track. The field was situated in the valley a couple hundred feet below Ridgewood. It was named in memory of a former student, Robert Hanson, an ace fighter pilot during World War II who was shot down over the Pacific. Hanson Field was built on an unstable part of the hillside and sections of the flat would collapse during the monsoon. One year, when a huge landslide covered part of the field, the track was kidney shaped.

On Sports Day each class had its own flag and uniform, with matching stripes on our shorts. For several years our class flag had a rampant leopard on a turquoise background, with a '74 in the corner, but that was eventually changed to a psychedelic patchwork of flowers and peace symbols. Sports Day began with a march-past in the morning—Mr. Hilliard barking out commands and each of the captains chanting, "Left, Left, Left, Right, Left." As we went by the bleachers Jamie Gilmore would call out, "Class of Seventy-four, eyes right!" and all of us would snap our heads around and look at the crowd of parents and teachers cheering from the steps. The band played John Philip Sousa's "Stars and Stripes Forever," while each class marched once around the track, then lined up in the middle of the field to form a *W*.

Over the loudspeaker system Frenchie Brown announced each of the events and the day was punctuated by the sharp report of Ron Kapadia's starting pistol and a volley of cheers as the runners sped around the gravel track. Diana Biswas always supervised the shot put and long jump, standing in the middle of the field with her clipboard and measuring tape. Even though there was a competitive atmosphere it was also a leisurely day, and by the afternoon one race blurred into the next. I ran the 880 and the mile, which were scheduled several hours apart, and most of my time was spent lounging in the sun with the rest of my classmates. Sports Day ended with a series of relay races, after which we waited expectantly to hear the final tally and find out which class had won.

Two weeks later was the Mussoorie Olympics, a track-and-field meet for all of the schools in town. This was a much more serious competition and the best athletes from each class were picked to represent Woodstock. The Olympics were the only occasion when all of the Mussoorie schools got together. Several thousand students congregated on Wynberg Allen Flat and it was like a carnival with food vendors and cold drink stalls. Woodstock provided the band which played for the march-past. The other schools had uniforms, blazers, and ties, while we dressed in our brown flannel sweatsuits with gold stripes on the sleeves. Our team mascot was the tiger and our school colors were brown and gold. Woodstock was always the scruffiest team on the field, marching out of step and waving to the crowd. The flag bearers carried the school banner in front of us, emblazoned with the symbol of the Lyre Tree.

. . .

Being the principal's son had its advantages and disadvantages. For one thing I didn't have to live in the dormitories and our house was close enough to the school so that my brothers and I were able to come home for lunch. Most of the time I didn't feel excluded or singled out because of my father's position, even though there were a lot of discipline problems at the school. Each semester a number of students got in trouble for one thing or another, and some of them were suspended or expelled. Once or twice I saw my father's name scrawled on the bathroom walls, but it was the high school headmaster and a couple of other staff members who attracted most of the criticism and resentment.

Like any school, Woodstock had its share of problems with tobacco, alcohol, and drugs. At the tea shops and paan wallahs in the bazaar we could easily purchase cigarettes or bidis, a cheap cheroot. Beer and spirits were somewhat more difficult to buy, but marijuana grew wild around the hillside. There was even a licensed vendor in the bazaar who sold hashish and bhang. Most of the chemists in Mussoorie didn't ask for a prescription and students were able to buy a variety of pills and capsules across the counter. With so many forbidden substances available it was surprising that there weren't more serious incidents at the school, though several students were expelled for taking drugs.

In ninth grade I had a classmate from Thailand, Sirilak Komutklang, who gave me smoking lessons. Lighting up a Charminar he demonstrated the different ways of holding it between his fingers and showed me how to blow smoke rings into the air. He also did a trick, where he put a burning cigarette on his tongue and took the whole thing inside his mouth, as if he'd swallowed it. Sirilak was a year or two older than I and considered himself a man of the world, telling me stories about massage parlors and prostitutes in Bangkok. One Saturday the two of us went into the bazaar and he offered to buy me lunch at a restaurant called Whispering Windows. The two of us sat upstairs, at one of the corner tables, the darkest section of the room, and Sirilak ordered two bottles of Golden Eagle beer. The proprietor of Whispering Windows, D. P. Singh, was a friend of my father's and I was afraid that we would get caught, but Sirilak kept calling me a coward and made me try some beer, pouring it into my glass of Coca-Cola.

By the time we left Whispering Windows, Sirilak had finished off three bottles of Golden Eagle and he could barely walk. Afraid that someone was going to see us, I hired a ricksha to take us home. Along the way, Sirilak kept falling asleep, and realizing that he needed a couple of hours to sober up I told the ricksha coolies to let us off at the Rialto Cinema. The only movie showing was a Hindi film, *Heer Ranja*, starring Raj Kumar. The picture had already started as Sirilak and I stumbled down the aisle and found our seats. Fortunately there was nobody from Woodstock in the audience and Sirilak was able to sleep off the beer while I watched the movie with a sense of guilt and apprehension.

Toward the end of our freshman year a group of my classmates got busted for smoking at a party on the hillside. I had been invited to join them but decided to go hunting on Witch's Hill instead. Afterward I was glad I hadn't attended the party because my father met with each student who got caught and they were straight-gated for the rest of the year.

Even though we already had a reputation for being a hippie school, the name "Woodstock" took on another meaning altogether with the rock concert in 1969. The movie *Woodstock* came out a year later and it was shown at the Rialto Cinema. All of us went down to see it and I remember Jimi Hendrix playing "The Star-Spangled Banner" and seeing Bob Dylan and Joan Baez on the screen. Many of the students at Woodstock dressed in bell-bottoms and flowered shirts, loose kurtas and Nehru jackets. Most of the boys let their hair grow out and the girls wore miniskirts. Dancing was now permitted at the school, after my father became principal, and every Wednesday night the high school students gathered in the hostel common room and danced to the music of Santana ("Abraxas"), Creedence Clearwater Revival ("Who'll Stop the Rain?"), and Crosby, Stills and Nash ("Woodstock"). Some of the couples danced together but most of the time it was each person by him- or herself, the lights turned low and the music shaking the hard cement floor. Sina Singh would sail about the common room, his mane of long hair flying behind him and his arms moving like a Kathakali dancer to the pulsing rhythm of "In-A-Gadda-Da-Vida."

Thanks to the Maharishi and Ravi Shankar, India was "in" and students at Woodstock adopted many of the counterculture symbols, learning to play sitars and tabla, wearing beads and medallions, which we could buy from the Tibetan shops in the bazaar. There was plenty of incense available and all of the paraphernalia that was being sold in novelty shops in America, water pipes and chillums, strings of beads and posters of Hindu gods and goddesses. This flowering of alternative lifestyles at Woodstock led to problems with the conservative Christians on the hillside and the issue came to a head in June of 1971.

By tradition, each graduating class had its flag pinned up on the curtains behind the stage during the commencement ceremonies. Most of these were simple banners with colored stripes and numbers, but a group of the students in the class of 1971 had designed a flag on which the symbol ॐ appeared. Om represented a sacred sound, a vowel, which invoked the presence of God, and it was often chanted as a part of Hindu prayers. To the conservative members of the class and their parents, Om stood for ignorance and evil, and they refused to sit beneath the ॐ. The rest of the class insisted that the flag should be displayed during their graduation. What began as a minor controversy escalated into a serious crisis, and this one letter of the alphabet divided the school and led to the cancellation of the graduation ceremony that year. No amount of compromise and conciliation worked to calm the tempers, and the year ended with a flood of bitterness and acrimony.

Soon afterward, some of the more conservative missions set up separate boarding facilities at Claremont and Dahlia Bank to protect their children from the corrupting influences in the Woodstock dorms. The divisions became even more acute and the students who were born-again Christians began to separate themselves from the rest of the school. Every Sunday afternoon they gathered for Bible Club at one of several houses near the top of the hill. They sang revival songs, listened to inspirational speakers, and prayed for the rest of us who were not there.

Around this time a number of hippies, or "freaks," as we called them, came wandering through Mussoorie, searching for enlightenment, nirvana, or simply a free meal and a cheap place to live. They gravitated toward the school and some of the missionaries took it upon themselves to convert these lost souls, many of whom were ill with dysentery and homesick for the West. These world travelers were vulnerable to the offer of a clean bed and the comforting ministrations of a motherly memsahib, chicken soup, a dose of Flagyl for their amoeba, and the seductive promise of being born again. Once they had been converted and regained their health these people hung around Landour and tried to share their newfound faith with those students who they believed had gone astray. One of these Jesus freaks was an Italian named Mario who was so obnoxious that my father had to ban him from the school.

Several evangelical groups from the States visited Woodstock, sponsored by the Bible Club. These were traveling troupes of Christian revivalists from the American heartland who flew around the world spreading their message of deliverance from sin and the redeeming power of the Holy Spirit. One group, called the Potter's Clay, put on a show in Parker Hall. Their performance began with several Christian songs, set to lively country-and-western tunes played on electric guitars. Their lyrics spoke of "the tender love of Jesus," "his close embrace," and "the soft caress of his forgiveness." It was seductive, toe-tapping music and the group was dressed in matching outfits, miniskirts and boots, cowboy shirts with rhinestone collars. The women, all of whom had blond curls and toothy smiles, moved with a suggestive eroticism, as if they were cheerleaders for Christ.

Between each medley of songs, different members of the group stepped up to the microphone and delivered a testimonial, explaining in earnest, confiding voices how their lives had changed once they accepted Jesus as their savior. The stories they told described the sinfulness of their early lives (smoking, drinking, sex) followed by an emotional epiphany, that moment when they finally saw the light of the Lord. Each testimonial offered a similar formula, and we were expected to follow their example and offer ourselves up for redemption. These performances had the opposite effect on me. I found the slick commercialism obscene and could not help but feel that we were being manipulated by the music, the costumes, and the persuasive voices of these born-again Americans. The prepackaged evangelism of groups such as the Potter's Clay only served to reconfirm my own rejection of Christianity.

*   *   *

I had heard of Frank Wesley long before he came to teach art at Woodstock. He was a well-known painter, an Indian Christian artist from Azamgarh, a small town in eastern Uttar Pradesh. As with many converts his family had adopted Western names. Mr. Wesley's paintings had been exhibited all over the world and his *Blue Madonna* was printed on one of the first UNICEF Christmas cards. My parents owned a watercolor of his, a mountain landscape with a thatch-roofed cowshed in the foreground. In 1969 he was hired to teach at Woodstock, and when I took my first class with Mr. Wesley I was in awe of him. He was a quiet, unassuming man, with an enormous mustache that twirled up at the ends. Somewhat hard of hearing, he could be impatient at times and was extremely demanding of his students, though he tempered his criticism with a wry sense of humor.

I had always been interested in drawing, even when I was in elementary school. During fifth grade, I began to copy cartoons from *Mad* magazine, which we used to buy in the bazaar. I also drew caricatures of my classmates and teachers which were passed around and got me into trouble more than once. But drawing was something that I didn't take very seriously until I began art classes with Frank Wesley. He taught us a variety of techniques, many of which were rooted in Indian artistic traditions. One of these was the Lucknow style of watercolor painting, which involved soaking the paper before applying a light, transparent wash. Some of Mr. Wesley's finest work was done in this style and the colors seemed to float above the surface of the paper. He also taught us how to paint frescoes, using the same process that was used in the Buddhist murals at the Ajanta and Ellora caves. On damp squares of plaster, we copied figures of Apsaras, lotus flowers, and elephants. Mr. Wesley was also a master of miniature painting, and he explained to us the subtle differences between Mogul miniatures with scenes of emperors and courtiers and the paintings of Kangra depicting the love play of Radha and Krishna.

As a young man, Frank Wesley had gone to Japan and studied painting and calligraphy. Whenever I got impatient with the exercises that he assigned, he would tell me that he had been forced to spend three months painting the same stick of bamboo again and again. He used to explain that the most important thing was not the act of painting itself but observing the subject long and hard enough, so that the image flowed effortlessly from the brush. I never achieved the discipline that Mr. Wesley expected of us, but I do remember working on a pen and ink drawing of a deodar tree for several days, trying to capture every detail. When I was almost finished with the picture, Mr. Wesley came up behind me and stood there for a minute or two, frowning at my drawing.

"What happened?" he said, with disapproval.

I looked up at him, confused.

"Tell me what's wrong with it," he said.

I stared at my drawing, trying to figure out what he was talking about.

"I don't know," I said.

"Look at the tree," he said, swatting me across the back of the head. "A deodar's branches always droop down at the end. You've drawn them so that they curve upward like a pine."

Saying this he reached down and tore the sheet of paper from my sketchbook and ordered me to start again.

Many of Frank Wesley's paintings depicted Christian themes and scenes from the Bible. Taking incidents from the life of Christ, he transposed them into an Indian context, painting a nativity scene with mud walls and thatch roofs, Mary dressed in a sari, surrounded by cows and buffaloes. One of his oil paintings was of Jesus in Banaras, dressed as a Hindu mendicant teaching a crowd of disciples on the banks of the Ganga. In almost all of his paintings the Christian iconography was grounded in an Indian setting and presented in an Indian style. One painting he did of Saul's conversion on the road to Damascus was similar to a Rajput miniature, with a turbaned figure on a horse approaching the red sandstone walls of a fortified city.

In many ways, Frank Wesley's paintings reversed the stereotypes of most Christian art, which tended to take the Scriptures out of context and portray Jesus and his disciples as Europeans. Even though I had no faith in God, I found Frank Wesley's vision of Christianity inspiring, a Lucknow watercolor of Lazarus as an emaciated beggar surrounded by pariah dogs, or the forgiving father embracing his prodigal son, who was dressed in a tattered dhoti. His Madonnas, of which he painted many, had the classical beauty of Gopis and Apsaras—*Madonna of the Mango Grove, Madonna of the Lotus Pool.*

While I was in his class, Frank Wesley began working on a

miniature of Saint Francis of Assisi. The composition of the picture was fairly simple, an ascetic figure dressed in saffron robes, seated on the ground in front of a ban oak. Surrounding Saint Francis were more than a hundred species of Indian birds. The painting was fifty-one by thirty centimeters and most of the birds were a fraction of a centimeter in size but accurately drawn. Mr. Wesley knew that I had recently started a bird collection, and as I sat and watched him working on the painting we discussed which different species should be included. Leafing through Salim Ali's *Book of Indian Birds*, the two of us chose the kalij pheasant that sat by Saint Francis's elbow, the egrets and brahminy ducks, as well as a bird of paradise flycatcher and a fork-tailed drongo. Working with brushes that were no more than a couple strands of sable, he re-created the brilliant plumage of each bird, picked out with the precision of a jeweler. Watching Frank Wesley complete that painting, over a period of several months, made me appreciate the spiritual side of his art, which transcended the boundaries of text and dogma. In addition to learning the discipline of painting I gained a greater understanding of man's place in nature, the image of Saint Francis, surrounded by a multitude of birds.

OPHRYSIA

The Mountain Quail—*Ophrysia superciliosa* (Grey)

Size: between a Quail and Partridge. Field Characters: Male: slaty grey-brown above tinged with olive. Forehead and prominent broad supercilium white, bordered above and below with black. Crown greyish brown with black streaks. Chin, throat, and face black, the last patterned with white. Under tail coverts black with broad white terminal bars. Short, stout coral-red bill (shaped rather like bush quail's), red legs, and relatively long tail for partridge make it unconfusable with any other game bird. Female: cinnamon-brown above, paler below, spotted and broadly streaked with black. Face pinkish grey; bill and legs duller red than in male. Distribution: known only in neighbourhoods of Mussoorie and Naini Tal. Last specimen procured near latter place in 1876. Habits: was found in patches of long grass and brushwood on steep hillsides, in small coveys of 5 or 6. Flew reluctantly almost when trampled on, heavily and for short distance, soon pitching into the grass again. Call: a shrill whistle.

Less than a dozen specimens exist in museums and nothing is known about its biology. All recent efforts to rediscover the bird have failed.

Ever since I first read about the mountain quail in Salim Ali's *Book of Indian Birds* it was my ambition to rediscover *Ophrysia superciliosa*. Nobody had seen this bird for almost a century and it was thought to be extinct, yet I firmly believed that one or two coveys still existed somewhere in the hills around Mussoorie. I was convinced that if I searched hard and long enough, surely I would find the mountain quail one day.

There was a colored illustration in the bird book, which I studied carefully, memorizing each feather, each distinguishing mark, the unusually long tail and coral red beak. I wanted to know exactly what Ophrysia looked like so that if I ever saw this rare bird, I would be able to recognize it immediately. The mountain quail was said to frequent grassy hillsides at altitudes between 5,000 and 6,500 feet. There were certain places I was sure Ophrysia could still be found—the southern slopes below Cloud's End and Benog Tibba, the valley between the villages of Patreni and Moti Dhar, or the abandoned fields at Cheli on the far side of Witch's Hill.

In seventh grade I started collecting birds with Scott Bunce and Fali Kapadia. Each of us had pellet guns and almost every day we would go hunting for specimens in the forests around Landour. Bob Fleming Jr., who was the biology teacher at Woodstock, taught us how to skin and mount the birds. He and his father, Robert Fleming Sr., were distinguished ornithologists and together they wrote the definitive field guide to birds of Nepal. More than anyone the Flemings were responsible for encouraging the study of natural history at Woodstock.

From the time that I began collecting beetles in elementary school, I had decided that I wanted to become a naturalist when I grew up. In my mind there was something noble and heroic about being a collector of rare and exotic specimens, an explorer discovering new species in the wilderness. At the beginning of ninth grade I joined the Woodstock Natural History Society, a club sponsored by the science department at the school. Among other activities, the WNHS published a book of field notes titled *Ophrysia*, a simple catalog of the flora and fauna of the Mussoorie Hills. The club also organized hikes in the mountains and trips to game sanctuaries on the plains. Our adviser, Joe Devol, was a graduate of Woodstock, who had returned to teach at the school. He himself had been a member of the WNHS as a boy and took a group of us on a field trip to Khanna wildlife preserve in Madhya Pradesh, where we saw tigers and gaur, the Indian bison. Each of us was expected to identify and collect different species of ferns and plants, bugs and butterflies, reptiles and birds. Through this process we learned the correct methods of taxonomy, the classification and preservation of scientific specimens. One of our incentives was that former members of the Woodstock Natural History Society had taken their bird collections back to America and sold the skins to museums in Chicago and Los Angeles.

In my enthusiasm, as a budding ornithologist, I set out to slaughter at least one pair of every bird in Mussoorie—scaly-bellied green woodpeckers, whistling thrushes, pygmy owlets, velvet-fronted nuthatches, red-billed blue magpies, and ashy drongos, all of which I killed in the name of science. Each of these had to be skinned and stuffed, a delicate process which involved parting the feathers on the bird's belly and making an incision from the vent up to the breastbone. After that I peeled away the skin, turning the bird inside out and removing any adhering bits of flesh, including the eyeballs and tongue. The specimen was then dusted with borax and stuffed with cotton wool, wrapped around a bamboo stick. The rarer birds, chir pheasants and bird of paradise flycatchers, were added to the Woodstock collection, which was displayed in a glass case along one wall of the biology lab. The rest of the more common birds were left to molder in my bedroom drawers and cupboards. Even with a generous amount of borax the specimens gave off a musty, decomposing smell, particularly during the monsoon, when their feathers were covered with a coating of yellow mildew.

I often dreamed of shooting *Ophrysia superciliosa* with my pellet gun and adding it to my collection. In my imagination I held the dead quail in my hand, running my fingers over the soft feathers on its breast and cutting it open with a razor blade. The flesh was still warm as I reached in and removed its crop, revealing the undigested seeds and berries that it had eaten. But the more I hunted for

Ophrysia, the more elusive it became. Whenever I was out in the hills, I listened for the telltale whistle, and the rustle of its wings as it took to the air. Though I felt its presence close at hand, my sixth sense telling me that it was near, I never saw Ophrysia. It remained an invisible spirit which lay beneath the surface of the wind, a feathered dream that permeated the landscape so that every movement of the grass, every sound conveyed its absence.

There were birds of prey in Mussoorie that must have hunted for the mountain quail as well, crested serpent eagles and giant lammergeiers which circled on the rising thermals, their feathers slicing through the clouds. Kites and kestrels hovered overhead on tremulous wings, searching the grassy slopes with eyes that could spot the slightest movement on the ground below. If Ophrysia was still alive their talons would have found the quail before I could, the raptors' beaks tearing apart its flesh and scattering its feathers on the wind.

One winter, when I was hunting with my father near the city limits beyond Jabberkhet, two birds flew out of the grass beneath my feet. Raising the shotgun to my shoulder I fired instinctively and one of them crumpled in midflight, dropping lifeless to the ground. For a few seconds I was certain that I had shot the mountain quail, though when I ran forward to pick it up I found a chukor partridge, similar in color, but larger, with a mottled breast and dull red beak. Another time, as I was walking home in the dark along the Eyebrow path, I shone my torch into the bushes at the side of the trail and noticed a bird huddled in the leaves. It was sitting absolutely still, dazzled by the light. For a brief moment the possibility crossed my mind that this might be the mountain quail, but stepping closer, I saw it was a pyura, a common hill partridge, about the same size but with different markings. As I reached out to catch the bird, it must have seen the shadow of my hand, and it flew off in a panic down the hill.

The name, Ophrysia, had an enigmatic quality, as if it were a mythological bird, something out of a Latin bestiary. Even though there were several specimens hidden away in British museums, I sometimes wondered if the mountain quail had ever actually existed, or if it was just the figment of an ornithologist's imagination, a Victorian explorer making up the names of unknown species as he went along. To those of us who searched for this bird, Ophrysia represented something larger than itself, as if it were a symbol of the tenuous balance in nature, a reminder of our own extinction.

*   *   *

On February 22, 1970, two members of the Woodstock Natural History Society, Fred Baur and Kenny Getter, died in an accident while they were traveling up to Mussoorie at the end of the winter holidays. I was waiting at the school gate for the first students to arrive on Coming Up Day when my father received a telegram to say that they had both been killed. Kenny was a senior and Fred a junior; both of them were in the Raipur party, returning from mission stations in the Chattisgarh area of Madhya Pradesh, where their parents worked. It was two days' journey from Raipur to Dehra Dun, and on the first night, soon after dark, the boys climbed onto the roof of the railway carriage in which they were riding. Passengers on the Indian railways often sit on the roofs of overcrowded trains, but along this route there was a low bridge across a river and one of the girders struck both boys and killed them instantly. Fred was knocked off of the train and into the water while Kenny fell backward onto the roof. Someone in the carriage below must have heard the sound and alerted the chaperons, who pulled the emergency alarm and stopped the train.

With this tragedy, the school was thrown into a state of shock and mourning. As each party arrived at the bus stand in Mussoorie they were told the news, and students walked through the bazaar, many of them in tears. Nothing like this had ever happened to us before and the new term began with the shadow of their deaths hanging over us. Up until that moment, we had always thought of ourselves as invincible, too young to die, yet in a fraction of a second, as the train rattled its way through the night, two of our schoolmates were killed, leaving the rest of us afraid and vulnerable. A memorial service was held in Parker Hall. My father and others spoke and prayed, trying to comfort and reassure us, though a sense of despair remained throughout the spring semester and on into the following year.

The Woodstock Natural History Society established a memorial fund to buy camping equipment, which students could sign out for weekend hikes. That same year we published a new edition of *Ophrysia*, which contained a dedication to Kenny Getter and Fred Baur. Even though I was several years younger and didn't know either of the boys very well, their deaths affected me more than I expected. I had never imagined that anything like this could take place at Woodstock. We seemed to live a charmed existence, invulnerable, untouched by danger, but after the accident I realized how often we took risks, whether it was climbing the cliffs around Mussoorie or riding in crowded buses along the precipitous mountain roads. Death had always seemed to be something far away, removed from our experience, but here it was, arriving with the start of school.

*   *   *

The subject of evolution was generally avoided at Woodstock and I only learned about Darwin's theories indirectly. The more liberal missionaries, such as my parents, found no contradiction between Darwin's ideas and Christian teaching. For them Scripture and science presented intersecting sets of myths and metaphors that only added resonance to the mystery of our origins. But there were many on the hillside who saw this as a form of heresy, and at least two of my science teachers were hard-bitten creationists.

Most of what I learned about Darwin's theories came from articles in magazines like *National Geographic*, and I gained only a superficial and incomplete knowledge of concepts such as natural selection. The only point at which the controversy over evolution really came to the surface at Woodstock was when we were shown a film in Parker Hall, *Inherit the Wind*, based on the Scopes Monkey Trial. Some of the more conservative students were not allowed to watch the movie because of their parents' fundamentalist beliefs. It may have been that the Landour community was so divided on the issue of creation that there was no room for any logical discourse. Instead of learning about dinosaurs and fossils, early hominids and Darwin's travels to the Galapagos Islands, we busied ourselves collecting and identifying as many different Himalayan species as we could. Being a member of the Woodstock Natural History Society, I learned the basics of taxonomy, the general order of things, but my voyage into science carried me aboard Noah's Ark instead of Darwin's *Beagle*.

Our pursuit of natural history had a destructive, predatory aspect. Most of my collections involved killing things in order to preserve them. An empty bottle, in which I placed a wad of cotton wool soaked in ether, served as an execution chamber for hundreds of butterflies and beetles. The magnifying lens with which I studied the colors on a grasshopper's wing could just as easily be turned at an angle to the sun, focusing the rays into a searing pinpoint of light that made the insect leap with pain. As a junior scientist, I was as much a torturer as I was a naturalist, impaling butterflies and moths with pins, bursting the egg sac on a spider, or pulling off the wings on dragonflies.

At every chance we got, Scott Bunce and I would hike out to Flag Hill or the Haunted House above Jabberkhet and search for snakes and lizards, turning over rocks and boulders. The most common species were brown and yellow grass snakes, which were not poisonous. We also caught graceful dhamans, sleek green serpents that grew to three or four feet in length. There were several poisonous snakes as well, particularly the Himalayan pit vipers, which were a rusty brown color and had a diamond-shaped head. When I was in fifth grade, my friend Craig Wertz was bitten by a pit viper.

His father, who was the doctor at the Landour Community Hospital, tied a tourniquet around Craig's forearm and cut an X on his hand to suck the poison out. A pit viper's bite is seldom fatal, though Craig's arm swelled up to twice its size and his fingers turned a greenish hue, the color of a peacock feather.

Several years later, when I was walking on the Eyebrow with Betsy Scott, we came upon a pit viper sunning itself in the middle of the path. Using a stick I was able to pin down the snake's head, and I asked Betsy to go back to her house to get an empty bottle to put it in. Soon after she returned, Alfred Powell, who used to manage the Presbyterian properties on the hillside, came around the corner. I was just about to grab the pit viper behind its head and try to slide it into the bottle when Mr. Powell began to give me instructions, waving his walking stick about like a baton. By this time my hands were shaking badly, but I couldn't very well back down, with Betsy watching me, and Mr. Powell making it sound as simple as tying your shoelace.

I did finally get the snake inside the bottle and took the pit viper to school the following day. We kept it in an aquarium in the biology lab and I trapped mice and rats in our attic to feed the snake. Dropping a live mouse into the aquarium I watched as the pit viper slowly raised its head three or four inches, poised and ready to strike. The snake moved faster than the human eye and all I heard was a snapping sound as the mouse fell backward, stunned and quivering. A few weeks later, the pit viper itself eventually died, and I put it in a jar of formaldehyde, curled up like a question mark.

In ninth grade I got interested in botany and started a fern and leaf collection, mounting the dried specimens on sheets of paper, which I kept in loose-leaf folders. For a while I also had a mushroom and lichen collection, until a pet kitten of ours ate several of my specimens and died. In biology class we used a book called *Keys to Mussoorie Plants* by Winfield Dudgeon. It was a thin volume, published in 1929 and intended "to enable the plant-lover who is untrained in botany to find the names of the more common and conspicuous trees, shrubs, climbing plants, and herbaceous flowering plants about Mussoorie." The system of identification used by Dudgeon, who had been a professor of biology at Ewing Christian College in Allahabad, was relatively simple. He had a list of numbered traits by which we could differentiate one specimen from another. For instance, the first choice under the category of trees was:

1) leaves relatively broad (more than 1/4 inch broad)—2
1) leaves very narrow (not more than 1/10 inch broad)—49

Studying the specimen in my hand I moved on to the corresponding number and matched the different traits: juice milky—5, juice not milky—7; leaves white or distinctly whitish beneath—11, leaves green beneath—12. Finally, through a process of elimination, the specimen could be identified:

11) leaves with a layer of fine cottony hairs beneath: Quercus *incana* (ban oak).

Once I got used to the key it was possible for me to identify most of the flowers, shrubs, and trees in Mussoorie. Many of these plants I already knew, like *Strobilanthes dalhousianus*, the "purple poppers" which I used to burst against my forehead as a child. They made a snapping sound and left an inky stain on my skin. After I had used Dudgeon's *Keys* for a year or two, I discovered another book, *Flora Simlensis*, which was a guide to the botany of Simla, published in 1902. It contained more detailed information, as well as line drawings of a number of different species. The author of *Flora Simlensis* was Colonel Sir Henry Collett, K.C.B., F.L.S., of the Bengal army. His description of a ban oak was full of cryptic details:

Quercus incana, Roxb.; *Fl Br, Ind* v.603. Leaves stalked, ovate-lanceolate, 3-51/4 - 2 in., Spinous-toothed towards the tip; upper surface glabrous, lower white-tomentose. Male flowers: stamens 3–5. Female flowers: styles 3. Acorns single or in pairs; cup at first almost covering the nut, but only about half of it when mature; scales imbricate; nut ovoid, white-tomentose when young, ultimately glabrous, brown. (Fig. 154)

Most of this meant nothing to me, for I had never studied Latin and I did not understand the archaic botanical terms. The accompanying illustration of leaves and acorns, however, was unmistakable. According to the title page of the book these drawings were sketched by Miss M. Smith, "artist at the herbarium, Royal Botanic Gardens, Kew."

In this way I learned the names and characteristics of many different species of Himalayan plants. Winfield Dudgeon's precise, yet time-consuming, system of identification forced me to follow through a sequence of careful observation that led me to the English and Latin names. The fact that I began without the aid of any illustrations was important, for I was forced to look closely at the specimens themselves and determine how they were different from each other. Sir Henry Collett gave me a broader, more comprehensive understanding of the formal rules of botany: the class, the order, the genus and species. His book contained a precise encyclopedia of facts, a regimented approach in which every plant was assigned its place in nature, much like the soldiers he must have commanded in the Bengal army, standing at attention in their ranks. The artist, Miss M. Smith, virtually anonymous in the simplicity of her name, provided me with illustrations and brought the plants to life on the page, resuscitating those dry specimens which Collett had gathered and carried back with him to the Royal Botanic Gardens at Kew. Two hundred of her drawings were scattered through the leaves of *Flora Simlensis*, each of which confirmed for me the names of those plants I had already identified. As she dipped the nib of her pen into the jar of India ink and drew the exact shape of the ban oak leaves (ovate lanceolate) with their "spinous toothed" edges it seemed to complete my knowledge of this tree.

There was only one thing left for me to learn—the Garhwali names for trees and plants. "Ban" oaks, like many of the other species in Collett's book, derived their English names from corrupted versions of Hindi or Garhwali words. Just as the mansura bush had been changed to "Mussoorie" by the British, "ban" oak was a mispronunciation of banj or banch, the name by which this tree was commonly known in the villages of Garhwal. It was an important tree for dairy farmers, who cut the leaves as fodder and used its branches for firewood and timber. I learned a great deal about the botany of Mussoorie from a man named Dil Das, with whom I hunted in the forests surrounding Patreni, a village five miles east of Mussoorie. He explained that there were three different kinds of oaks—banj, kharsu, and moru—each of which had a slightly different leaf. In the course of our wanderings through the jungle, Dil Das taught me many of the Garhwali names for other trees like sinyaru (waterwood), burans (rhododendron), and semla (bauhinia). Living in the forest, he knew the use of every tree, how the moru and bhimal leaves provided the best fodder for his cattle; the strongest timber came from semla trees, which were used for making wooden plows; and the smooth, round trunk of a tun was carved into drums that were used in festivals. For Dil Das these trees were not something that he collected or classified as a curious naturalist. Instead, they were a useful part of the world around him, like the ringal bamboo which he and his uncles wove into baskets, the kaphal berries and other wild fruits that grew in the forest, the anchu roots that he used to ferment his homemade liquor.

*   *   *

When I was in high school, I saw no contradiction between being a hunter and a naturalist. One of my favorite authors was Jim

Corbett, who wrote a series of shikar books including *The Man-eating Leopard of Rudraprayag*, *The Temple Tiger*, and *Jungle Lore*. The son of a postmaster in Nainital, a hill station to the east of Mussoorie, Jim Corbett was born in 1875 and grew up in the forests of Kaladunghi, a small settlement in the Terai. His success as a hunter and his fame as a naturalist gained him worldwide recognition. Corbett's books were wildlife classics and he received numerous medals and awards. In 1968 a newly discovered variety of tiger was named *Panthera tigris corbetti*. The Indian government issued a commemorative postage stamp, and a game sanctuary near Kaladunghi bore his name. Even though he was a hunter, all of Corbett's books contained impassioned arguments and appeals for protecting India's wildlife and natural habitat.

When I was very young, my mother and father used to read Jim Corbett's stories aloud to me, and as I grew older I reread his books many times over, the images of the jungle imprinted in my mind. Listening to chapters from *The Man-eating Leopard of Rudraprayag* before I fell asleep each night, I could picture myself seated in the branches of a mango tree, looking down at the remains of a human victim, waiting for the man-eater to return and devour its kill. As I drifted into dreams, I could hear the cries of birds and animals, which Corbett described, kalij pheasant, langur monkeys, and barking deer, their alarm calls signaling the predator's approach. One of my favorite stories came from *Man-eaters of Kumaon*, his most famous book. While Corbett was tracking a man-eating tigress down a narrow ravine, he discovered a nest which contained a clutch of nightjar eggs. Being an avid collector, he picked up the delicate eggs and placed them in the palm of his left hand. In the other hand he was carrying a rifle, and as he turned the next corner of the ravine, Corbett came face-to-face with the tigress, crouching in the sand. His first instinct would have been to raise the rifle quickly to his shoulder, but because he was holding the eggs, he froze as soon as he saw the man-eater. She watched him with "a smile similar to that one sees on the face of a dog welcoming his master home after a long absence." Very slowly, inch by inch, Corbett swung the rifle around and tilted the muzzle upward until it was aligned with the man-eater's head. When he finally pulled the trigger, his bullet struck the tigress right between the eyes. As Corbett tells the story, he himself would have been killed if he hadn't been holding the eggs. The tigress was no more than a few yards away and she would have charged at the first sign of any sudden movement. The story ends with Corbett retracing his steps and putting the nightjar eggs back in their nest, returning them to their rightful owner.

I had always been interested in hunting, from the time I started shooting doves and rabbits with a slingshot in Etah. Collecting birds with my pellet gun prepared me for stalking animals and helped sharpen my aim. By the time I entered high school, my father let me use his shotgun and rifle, provided I was accompanied by an adult. One of the chokidars at school, Shyam Singh, was a keen shikari and he often took me hunting on Witch's Hill and the ridges above Kimoin. Later on, I met Dil Das, with whom I shot barking deer and ghoral, a kind of goatlike antelope similar to the European chamois. Hunting season in the hills extended from the middle of September through the fifteenth of March, but I did most of my shooting during the winter holidays, when school was closed.

Winter was my favorite time of year in Mussoorie, when most of the houses on the hillside were deserted and many of the shops in town were closed. Only a few of the families at the school remained in Landour throughout the winter break. There wasn't much to do at this time of year except to go hunting, and I spent almost every day in the jungle, with one or another of my friends, Sundar Singh, Ajay Mark, and Fali Kapadia. We never shot very much, an occasional pheasant or partridge, and sometimes a barking deer or ghoral, but most of the time I came back empty-handed. The hunting in Mussoorie was difficult because of the steep terrain and the dense forest cover. Many times the animals were out of range before we saw them and I seldom got more than a glimpse of movement in the underbrush.

During the winter of 1971, Ron Kapadia, Fali's father, shot a bear on the north side of Kimoin Ridge. Shyam Singh, who had been hunting with him, arrived at our door soon after dark and told my father that they needed a jeep and trailer to fetch the bear. It was a huge animal, and it took us several hours to haul it out of the valley and up to the Tehri Road. By the time we got the bear back to the Kapadias' house it was ten o'clock at night. With Shyam Singh's help, Fali and I began to skin the bear, just as we had done with the birds we collected, slicing open the belly, all the way up to the white V on its chest. The heavy coat of fur made it difficult work and the skin was so thick that we had to keep sharpening our knives. News of the bear had spread all over the hillside and a crowd gathered on the veranda where we were doing the skinning, under the light of a dim yellow bulb. In Garhwal, bear's fat was considered a cure for ailments such as arthritis and rheumatism. As Fali and I cut away the white slabs of lard, Shyam Singh apportioned this precious substance to each person in the crowd. By the time we were finished with the skinning my arms and clothes were covered with blood and grease. The gamy, pungent odor of the bear was overpowering and I had to take two or three baths before I finally got rid of the smell. The next day we tried to cook up some of the flesh in a curry but it was like chewing on a rubber tire and most of the meat and bones went to feed the dogs.

•   •   •

On my thirteenth birthday, my parents had given me a cocker spaniel puppy as a present. He was a light tan color, with long ears and mournful eyes. I named him Schnapps because of my favorite TV show, *Hogan's Heroes*, which I used to watch in America. One of the characters, Sergeant Schultz, was always drinking schnapps and I liked the sound of the name, even though my parents were teetotalers. We had owned several dogs before, including Penny, a mixed-breed female who had to be put down just before we went on furlough. Schnapps was my pet and he slept in my room at the foot of my bed, an affectionate, unkempt dog with matted fur. As he grew up, Schnapps developed an obsession for hunting and loved to go out into the forest with me. Even though I never trained him properly he had the natural instincts of a bird dog and learned to flush pheasant and partridges. He wasn't the best retriever but he had a keen nose, and I could tell whenever there were birds around because the short stump of his tail began to twitch like a Geiger counter.

Schnapps was completely fearless and loved the sound of a gun being fired. On the Fourth of July and during the festival of Diwali, when my brothers and I exploded fireworks in our front yard, he would race about excitedly, barking whenever a bomb went off and catching the bottle rockets in his mouth. At the sight of a shotgun, Schnapps would go wild with delight, pawing at the front door in his eagerness to go hunting. On those few occasions when I left him at home he would sit in my room and howl with disappointment. The two of us spent hours together in the jungle. Setting off before dawn, we would circle the game trails on Pari Tibba, starting from Dhobighat and working our way across to the fields at Panyala, over to Khetwalla and Cheli, returning via Naina ki Chaan along the middle road, or Beech ka Rasta. Schnapps would range up and down the khud in front of me and whenever he got a scent I could see him darting into the bushes, his tail wagging furiously. A couple of seconds later I'd hear him bark and the kalij pheasant would come rocketing down the hill. Their shrill alarm call whistled in my ears as they fixed their wings and flew past me like guided missiles. I was never a very good shot and often missed, though Schnapps was a forgiving companion and always led me on to the next covey of pheasants, around the hill. By instinct he ignored the laughing thrushes and scimitar babblers, responding only to the scent of game birds. One winter, when I was hunting with my father above Patreni, Schnapps flushed a bear and chased it down the path toward me. I had to save myself by scrambling up the khud, as the bear came charging in my direction, a ferocious cocker spaniel nipping at its heels.

Leopards were the only real danger that our dogs faced and we would have to be careful in the evenings after dusk, making sure that Schnapps was kept indoors. Quite a few dogs on the hillside were killed and eaten by leopards, particularly during the winter, when there were fewer people on the hillside. Schnapps was attacked a couple of times, once while he was with my father and my brother Joe on Witch's Hill. Following a scent into a dense thicket of ageratum bushes Schnapps came face-to-face with a leopard, which grabbed him by the head.

Cocker spaniels have very loose skin and Schnapps must have jerked aside as he was bitten, so that all the leopard got was a mouthful of fur. My father heard a yelp, and a few seconds later Schnapps came hurtling out of the bushes, dripping with blood. He didn't seem to be in pain and even though my father whistled and called him, Schnapps headed off in search of more pheasant. The leopard slunk away, growling in disappointment. When Schnapps got home that evening we were finally able to examine the wound, and I discovered four holes in his head, where the leopard's canines had punctured his skin. A carnivore's teeth are tainted with decaying bits of flesh and a leopard's bite is very likely to go septic. By the next afternoon, Schnapps's head had swollen up to twice its normal size and we had to give him a dose of penicillin and pour disinfectant into his wounds. The swelling took a couple of weeks to subside, but even after the scars healed, Schnapps had a lopsided face.

Leopards were declared a protected species by the time I started hunting and I never had any interest in shooting one. They were difficult animals to see, and usually moved about at night, though it wasn't unusual to find their pug marks on the paths around Landour. One winter, we got word that a leopard had killed a horse in the valley below Dhobighat. Fali Kapadia and I went down with our cameras and telephoto lenses to try and get a photograph. The leopard was an old male who had taken several dogs from the hillside. Unable to drag the dead horse into cover, he had left the half-eaten carcass lying in the middle of an abandoned field. As Fali and I approached, we could tell that the leopard was still nearby because the vultures were sitting in the trees, afraid to settle on the dead horse. The two of us crept around the edge of the field and climbed up the opposite ridge, about fifty yards away from the kill. After we'd been sitting there for half an hour, several vultures flew down and began to tear at the entrails of the horse. The others followed, and within a couple of minutes there must have been at least twenty or thirty of the huge birds squabbling and hissing at each other. I was sure that the leopard must have seen us and gone away, but just as I was about to give up, we heard a low, guttural cough and out of the bushes came a streak of yellow fur. The leopard charged into the middle of the vultures, who scattered in confusion, flapping their wings. Several of the birds had trouble getting into the air, and as we watched, the leopard stood up on his hind legs and knocked two vultures to the ground with his claws, just like a boxer, swinging right and left. All of this took place within a couple seconds, and after sniffing at the dead vultures the leopard sat down to guard his kill. Fali and I were so startled we almost forgot to take pictures, and all I got was a blurred photograph of the leopard lunging at the vultures.

.　.　.

Mussoorie's ecology was rich and diverse but it was threatened by many different forces, including the hunting which I did. The most obvious threat to the environment was limestone mining, which had been going on since the early sixties, and there were a number of strip mines along the road to Dehra Dun. Some of the largest quarries lay just above my aunt and uncle's home in Rajpur, where I could see ugly white gashes in the ridge, as if the mountains had been chewed away to the bone. Rough unpaved roads criss-crossed the open mines and millions of tons of limestone were hauled down to Rajpur in Chevrolet Power Wagons, or "gattus" as they were commonly known. Even though these trucks dated back to the Second World War they seemed to be the most powerful vehicles ever built, capable of negotiating nearly vertical roads with a full load of rocks. The sound of the gattu engines and the grinding of their gears carried across the valleys and I would watch them crawling up the ridges like mechanical termites. From a distance I could see the miners blasting sections of the mountain, white puffs of dust erupting with each explosion. It took several seconds for the sound of dynamite to reach my ears, long after the cliffs collapsed into a scree of rubble. Gangs of men worked in the mines, using crowbars, pickaxes, and shovels, chanting as they broke the rock into smaller pieces. Perched atop the trucks, these miners rode back and forth from the quarries to the limestone depot at the foot of the hill. Their clothes, their skin, their hair were covered with white dust, so that they looked like ghosts, riding the thundering Power Wagons out of the hills.

Most of the mining operations near Mussoorie were finally stopped in the late seventies, after a number of environmental groups protested and the Supreme Court intervened to shut them down. By that time, however, broad sections of the ridges had been laid bare and some of the lower hills were almost as white as the snow peaks to the north. One summer, when the prime minister, Indira Gandhi, came to visit Mussoorie by helicopter, the mining contractors were so worried that she would see the strip mines along the motor road, they painted the rocks green in an attempt to hide the scars from view. Fortunately, this ruse didn't work, for the color they chose was a bright parrot green and it stood out like a livid stain on the mountain, highlighting the destruction.

During the late sixties and early seventies a series of phosphate mines were also excavated on Witch's Hill and farther east of Mussoorie. Unlike the limestone quarries, these mines tunneled into the ridges, penetrating several miles underground. Most of them were shut down a few years after they were started, though a large phosphate operation continued at Durmala, twelve miles out the Tehri Road.

The other annual threat to the environment was forest fires. During May and June, before the monsoon arrived, the Tehri hills became parched and brown. I could always tell when the fires were going to start, a dry, brittle feeling in the air. It was as if the elements had reached a critical point of combustion, leaves wilting on the trees, grass turning into tinder, and the sun magnified through an opaque haze of dust. One morning I awakened to the first scent of smoke filtering through the screens on my bedroom window. The fires often started on the ridges below Nali, in the forests of long-needle pines, where the carpeting of dry needles required only a cigarette butt or the smoldering remains of a bidi to ignite them into a blaze. From the top of the hill we would see fires on Nag Tibba, sweeping across the slopes of grass, fingers of smoke in the valleys.

On the ridges near Moti Dhar and Patreni the fires raced up the mountain like tornadoes, blackening hundreds of acres in a matter of hours. The fires moved fastest when they swept uphill, fanned by the wind. We watched the flames jump from tree to tree, an orange blaze surging upward like a volcanic eruption. When the fires reached the tops of the ridges they crossed over and began their descent, creeping downward like a ribbon of molten lava, with a dark wall of smoke in their wake. At times a burning pinecone was dislodged and rolled down the hill, scattering embers as it tumbled into the valley. In this way, dozens of smaller conflagrations were started, each of them rushing back up the hill to meet their source.

As the forest fires approached Landour we got ready to protect our houses and the buildings at the school. On the north side of the hill was a fire line but it was ineffective, especially if the wind was blowing. The men on the hillside and teams of high school boys organized themselves into fire brigades. The Indian army also

sent up troops from Dehra Dun to protect the cantonment properties in Landour. Lines of soldiers patrolled the Chukkar, carrying
picks and shovels, jeeps racing back and forth, as if there were a war
going on. In 1965, when I was in third grade, an American anthro-
pologist who was studying at the language school was killed in
a forest fire below Sisters' bazaar. He got separated from the other
firefighters and was caught in a ravine, engulfed by smoke and
flames. His death made the fires seem all the more threatening and
dangerous. My mother took me to the funeral service at Kellogg
Church and as I sat there listening to the hymns and prayers I could
smell the bitter, acrid scent of burning oak leaves in the air.

Many years later, while fighting a fire below Oakville and Jabberkhet, I worked my way down to the stream in the valley, where
the flames had crossed over during the night. Most of the fire had
burned itself out but a few of the trees were still smoldering and I
could hear an occasional crackling sound as the green sticks burst
and popped. The few flames which were still burning on Flag Hill
had a metallic color in the hazy sunlight, like cheap tinfoil. As I
reached the stream, I saw what looked like bits of white ash floating above the shallow pools of water. It took me a few moments to
realize that hundreds of butterflies were swarming through the
smoke. They were mostly cabbage whites and common emigranty.
Usually at this time of year the butterflies were attracted to the
chestnut trees, farther up the hill, but they had been trapped in the
valley by the flames and I could see that they were dying, suffocat-
ing in the heat. The surface of the stream was covered with dead
butterflies, their pale translucent wings like a shower of chestnut
blossoms falling through the smoke.

ROAD TRIPS

The Hindustan Landmaster, which we had owned since the year after I was born, was eventually sold. The car had been through a lot of rough use on village roads around Etah and climbing up and down the mountains. Its engine barely had the strength to make it up Mullingar Hill and whenever the car overheated we had to wait at the side of the road until the vapor locks cooled off. The electric fuel pump gave us a lot of trouble and more than once I had to ride in the trunk, clicking two wires together to keep it moving. Driving up to the Chukkar one day, we nearly had a serious accident, when the brakes failed and the Landmaster began to roll backward down the steepest stretch of the road, just above Claremont. If my father hadn't spun the wheel and rammed the car into the side of the hill, we would have gone off the edge of the mountain and fallen several hundred feet into the valley below.

A new vehicle cost more than we could afford but my father had heard of a place called Motiya Khan, in a section of Delhi, where junk dealers specialized in reconditioning army disposal jeeps and trucks. During the winter holidays, we made a trip to Delhi, and my father took me with him to search for a secondhand jeep. We had some trouble finding Motiya Khan because there was no specific address or street, just an open field of makeshift sheds and workshops, with the constant sound of panel beating in the background, puddles of greenish oil on the ground, and the blinding flashes of welding torches. All around us were the chassis of military trucks, stacks of tires, and mountains of rusting parts. The air was redolent with the smell of diesel, paint, and burning rubber. Each of the junk dealers had a separate lot in Motiya Khan, with half a dozen young men or boys working on the vehicles, their clothes, arms, and legs covered in black grease. Motorcycles were being revved up and tuned, cylinders rebored and tires retreaded. Most of the vehicles dated back to the forties and early fifties. In one workshop I recognized a couple of the Chevrolet Power Wagons which were used for limestone mining in Mussoorie. In another section of Motiya Khan I saw half a dozen World War II Harley-Davidsons and Indian Chiefs, converted into motorcycle rickshas, which were used to ferry people around the streets of Delhi. The twisted skeletons of wrecked cars and buses lay about like rusting carcasses, scavenged for pieces, or bent back into shape. No matter how old or decrepit, nothing seemed beyond repair in Motiya Khan, and most of the workshops had lathes where replacement parts were being turned out, a brand-new axle or a set of tie rods custom-fitted on the spot.

The vehicle which my father chose was a 1952 Willy's jeep, with a side valve engine and a canvas roof. It was freshly painted a military green, and the junk dealer, a bearded Muslim in a starched white kurta and spotless churidar, claimed that the jeep was as good as new, even though the Indian army had already used it in two wars against Pakistan and the spare tire had an ominous bulge. I don't know how much we paid for the jeep, but I do remember the excitement of hearing the engine start up for the first time and sitting in the front seat as my father drove it around the unpaved lanes of Motiya Khan, testing the four-wheel drive. There were no doors on the sides and the seats at the back were nothing more than a metal bench on either side.

The following day we drove the jeep from Delhi to Mussoorie, a distance of three hundred kilometers, ordinarily an eight-hour journey. A series of towns and villages were clustered along the narrow two-lane highway. Passing through each of these we had to slow down and edge our way between crowds of pedestrians and bicycles, tractors and bullock carts. My father kept his hand on the horn most of the time. Even the open stretches of the road were slow driving, with railway crossings where we had to stop, sometimes for half an hour, waiting for a train to pass. In several of the towns, Modinagar, Daurala, and Muzzafarnagar, there were sugar mills and sections of the road were blocked by lines of buffalo carts hauling sugarcane. The smell of the sugar mills was overpowering, a sewagelike stench that filled the air for miles around. The most crowded town of all was Meerut, a winding bazaar with endless traffic jams, buses and trucks cutting in upon each other, a cacophony of horns and clouds of diesel exhaust, bicycle rickshas ringing their bells, and the cries of hawkers selling everything from peanuts and fruit to gaudy underwear, pink and white brassieres that looked like funnels of lace. On the other side of Meerut lay a military cantonment and a prisoner of war camp, where Pakistani soldiers were held captive. As we passed by the barbed-wire fences, the gates and watchtowers, one of the sentries saluted our jeep, mistaking it for an army vehicle.

The jeep had a top speed of fifty miles an hour, though we seldom went that fast. Because the engine had recently been rebored and fitted with new rings and pistons, we had to stop every hour or so to let it cool down. In Khatauli, a small village ten miles beyond Meerut, was a bridge across the canal where we used to stop for picnic lunches while driving up from Etah. A grove of shesham and babool trees shaded the embankment and it was a quiet, secluded place. Recently a tea stall had been opened on the canal bank, which became a popular halfway stop on the road to Mussoorie, selling omelettes and somosas. A few years later the tea shop expanded into Cheetal restaurant and the forestry department set up a small zoo, with caged deer and black buck.

Our jeep worked well for most of the drive and even though it was uncomfortable sitting on the backseats, my brothers and I enjoyed the trip, eating peanuts and throwing the shells out of the canvas flaps. My mother did not drive but rode in the front seat next to my father, with a picnic basket full of fruit and snacks at her feet, from which she passed us cookies and oranges. The winter air was cold and the temperatures dropped as soon as the sun began to go down. We huddled together in the open jeep, bundled up in jackets and scarves, watching the sugarcane and mustard fields slip by, the jamun trees that lined the road, their branches extending over the highway like a leafy tunnel. I could smell the sweet smoke of cow dung fires from the villages we passed, a scent that made me nostalgic for the winters we spent in Etah. As we came into Roorkee, where the road to Hardwar divided, we crossed the canal again and I was able to see the mountains for the first time, their gray outlines profiled against the twilit sky. The Himalayas looked so far away, like a line of distant tents, a shadowy encampment.

It was already dark by the time we reached Chutmalpur, where we stopped for a cup of tea to warm ourselves. Ahead of us were the Siwalik hills, another hour and a half to Dehra Dun. This section of the road passed through the Rajaji game sanctuary in which there were wild elephants and other animals. The jeep's headlights illuminated the lines of sal trees on either side of the road and we could see the eyes of deer and jackals crossing in front of us. There was very little traffic and my brothers and I were falling asleep, when the jeep's engine began to choke and sputter, taking us a few hundred feet farther into the forest before dying out with a consumptive cough.

My father pulled over to the side of the road and switched off the headlights. The night was completely dark and silent, no sign of any other cars on the road. The nearest village was two or three miles away. Anxiously, we got out our flashlights and opened the hood of the jeep. My father fiddled around in the engine while I held the light for him. There didn't seem to be anything wrong with the carburetor or the spark plugs and all of the wires were attached, but when my father tried the starter it made a futile, whining sound. Afraid of draining the battery, we tried the crank, a procedure which my brothers and I would get used to over the years. Each of us took turns at the "handle," as it was called, but the engine wouldn't start. We even tried to push the jeep while my father popped the clutch but nothing worked. Eventually, we decided to check the petrol tank. Soon after leaving Delhi we had realized that the fuel gauge wasn't working, but after filling up in Meerut we figured there was enough fuel to take us all the way to Dehra Dun. Opening the cap and pushing one end of the crank inside, we discovered that the gas tank was completely dry.

A few cars and buses had gone past, their headlights blinding us at the side of the road. Finally, we hailed a truck that was headed into Dehra Dun. My father hitched a ride to the nearest petrol pump while the rest of us waited in the jeep, imagining wild elephants or leopards and tigers coming out of the forest to attack us. We had heard stories that there were dacoits in the Siwalik hills who waylaid travelers in the dark. Every sound we heard made us think of bandits sneaking up on us. Gathering a pile of sticks we lit a fire to warm ourselves, and my mother rationed out the last of the cookies. Two hours later my father returned, in another car, with a jerry can of fuel. Once the tank was filled with petrol the jeep started up right away and we got home to Landour around midnight, after being on the road for fifteen hours.

.   .   .

Uncle Jim and Aunt Barry lived in Rajpur, a small town at the foot of the mountains, fifteen miles below Mussoorie. They had three children, my cousins Marty, John, and Tom. Our families were very close—as my aunt would say, she had six children with two sets of parents. Uncle Jim and Aunt Barry ran the Christian Retreat and Study Center in Rajpur, a Christian ashram which they founded on the site of an old glass factory. It was a large compound, encircled by a high stone wall, with several old bungalows, a chapel, and a library. In one section was an orchard of fruit trees, guavas, mangoes, and litchis, enormous stands of bamboo, and even a pipal tree which had been planted by Mahatma Gandhi. The flower beds, which overflowed with sweet peas, phlox, and cornflowers, were lined with chunks of purple and green glass, remnants of the original factory. I used to think that these were giant sapphires and emeralds, their gnarled shapes glinting beneath the coxcombs and zinnias.

Dozens of Hindu ashrams were located in Rajpur, spiritual retreats where people came to meditate and spend their time in quiet contemplation. The Christian Retreat and Study Center was a place where conferences and seminars were held on interfaith dialogue or other theological issues and Christian scholars came for research and reflection. There was a peaceful feeling of sanctity about the Rajpur center but for me it was the perfect setting for adventure and exploration. There were corners of the compound which were wild and untended, ruined sections of the old glass factory where my brothers and I would go searching for monitor lizards and snakes. In the middle of the garden was a map of India made of stones and cement, with the mountains rising up in bold relief. When we were very small we used to climb about on this map, and during one of our many visits to Rajpur, my brother Joe fell off the Himalayas and broke his leg. On the lawns in front of my aunt and uncle's bungalow, our cousins Tom and John played games of cricket. Joe, Andy, and I were recruited as fielders, dodging the hard red balls as they went flying for a generous six runs beyond the jacaranda trees that bordered the driveway.

My aunt and uncle had a jeep station wagon and we often went for camping and fishing trips with them to forest bungalows in the

Dehra Dun Valley. These expeditions were preceded by elaborate preparations, lists of food and supplies, mountains of gear to be packed into the jeeps and trailers, tents and sleeping bags, fishing tackle, picnic baskets and thermos flasks. It often looked as though we were setting out to spend several months in the wilderness instead of going on a weekend camping trip. Most of the forest bungalows where we stayed were only fifteen or twenty miles from Rajpur, Khansrao, and Satya Narayan, on the Song River, a tributary of the Ganga. We also had a favorite camping spot near Paonta Sahib, at the confluence of the Jumna and Giri Rivers. To get there we had to cross the Jumna on a ferry. Only one jeep could go across at a time, driving up two planks of wood and onto the rickety wooden boat. The ferry was attached to a pulley on a cable that was stretched across the Jumna and the current swung the boat in an arc downstream, before it landed on the other side. Our overloaded jeeps and trailers seemed so precariously balanced on the ferryboat that they looked as if they were going to fall into the river. My cousins and I rode back and forth on each trip across the Jumna, watching the ferrymen leaning onto their poles and the pebbled river bottom disappearing into the swift, green current as we were swept away from shore.

Uncle Jim was a fisherman and he gave me my first rod and reel one Christmas, when our two families went on a camping trip to Satya Narayan, near the confluence of the Song River and the Ganga. Each morning, I followed my uncle down the weedy trail from the forest bungalow at Satya Narayan to the rocky banks of the Song. There were two bridges across the river, one for motor vehicles and the other for trains that ran between Hardwar and Rishikesh. Most of the year, the Song was a clear, meandering stream about thirty yards across, though in the monsoon it would flood to three or four times its width. A broad, open margin of bleached white rocks lay on either side of the river, marking the flood level of the Song. While fishing Uncle Jim wore a floppy Gurkha hat and he would stop from time to time to light his pipe, the smell of Macropolo tobacco mingling with the scent of lantana bushes that grew along the riverbank.

The first two days at Satya Narayan I didn't catch a thing, so on the third morning, while Uncle Jim was fishing near the railway bridge, I made my way upstream, determined to try a different spot. For an hour or two I kept fishing without a strike, discouraged and impatient. I had almost given up when I saw a sadhu, dressed in saffron robes, seated on the opposite bank, under an arch of the motor bridge. He was an old man with thin gray strands of hair gathered into a loose topknot above his head and a scraggly beard.

As I walked under the bridge, he gestured to me. I was across the river from him, and calling out in Hindi he said that he would show me where to catch a fish. Hesitantly I walked down to a point directly across from where the sadhu was sitting. The day before I had fished this pool for a couple of hours without any luck, but the old man raised his finger and pointed to a spot near the center of the river. Using a brass Mepps spinner, I cast toward the place where the sadhu had directed me. Before the lure had even touched the water a fish leaped out of the pool and hooked itself. I was so surprised I nearly forgot to reel in my first mahseer, twelve or fifteen inches long. Unhooking it I laid it on the riverbank, where it flopped about among the rocks. The sadhu was smiling at my excitement and now he pointed to another spot about ten yards above where I had hooked the fish. I cast again and the same thing happened. Another mahseer jumped out of the water and grabbed the spinner. I reeled it in as quickly as I could and dropped the second fish beside the first, turning to see where the sadhu would direct me now, convinced he had some magical powers. But this time, instead of pointing at the river the mendicant gestured toward the two fish that I had caught.

"Now," he said, raising his voice, "I want you to throw them back into the water. You must release them before they die."

I looked at him in disbelief but the sadhu's expression was stern and I knew that he expected me to do as I was told. My fish lay in the sand, their gills opening and closing helplessly. I weighed the consequences; if I disobeyed him the sadhu might put a curse on me. At the same time, fifty feet of water lay between us and there was no way that the elderly sadhu could reach me. For a minute or two I did not move, and he called to me again, his voice insistent:

"Quickly, put the fish back in the water."

Reaching down I picked up the mahseer, hooking my fingers underneath their gills, and then, allowing reason to overcome my superstitions, I turned and ran as fast as I could go, leaping over the rocks and driftwood on the shore. Behind me I could hear the sadhu cursing angrily but I ignored him, carrying the two fish in one hand and my spinning rod in the other. I didn't stop until I reached the railway bridge, where Uncle Jim was waiting for me in the shade.

. ▪ .

Another place our family often went on holidays was Corbett National Park, a wildlife sanctuary about 150 miles east of Mussoorie. It was a full day's drive, along unpaved forest roads, and on these trips our families would often split up between the two vehicles. I preferred to ride with Uncle Jim and Aunt Barry because they carried more snacks to eat, brownies, banana bread, and glucose biscuits. My uncle was a diabetic and had to keep his blood sugar balanced. In many ways these were the closest times we spent together as a family, crowded inside the jeeps and driving for hours over rutted roads. We would sing songs, talk and joke, or fall silent for long stretches of the drive, content and secure in the company of our extended family. One jeep would follow the other, usually at some distance to avoid the clouds of dust. Every hour or two we would stop to change a flat tire or to use the facilities of the jungle. Uncle Jim would light his pipe and cups of coffee were poured out

on the hood of the jeep, biscuits passed around, and distances calculated, each of us trying to figure out how much farther we had
to go.

As with our journeys across America, these road trips were
family rituals and each person knew his or her role. My father did
the driving and if the jeep broke down, which often happened, he
was responsible for fixing it. My mother organized the food and
other supplies, decided on the menus, made lists, and supervised
the packing. She put up with a lot of inconveniences and was end-
lessly tolerant of the primitive conditions and discomforts on our
camping trips. Andy, Joe, and I would fetch and carry things, roll
up the sleeping bags, and count the tent pegs to make sure we had
enough. Our other duty was to push the jeep whenever it refused
to start, the three of us leaning against the tailgate and trying to
pick up enough momentum before my father popped the clutch. If
that method didn't work, there was always the dreaded crank,
which left calluses and blisters on our hands and had a nasty habit
of kicking back, hard enough to dislocate a person's shoulder.

Corbett Park was located in the Terai, an area of dense jungles
and open grasslands at the foot of the Himalayas. The Ramganga
River, which flowed out of the mountains of Kumaon, passed
through the sanctuary. During late December and early January,
right after Christmas, our family often reserved one of the forest
bungalows in Corbett Park. The places we preferred to stay were
Sarapdulli or Ghairal, on the banks of the Ramganga. These bungalows had two suites of bedrooms, a kitchen and a dining area, as
well as a broad veranda. The accommodations were spartan, no
electricity or running water. We pitched our tents in the yard and
my cousins, my brothers, and I slept outdoors.

The Ramganga was the most beautiful river that I had ever
seen, an unspoiled mountain stream which flowed between the
forested ridges of the lower Himalayas. At points it broadened into
deep green pools, as if gathering strength for the whitewater rapids
that lay downstream. During the winter months the water was

crystal clear and the broad banks were covered with round white boulders. Two different species of crocodiles sunned themselves on the rocks, the broad-nosed muggermuch and the giant garial with its rapierlike snout. Despite their presence we would go swimming in the Ramganga, floating down the river on inner tubes and air mattresses. Whenever they saw us coming the crocodiles would dive for cover.

I never had much luck with fishing in Corbett Park though we could see schools of mahseer gliding through the water and the heavy-bodied goonch, a kind of freshwater shark, lying like motionless shadows on the bottom of the deepest pools. Tom once caught a ten-pound fish near Sarapdulli, and many years later I helped land a thirty-five-pound mahseer below Ghairal, but most of the time we never got a bite. On one of our first trips to Corbett Park, my father was casting and hooked Joe in the side of the face with a spinner. Two barbs on the treble hook had to be cut off and pushed through his cheek, an operation that was performed with a pair of pliers from the toolbox in the jeep. The pliers were boiled for half an hour to disinfect them, and while my mother held Joe's feet, my father twisted the hooks around and pried them out of his mouth. I couldn't bear to watch, it seemed so painful, but Joe didn't make a sound.

During the mornings and evenings we would drive out in our jeep with the roof down, trying to spot game along the forest roads. There were hundreds of chital in the grasslands, hog deer and sambar, wild boar and leopards. During winter the peacocks performed their courtship dance, the gaudy males spreading their plumes and stamping their feet as they turned in circles. At Dikhala, the park headquarters, we were able to hire elephants to take us into the jungle to look for animals. Four of us would climb onto the back of each elephant along with the mahout, who carried a sharp metal goad and sat on the elephant's neck, just behind its ears. One of the elephants in Corbett Park was named Melancholy—the mahouts pronounced it "Milan-Kali"—and we always asked to ride on her. Afterward, as a reward, we fed her sticks of sugarcane that she would take delicately in her trunk and chew on slowly, the sweet juice dribbling down her neck.

Corbett Park was one of the few places in India where we could still see tigers in the wild. When I was in my junior year of high school, I saw three tigers in one day near Ghairal bungalow. One of these came swimming across the river while I was fishing, shook itself dry, and ambled into the jungle hardly twenty feet from where I was crouched behind a rock. The tigers weren't really dangerous unless they were disturbed, and I was much more frightened of the wild elephants in Corbett Park. Most of them lived in herds but there was a lone male who became a rogue. He was called Der Danth (one and a half teeth) because he had a broken tusk. During a rampage he destroyed the barbed-wire fence around Ghairal bungalow and smashed one of the pillars on the veranda. The Campbells, friends of ours from Delhi, had been charged by Der Danth, who left an impressive dent in the side of their Land Rover.

. . .

One summer we took a trip to the Kulu Valley, an area of the Himalayas which I'd often heard about but never visited, about a hundred miles to the west of Mussoorie, beyond Simla. As usual our jeep was heavily loaded, with a canvas tarpaulin tied over the trailer that carried our gear. This time there were only the five of us, and Chandu, who came along to do the cooking. The monsoon had just started and we set off in a downpour, streams of water leaking through the seams in the canvas roof and between the cracks in the windscreen.

The rain continued until Dehra Dun, where we stopped and bought a crate of litchis, which we peeled and ate as we drove along, spitting the seeds out the back of the jeep. Joining the Grand Trunk Road in Saharanpur, we drove through Ambala, then on to Chandigarh. It was warm and humid on the plains, though it rained in patches along the way. We watched the kilometer posts go by, the names of the towns and cities along the route written alternately in English, Hindi, and Punjabi. We calculated the distances in miles, multiplying the kilometers by six, then dividing by ten. Outside of Chandigarh we stopped at a dhaba, a roadside restaurant, where we ate subzi and tandoori rotis for lunch. The food was heavily spiced and made our faces stream with sweat. The Sikh truck drivers eyed us with amusement. To them we must have looked like a family of refugees, our trailer loaded high with camping equipment. As we ate our meal, a group of children gathered around, pointing and laughing. One or two of them tried to speak to us in English, phrases they had learned in school, "Good afternoon," "Time please?" and "Which country are you from?"

It took us a day and a half to reach the Kulu Valley. We spent the night in a circuit bungalow, somewhere in the foothills, then headed back into the mountains, driving along the Sutlej, one of the five rivers that flow across the Punjab. At places the road cut through narrow gorges, a treacherous passage carved out of the cliffs. Instead of going to Manali, the main town in the Kulu region, we headed up the Parvati River, a tributary of the Sutlej. At one point we had to cross over a narrow bridge, which looked as if it was going to collapse, barely wide enough to take the jeep and trailer. All of us got off except for my father, and we watched as he inched his way across. The road was unpaved from there and we drove another eight or ten miles up the valley until we came to a grove of deodar trees at a bend in the river, which seemed an ideal place to set up camp. There were no buildings or villages in sight, only the mountains rising up on either side of us, cragged walls of rock that disappeared into the clouds. Later, when the sky began to clear at dusk, we could see a single snow peak at the head of the valley, a jagged triangle of gold, burnished by the setting sun.

We pitched our camp on the banks of the Parvati River, the deodar needles providing a soft carpeting underfoot and a resinous fragrance in the air. As we unloaded the trailer, I had a feeling that nobody had ever camped at this spot before and we were like homesteaders putting down our roots, driving tent poles and stakes into the virgin soil, claiming this patch of land for ourselves. We had everything we needed there: food and shelter, firewood and water, all of the elements for our survival. I believed it was a place where we could live forever.

The Parvati River was named after the wife of Siva, the Hindu god of creation and destruction. Parvati was the mother of Ganesh, the elephant-headed deity, and a powerful goddess in her own right. The river was swollen with snowmelt, a swift, chalky current that licked at the roots of the deodar trees along the bank. Within the confines of the valley, the sound of the water was so loud we had to shout to make ourselves heard, as we pitched tents, assembled camp cots, and set up the kitchen, using our trailer as a windbreak. We had three tents, one for my parents, one for Joe, Andy, and me, and the third for Chandu, which also doubled as a kitchen when it rained. By late that afternoon we had settled in, gathered firewood, and established the camp. Sitting under the canopy of deodar branches, the steady roar of the river drowning out all other sounds, I felt as if we had traveled much farther than we actually had, a sense of loneliness and escape, as if we were castaways in a remote and unknown valley, abandoned by the world.

Five or six miles upstream, where the jeep road ended, there was a small village and pilgrim center called Manikaran, where Hindus came to bathe in the hot springs and to pray at the temples. One day we hiked up to the ridge above Manikaran, onto the bugiyals, or meadows, that overlooked the valley. Halfway to the top we rested under a massive deodar tree which was so broad that all three of us, Andy, Joe, and I, could barely reach our arms around the trunk, clutching at each other's fingers. Buried in the coarse bark of the tree was a brass trident, the symbol of Siva, which must have been left there by a devotee. We climbed on up the sloping meadow toward the crest of the ridge. There was no path but I scrambled ahead of everyone else, pulling myself up the hill by grabbing tufts of weeds and wild anemones. The palms of my hands were soon stained green and bore the scent of grass and herbs, caraway and sorrel.

I was carrying a rucksack with our lunch and thermos flasks of tea. When I reached the top of the ridge I was exhausted, and taking out a tin of sweetened condensed milk I punched two holes in it and began to suck the rich, syrupy contents into my mouth. The milk was so sweet it made my throat ache but I couldn't stop myself and before I knew it the tin was empty. When my parents and my brothers arrived, half an hour later, they were furious with me because no milk was left to mix with their tea.

Across the river from our camp, we had noticed a stone hut tucked into the hillside. At first we thought it was uninhabited, but a day or two after we arrived I saw a figure emerge from the hut. I could see that he was a sadhu, with oiled black hair and beard, dressed in saffron robes. With the noise of the river, there was no way that we could speak to him, and he watched us from a distance. A few days later, while my brothers and I were trying to build up our courage to swim in the freezing waters of the Parvati, we saw the sadhu beckoning to us and pointing downstream toward a crude rope bridge across the river.

Half an hour later we were on the opposite shore, waving to my parents, who didn't know where we had gone. The sadhu was a quiet, friendly man who showed us a hot spring bubbling out of the side of the hill near his hut. The water was boiling as it emerged from a crevice in the rocks, which were encrusted with yellow minerals. The spring flowed into a slate-lined channel and from there into a square tank which was also paved with smooth pieces of slate. The tank was about three feet deep and just big enough for one person to sit inside. The sadhu told us that we were welcome to bathe there if we wished. The water was scalding hot but each of us took turns lowering ourselves slowly into the thermal pool until we were submerged up to our necks, feathers of steam rising off the surface. In front of the tank was a sandy beach that sloped down to the river. My brothers and I dared each other to dive into the icy current after sitting in the hot spring. Joe was the first to try, leaping out of the pool and plunging headfirst into the river. I followed him a few minutes later and the freezing shock made me feel as if my skin was contracting around my bones.

During the rest of our stay in Kulu, we visited the sadhu every day and gave him a few of our supplies, flour and sugar, some vegetables. He seemed pleased with these and showed us how he boiled potatoes in the hot spring, where the water came out of the rocks. Within half an hour they were cooked and had a salty taste from the minerals. I asked the sadhu how long he had lived there, and with an uncertain gesture of his hands he said he couldn't remember, four years, maybe five. He told us that he had built the hut himself, gathering the slabs of slate from the cliffs nearby. It was a simple structure, a single room, with an open door, more like a cave than a house. The sadhu lived by himself and he said that villagers and pilgrims gave him food. When I asked him his name, he laughed and said he didn't have one. I could call him Baba, if I wanted. He wasn't from the hills originally but wouldn't tell us where he came from.

"I've left all that behind," he said. "The only thing that matters is that I am here."

"Don't you have a family?"

He shook his head and asked, "What about you? Where are you from?"

"Mussoorie."

"I've been there once," he said. "And you are English?"

"No. American," I said. "But I was born here in this country."

"I know some English," said the sadhu, picking up a stick and scratching in the sand. Very carefully, he wrote the first three letters of the alphabet, then laughed and brushed them away with his hand.

．　．　．

My father was born in Kashmir and when he was a child his family spent several months each year camping at Nasim Bagh, a chinar grove outside of Srinagar. From my grandmother I had heard stories about their summers in Kashmir, houseboats on Dal Lake, promenading along the Bund, and hiking trips above Pahalgam. During the twenties and thirties my grandparents had been posted in Jhelum, Abbottabad, and Rawalpindi, towns in the Punjab and Northwest Frontier Province, which were now a part of Pakistan. After independence and partition in 1947, Kashmir remained a disputed area. India controlled most of the valley, while Pakistan held on to a smaller section called Azad Kashmir. Two wars had been fought over the region, and tensions remained high, for it was the only state in India with a majority Muslim population.

In the summer of 1972 we drove to Kashmir with Uncle Jim and Aunt Barry. My cousin John was living in India at the time, doing alternative service as a conscientious objector from the war in Vietnam. He was teaching at a college in the Punjab. Tom was also back in India, working as the social activities director at Woodstock. He and Ajay Mark, a family friend, borrowed an old BSA motorcycle from one of the teachers at the school and decided to drive it to Kashmir. Heading out from Mussoorie and down onto the plains, we traveled together in a convoy across the Punjab. The first night was spent in Pathankot, a large military cantonment, which lay only a few miles from the border. Army vehicles were everywhere and we passed through several checkpoints where we had to show our passports and foreigner's registration papers. The following day we drove on to Jammu and climbed up to the Banihal Tunnel, from where we had our first view of the Kashmir Valley.

The scenery was even more picturesque than I had expected, a broad, green swath of rice paddies and cherry orchards, saffron fields and groves of stately walnut trees, cupped between the Himalayas and the Pir Panjal. The roads were lined with poplar trees, and weeping willows leaned over rippling brooks. There was something vaguely European about the landscape, a cultivated, orderly feeling that was very different from other parts of India that I knew. When we arrived at our camp, on the meadows above

Pahalgam, the scenery made me think of the Swiss Alps, steep snow-capped peaks descending into evergreen forests and meadows full of wildflowers, like landscapes in *The Sound of Music*. Our friends the Campbells used to camp at Pahalgam every summer and with their help we rented tents from a local tour operator. Our stay in Kashmir was much more organized and luxurious than our other camping trips. Both Prem and Chandu had come along to do the cooking and we even had a dining tent with tables and chairs. The Lidder River flowed below our camp and we fished for rainbow trout in the tumbling rapids. We hired ponies and went riding on the bridle trails that circled through the deodar forests. There was plenty of time for sitting around and reading, and playing games of Frisbee, cricket, and touch football on the grassy field in front of our camp.

A few days after we arrived in Pahalgam we took a trek up to Kolahoi Glacier. This was a place I'd heard about for years, part of the Alter family lore. In the 1920s my grandfather and his brother, my great-uncle Joe, had a climbing accident on Kolahoi. They were trying to scale the peak above the glacier when my grandfather slipped and fell headfirst into a crevasse. He was rescued but suffered a serious head wound and lost a lot of blood. When he was finally carried down to Pahalgam, the only available doctor was a veterinarian who sewed my grandfather's scalp back on. Our trek to Kolahoi Glacier was much less eventful, though on the way back we got caught in a heavy rainstorm. The road was washed out by a flash flood and we had to wade through muddy water up to our waists.

While we were camping in Pahalgam, a girlfriend of mine from school, Sue Collins, was staying with her family on a houseboat on Nagin Lake in Srinagar. I had been wanting to visit her, and my parents finally agreed to let me go down for the day. It was a two-hour bus ride and by the time I reached Nagin Lake it was almost noon. Sue's parents invited me to spend the night, which I was happy to do, even though I had promised my mother and father that I would be back in camp that evening before dark. Kashmir is famous for its romantic atmosphere, to which I was susceptible. Just before sunset, Sue and I went for a shikara ride on the lake, reclining on a cushioned seat while the boatman, with his heart-shaped paddle, guided us through the lotus blossoms. The last bus to Pahalgam had already departed and there was no way to get in touch with my family, even if I'd had the inclination.

Meanwhile, my parents were getting worried. Afraid that I might be lost or stranded, they set off in the jeep to look for me. Around ten o'clock that evening, as Sue and I were holding hands on the porch, watching the moon rise above Nagin Lake, I heard a knock on the door of the houseboat. My mother and father walked in and even though they said very little, I could tell that they were angry. On the long drive back to Pahalgam I tried to apologize and explain what had happened but my parents maintained a reproachful silence. Worst of all, however, I had to endure the teasing of my cousins and my brothers for the rest of the trip.

At the end or our stay in Kashmir, we moved down to Srinagar and spent three nights in a houseboat called *The New International*. These boats were made of deodar wood, which gave off a pleasant cedar smell. Intricate carvings surrounded the window frames and paneled walls. The boats were like floating guesthouses, rented out by the day or week, including room and board. The food was disappointing, though, bland and badly cooked. Our first morning on the houseboat we saw a pair of ducks floating by our window and in the evening both of them were on the table, roasted to a crisp and surrounded by a pile of boiled carrots and potatoes. Most of us got sick and we discovered later that the water which we drank was drawn directly from Nagin Lake, into which the sewage from all of the houseboats drained.

On one of the larger boats near us there was a contingent of UN military observers who were supposed to be overseeing the border dispute with Pakistan. The Indian authorities wouldn't let them near the line of control, so they spent most of their days sunbathing and water-skiing. Each of the houseboats and shikaras had fanciful names—from the grandiose, *New Glory, Omega,* and *Emperor's Choice,* to the ridiculous, *Lover's Delite* and *My Fair Lady.* Even some of the merchants in Kashmir had nicknames, like "Cheerful Chippendale," "Mr. Marvelous," and "Suffering Moses," who owned a handicrafts emporium where my grandmother used to shop in the thirties and forties.

By this time, the romance of Kashmir was wearing thin. Sue Collins and her parents had already left and I was bored and sullen, even though we went water-skiing on the lake and visited Shalimar Bagh, built by the Mogul emperor Jehangir. I hated Srinagar because there were so many tourists around and I felt as if I was being cheated whenever I went out. A constant string of vendors came by our houseboat, paddling up in their shikaras, selling handicrafts and flowers, fur hats and jewelry boxes made of papier-mâché. There was a commercial, mercenary quality about Kashmir and wherever we went I was surrounded by touts who offered cheap rates at hotels, guided tours of the floating gardens, lotus blossoms carved from walnut wood, or postcards of shikaras silhouetted against the sunset.

Even though I was a tourist I didn't want to be treated like one. It made me feel acutely aware of being a foreigner, and when I tried to speak to the Kashmiris in Hindi they looked at me with disdain. At the handicrafts shops in Srinagar the prices were inflated and I felt as if everyone I dealt with was out to gyp me. Walking along the Bund, an embankment overlooking the Jhelum River, I kept having to wave off young boys who wanted to sell me souvenirs or buy dollars. By the time we finally loaded up our jeep and drove away from Kashmir, I was ready to go home.

THE INNER LINE

The closest and most prominent of the snow peaks that we could see from Mussoorie was Bandar Punch (the monkey's tail), a broad massif with twin summits that rose twenty-two thousand feet above sea level. Hidden from view on the north side of the mountain was a third summit, called Black Peak. This section of Bandar Punch was only visible by hiking up the Har-ki-Dun Valley, which circled around behind the mountain. From our perspective in Landour, Bandar Punch appeared to be the largest mountain in Garhwal, even though it was actually not as high as some of the other peaks—Nanda Devi or Trisul, Chaukhamba and Kedarnath. Bandar Punch got its name from Hanuman, the monkey god, who came to the Himalayas after the epic battle of Lanka and plunged his burning tail in the snow to put out the flames. Gangotri and Jumnotri, the two main sources of the Ganga and Jumna, lay on either side of Bandar Punch. The glaciers from which these rivers flowed were considered sacred by Hindus, a place of pilgrimage.

On a clear day the snows stood out like jagged shards of broken porcelain, imposing and inaccessible. Often the mountains were obscured by dense banks of clouds, only a single peak or two floating in the mist, as if detached from the ridges in the foreground. The foothills unfolded beneath the higher mountains like pleated canvas. Forested with oaks and pines, their lower slopes were creased by terraced fields and dotted with villages. As the crow flies, Bandar Punch was no more than forty miles away, but with the intervening ranges, it was at least a five-day trek to reach the snow line.

Among our family photographs we must have had several hundred pictures of the snows, countless slides and prints of Bandar Punch, framed by oak or deodar branches, snapshots clicked at every hour of the day, from sunrise to sunset. There were even a few time exposures taken by moonlight in which the mountains had a pale, spectral quality, like cobwebs against a darkened windowpane. In many of the photographs my brothers and I were forced to stand in the foreground, squinting into the sunlight. The snows provided a backdrop for my childhood in Landour, much like the painted curtains which street photographers used to frame their portraits. Bandar Punch and the other mountains remained unchanged in each of the pictures, as I grew taller every year, and more self-conscious posing for the camera.

When I was in high school I got interested in photography, and for several years I tried to take an accurate picture of the snows. This seemed the easiest thing to do, but in fact it was impossible. With an ordinary camera lens, the Himalayas shrank into obscurity and almost disappeared from view. Instead of the dominant white profiles which stood against the sky, the mountains became indistinct and miniature in photographs, like an uneven line of molars, protruding above the foothills. Using a telephoto lens, with filters, I could very nearly make Bandar Punch appear the way it looked to my naked eye, though I was never satisfied with the scale and perspective in any of the photographs I took. Every time I watched the shapes emerge in my developing trays, those familiar outlines darkening on sheets of Agfa paper, I felt a sense of disappointment, realizing that I would never be able to capture a precise image of the snows.

Sometimes, in my frustration, I wondered if the mountains were nothing but an optical illusion, their scale and dimensions skewed by the angle of the sun or a deceptive depth of field. The Aglar valley, behind Landour, fell away so sharply that it could have made the snows appear much larger than they actually were, exaggerating their elevation. But as I squinted through the viewfinder of my camera, trying to compose a perfect picture, it was clear that no matter where I stood or how carefully I adjusted my lens, in reality those mountains would always be much greater than any photograph I tried to take.

*   *   *

In 1962, after India's war with China over mountain borders, the government established what was called the "Inner Line," beyond which foreigners were not allowed to travel. This boundary made it impossible for us to hike back into the snows, and throughout my years in school, I was continually frustrated because the higher Himalayas were cut off for me. We were not permitted to trek any farther than the first range of hills to the north of Mussoorie, and places such as Gangotri and Jumnotri lay well beyond the Inner Line. Bandar Punch and Har-ki-Dun were also out of bounds, which meant that the Black Peak itself remained obscured from view. Years later, when these restrictions were finally lifted, I was able to trek up to many of the glaciers and valleys in Garhwal, but the Inner Line would always remain a part of my subconscious, an invisible border that defined me as a foreigner.

I barely remember the war between India and China, though in the years that followed there was a residual sense of anxiety, as if the Chinese army might invade across those mountain passes once again. There were rumors after the war that advance parties of Communist soldiers had made it as far as the tea stalls at Burans

Khanda, only eight miles out the Tehri Road. I doubt if there was any truth in this, but these were the stories people told, and it kept the threat alive. Some of the missionaries in Landour had "China connections." Either their relatives had worked there before Mao threw them out or they had lived as children in Shanghai and Canton. Once, I even heard a rumor that John Birch (an American missionary who was killed in China and after whom the virulently anticommunist organization is named) was born in the Landour Community Hospital, again unlikely, but a symptom of the suspicions and hatred that some of the missionaries felt for the "Red Chinese." Within the Christian confines of Landour there were those who harbored an acute sense of fear and paranoia toward the Communists, believing in the dangers of a yellow peril.

One of the main reasons for the war in 1962 was that the borders between India and Tibet were never clearly demarcated. Though the British mapped the Himalayas with fastidious precision, charting every ridge and stream, the northern boundaries of India remained ambiguous. Perhaps the British imagined that some day their dominions would extend even farther into central Asia. An aura of intrigue and subterfuge surrounded "the Great Game," when Britain was competing with the Russians for influence in the mountain kingdoms that lay along the upper margins of their empire. During the nineteenth century sections of the Aksai Chin Plateau, which lay beyond the Himalayas, were claimed by the British, though they never really controlled this region. In 1947, at the time of independence, the status of these remote and desolate areas was left unresolved in the transfer of power, despite the Macmahon Line, an arbitrary frontier that was drawn across the maps. Most of India's mountain borders lay at altitudes of fifteen and twenty thousand feet, in areas where no one lived and no one dared to go, except for mountain climbers and a few nomadic traders carrying salt and flour back and forth between the Tibetan plateau and the upper reaches of Garhwal. The Himalayas were perhaps the most futile and forbidding place to fight a war, those invisible, shifting borders constantly realigned by avalanche and blizzard. The lines on the maps were no more rigid than the glaciers that they crossed; they moved and cracked and eventually melted into mountain streams.

The only clear memory I have of the war with China is that everyone in Landour was knitting woolen socks for the Indian troops, to protect their toes from frostbite. I remember more clearly the other wars with Pakistan, which were also fought because of disputed borders. We had to put black-out paper on all the windows in our houses, and every day the fighter jets would break the sound barrier overhead. The Mirages and Migs from the Indian air force station in Ambala circled over Mussoorie, their dartlike silver shapes screaming across the sky and leaving vapor trails that led toward the snows. Each sonic boom sounded as if a bomb had landed and all the windows in our house would rattle. That was as close as the wars ever came to us, though the newspapers and radio carried reports of casualties and bloodshed, territory gained and lost.

Sometimes I tried to imagine what would have happened if the Chinese had actually captured Mussoorie, and I wondered whether we, as Americans, would have been slaughtered or ignored. The United States was helping India at the time, unlike the wars with Pakistan, when Washington took the other side. I imagined that the Chinese would round us up and put us into concentration camps, surrounded by barbed wire and sentries, all of Landour converted into a prison. In my fantasies, I pictured myself escaping through the Tehri hills, hiding in the caves on Witch's Hill, eluding the Communists and living off the land.

During the late fifties, a number of Tibetan refugees came across the border into India, escaping from the Chinese troops, who took over Lhasa in 1959. The Dalai Lama and many of his people settled in hill stations like Mussoorie, Simla, and Dharamshala. A refugee colony was established in Happy Valley, at the opposite end of Mussoorie, beyond Library bazaar. The Tibetans built a Buddhist temple and many of the refugees sold handicrafts along the Mall. There was also a Tibetan school in Happy Valley and we competed against them in cross-country and other sports. A small number of Tibetan students were enrolled at Woodstock, and there was a girl in my class named Dachen Samchok who had escaped from Tibet with her mother and an older brother and sister. Her father remained in Lhasa as a political prisoner. When I was in second grade the Dalai Lama came to attend an orchestra concert in Parker Hall. I remember all of us stood up as he was escorted down the aisle, a young man with glasses, dressed in ocher robes.

The Indian government allowed the Tibetan refugees to settle in the hills, and several European aid agencies set up rehabilitation programs in Mussoorie. Even though the Tibetans seemed to adjust to their exile and most of them did well as merchants and traders, they did not give up their hope of returning home. All of the Tibetan shops and restaurants in Mussoorie had pictures of the Dalai Lama and the Potala Palace on their walls. At certain times of the year, demonstrations were held in Happy Valley during which the refugees performed inspirational plays and tableaux, depicting battles with the Chinese, shadowy figures of men with guns and loud explosions, as well as monks wearing grotesque masks, dressed up as mythical snow lions, dancing on an outdoor stage. We also heard a rumor, which was probably true, that the CIA had established a secret military camp for Tibetan guerrillas in the nearby hill station of Chakrata, where they were being armed and trained to take back their homeland.

Out the Tehri Road a couple of miles was a ridge called Flag Hill. It was a place where we often went for picnics, less than an hour's walk from school. At the top of Flag Hill was a level clearing with an unobstructed view of the snows. The Tibetan refugees had turned the hill into a shrine, where they came to pray for their return across those mountain passes. Draped on all of the trees that surrounded the summit were square cloth flags on which were printed Tibetan characters and images of Buddhist deities. The prayer flags were strung on long pieces of twine and fluttered in the breeze like the pennants on a sailing ship. Some of them were frayed and faded, others new and freshly printed with prayers. Standing at the top of Flag Hill, looking at the snows, I could not help but feel my own ambiguous sense of exile. The mountains seemed so close yet so impossibly far away.

.　.　.

Because of the Inner Line, the highest mountain that we could climb was Nag Tibba, just under ten thousand feet. Usually it took four days to get there and back. The first time I tried to climb this peak, we didn't make it to the top, though I returned to Landour with my companions and we lied about it for a while, claiming that we had conquered the mountain. After that I climbed Nag Tibba three more times. There were grassy meadows at the top and a cairn of rocks with a wooden pole to mark the summit. Supposedly, if a person climbed onto the cairn and shinnied up the pole, he reached an altitude of ten thousand feet. Nag Tibba was difficult to climb because there was very little water along the path, which ascended straight up the face of the mountain. It was also a deceptive hike because there was a false peak and a confusing maze of trails near the top of the ridge. Several groups of students from the school got lost on the mountain, particularly when the mist rolled in, and they had to bivouac for the night.

On the far side of the mountain was a deserted forest bungalow and a small wooden temple in which there were stone images of Nag, the cobra deity, from which the mountain got its name. A square pool of water lay in front of the temple, but it was a green, murky color. I once drank from this pool in desperation, having emptied my canteen while climbing up Nag Tibba. The water tasted like algae and I had to spit most of it out. In 1973, my brother Joe and a classmate of mine, David Buckner, set the record for hiking to the top of Nag Tibba and back in less than twelve hours. They headed off early in the morning, before sunrise, and ran most of the way, a distance of over forty miles, taking shortcuts and carrying only canteens and chocolate bars.

The shortest route to the top of Nag Tibba was from the south, passing through the village of Mangalori. I also climbed the mountain from Deolsari and Untar, which was a longer but less strenuous hike. My last trek to the top of Nag Tibba, I approached the summit from a different direction, following the crest of the ridge across from Lurntzu and climbing the northeastern face of the mountain. There wasn't much of a path and the ridge I followed was heavily forested with moru oaks. A few miles from the top I came upon a Gujar camp. Nomadic Muslim shepherds, the Gujars migrated from the higher pastures in the summer to the Siwalik hills beyond the Dehra Dun Valley during winter. Throughout Garhwal, Himachal Pradesh, and Kashmir, there were tribes of Gujars who herded their buffaloes back and forth through the mountains.

Their appearance was striking, especially the men, who wore embroidered hats with tufts of bright colored wool. Many of the older men dyed their beards with henna, a rich orange color, signifying that they had been to Mecca on pilgrimage. Most of the villagers in Garhwal were Hindus, and the Gujars, being Muslims, generally kept to themselves. Many times when I was hiking I came across a group of Gujars on the move, the women leading a train of ponies or mules loaded down with their belongings. The men would follow herding the buffaloes, clumsy black beasts with sweeping horns, making their way up the narrow trails. The Gujars also raised bhootia dogs, Tibetan mastiffs, with matted fur and tiny, vicious eyes. The dogs wore metal collars with spikes to protect them from leopards and bears.

On my way back down from Nag Tibba I stopped at the Gujar camp to buy some milk. As I approached the cluster of straw huts the bhootia dogs began to bark, but the Gujars told me that they would not attack unless I went near the buffaloes. Pouring milk into my canteen, one of the old men, with a hennaed beard, told me about his pilgrimage to Mecca and how he had ridden in an airplane for the first time, from Delhi to Saudi Arabia. The ticket, by his calculations, cost him the value of two buffaloes.

I remember being fascinated by the Gujars because of their nomadic life and the way they moved unhindered through the mountains. Many of them were fair skinned and a few of the Gujars had eyes as blue as mine. I often thought that I could easily disguise myself as one of them and travel undetected, back into the highest pastures, beyond the Inner Line.

. . .

Hiking was a popular activity at Woodstock, and whenever we had a long weekend or holiday, groups of students set out along the Tehri Road for places like Dhanaulti, Sirkanda Devi, Nali, and Deolsari. The school even had its own hiking song, composed by Dr. Fleming. The tune was based on the cry of the Himalayan cuckoo, a familiar birdcall in Mussoorie.

Toward the end of tenth grade, a group of us decided to take a "mixed hike," boys and girls together. Because we wanted to camp overnight we needed a chaperon, and high school headmaster Bob Morris and his wife agreed to accompany us. Mr. Morris had been our homeroom teacher in ninth grade, a Canadian who worked for the BMMF.

There were four couples in our group, including Sue Collins and myself. We didn't plan to go very far and the hike was more of an excuse to get away from Woodstock and spend some time together. I suggested that we go to a place called Seraghat, which was only five miles from the school. It was down in the valley below Witch's Hill and there was a stream with terraced fields nearby, which hadn't been cultivated for years, an ideal spot to set up camp. Just down from the fields was an abandoned water mill, where the stream had been diverted into a channel that was used to turn the grinding stone.

We set off after school on Friday, loaded down with tents and sleeping bags. Passing through the Dhobighat I saw lines of laundry drying in the sun and heard the familiar sound of washermen beating clothes against the rocks. The path to Seraghat dropped steeply into the valley and followed the stream. Each of the couples walked together, holding hands at the wider stretches of the trail and following single file on the narrow sections. I knew this path by heart because I often went hunting near Seraghat during the winter holidays. After a couple of miles we passed above a grove of wild cinnamon trees that grew beside the stream, and farther on we came to a cowshed and some potato fields surrounded by a fence of thorns to keep out porcupines and wild boars.

Most of the hike was downhill and we got to Seraghat an hour before dark, with plenty of time to set up our tents—one for the girls and one for the boys and a small pup tent for our chaperons. Everyone was in high spirits and we made rice and dal for dinner and sat around the campfire afterward. Sue and one of the other girls began to sing, mostly gospel songs and Christian ballads. "Michael row the boat ashore, alleluia!" Sitting close to my girlfriend, our legs touching, I hummed along because I didn't know the words. For the past few days, Sue had been upset with me because I had told her that I didn't believe in God. She was a devout Christian and this troubled her. We had talked about it quite a bit and Sue had tried to convince me to go with her to Bible Club, but I kept making excuses.

Sparks from the fire shot upward through the smoke. The sky was clear and full of stars. I could see Orion and his dog overhead, one of the few constellations that I recognized. On the ridge across from us were the flickering lights of Chamasari village, a mile and a half away. After a while we ran out of songs to sing and started telling ghost stories. I told one about a churail, a witch who lured men into the forest. This was a story I'd heard while hunting with Dil Das. Churails were said to be beautiful women, with almond eyes and long black hair, but their feet were turned around in the wrong direction, so that they could walk backward while they beckoned to their victims. If a man fell under the spell of a churail he became gradually weaker and weaker until he finally wasted away. The only solution was to tie a spool of thread to her finger and in the morning, when she disappeared, you followed the thread as it led you deep into the center of the jungle to a secret place, a hidden ravine. When you finally reached the end of the string, all that you found was an old, dry bone, the bleached white joint from a woman's finger, which had to be burned on the spot to kill the churail.

After I finished the story someone asked me if that was how Witch's Hill had got its name, and I said I didn't know. Around ten o'clock Mr. and Mrs. Morris told us that they were going to bed and the girls decided to turn in as well. Since there wasn't any chance of rain I planned to sleep outside. One of the other boys joined me and the two of us lay awake for a while, listening to the girls' voices inside their tent, the glow of flashlights shining through the canvas fabric. I could hear night sounds in the dark, the faint call of an octave owl and the rustle of mice in the grass. The fire had died down to embers and the stars filled the space between the dark outlines of the ridges, which rose up on either side of our camp. Within a few minutes I fell asleep to the murmuring whisper of the stream.

The next day, after breakfast, we changed into our bathing suits and went swimming in a shallow pool just down from our camp. The stream was hardly deep enough to wade in and we spent most of our time sunbathing on the rocks, rubbing our skin with coconut oil. Each of the couples sat together and our chaperons kept a discreet distance, reading in the shade. As we were joking around one of the boys mentioned our fifth-grade hike to Bhatta Falls. I started to laugh, still embarrassed by the memory of Mr. Goodwin taking off his clothes. The girls asked us what had happened on that hike, but none of us would tell. There was no longer any reason to keep it to ourselves, but the more the girls began to pester us, the more secretive we became, refusing to reveal the truth.

A couple hours later, once the sun was high above us, I suggested to Sue that the two of us explore farther down the stream to see if there was a deeper pool where we could actually swim. She agreed and we set off together along an overgrown path that took us past the water mill and around a bend in the stream. Very soon we came to a narrow gorge, where the water poured over the lip of a rock and down to a pool about thirty feet below. Because of the undergrowth it was difficult to see what lay ahead, but farther on I could just make out the edge of a second waterfall, much larger than the one that blocked our path. Casting about in the weeds along the shore I found that the trail continued up the opposite bank and across the ridge. Taking Sue's hand I followed the path, which climbed for a ways, then descended toward the stream again and led us down to the top of the second waterfall.

At this point the gorge was no more than twenty feet across and there were cliffs on either side, with the branches of trees leaning over the top. Except for a patch of sunlight, where we stood, the valley lay in shadow. A strip of sand bordered the stream, which flowed over the pebbled bottom, no more than five or six inches deep. Farther up I could see the pool, which was about forty feet in length. Along one side was a shelf of rock, and the cliffs closed in around it like a grotto, the water clear and still as the surface of a mirror. By this time we were out of earshot of our friends and the only sound was the spattering of the waterfall below.

Sue was standing a couple feet away from me and when I turned to look at her I knew immediately that there was something wrong. She had a frozen expression on her face, staring straight into the gorge, as if she had seen a ghost. When I asked her what was going on, she didn't say a word, and I noticed that her skin was covered with goose pimples, even though it was a warm and humid day. As I reached out to put my arm around her, she turned abruptly and began to run. Surprised and puzzled, I called after her, but she kept going, scrambling up the path. Looking back into the gorge I couldn't see a thing, except for the shadows of the trees moving on the water. Hurrying after Sue, I caught up with her and tried to make her stop, but she was in a panic and brushed my hand away. By now I could hear the voices of our friends, and when we reached the camp, Sue disappeared into her tent. I kept asking her what was wrong but she refused to answer. None of the others had noticed what was going on between us, and I rejoined them on the rocks, anxious and confused.

Later in the afternoon, once we had eaten lunch, I decided to go back to the gorge by myself and see what I could find. By this time the sun had disappeared behind the hill and the entire valley lay in shadow. Cautiously, I made my way past the water mill and up the trail. This time I noticed that there was a pushta wall along one section, and I could tell that it had once been a more substantial path, though it obviously hadn't been used for years.

After I clambered down to the stream bed, I looked over the edge of the lower waterfall and saw that it dropped nearly a hundred feet, spilling into the air like fluted glass. The gorge seemed much darker now and more forbidding, though my curiosity overcame my fear. Taking off my shoes and wading across the stream I climbed onto the shelf of rock that overlooked the pool. The water was even deeper than I had expected, eight or ten feet at least. The upper falls, at the top of the pool, flowed through a crevice between the rocks, splashing me where I stood.

I was wearing a pair of jeans over my bathing suit, and stripping off my clothes I stood on the ledge for several minutes. Looking down into the pool, at the magnified shapes of submerged rocks, I felt a hint of uneasiness, though I was determined to prove that there was nothing to fear. Finally, taking a deep breath, I jumped into the pool. The water was cold, but as my head went under I felt a different kind of shock. It seemed as if my whole body had been embraced, an immediate sense of terror, as if an invisible python had wrapped itself around my arms and legs. The instant my feet touched the slick rocks on the bottom of the pool, I kicked myself upward in a panic, thrashing my arms and lunging out of the water and onto the safety of the shelf.

For the second time that day, I ran from the gorge, as fast as I could go. Clutching my shoes and clothes, I raced back up the path, stopping only when I got to the abandoned water mill. My heart was beating like a tabla and my mind was full of shadows, the dark shapes of rocks at the bottom of the pool. I had no idea what it was that had scared me but I knew it had to be the same thing that had frightened Sue.

As I got back to camp the others were already packing up to leave. I tried to speak to Sue, but she wouldn't look at me, and we hiked home in silence, climbing up the trail to Dhobighat and reaching the school at dusk. I myself was still too shaken by the experience to tell any of the others, and I had no explanation for what had taken place. After that hike my relationship with Sue was never the same, and the two of us broke up before the end of the year. Once or twice I tried to ask her what she'd seen and told her how frightened I had been, but she just shook her head and looked away.

The following winter, when I was hunting with Dil Das on the cliffs above Seraghat, I told him what had happened. He listened quietly and nodded when I described the gorge and the pool of water. Dil Das said it must have been a ghost, one of the bhoots that lived near the stream. He explained that the gorge was a burning ghat, where the villagers from Chamasari cremated their dead.

•   •   •

The mountains were full of mysteries like this, and the mythology of Hinduism added to their supernatural aura. On the walls of barbershops and tea stalls in Landour bazaar I saw devotional lithographs depicting Himalayan deities and the sacred sources of the Ganga. Some of these pictures were like schematic diagrams or maps, but everything was out of scale, a line of snow mountains at the top and drawings of temples and shrines, as well as pilgrim trails. There were images of Siva sitting cross-legged upon the Himalayas, an ascetic god with dark blue skin, absorbed in meditation. He was said to live on Mount Kailas, the most sacred peak of all, which lay beyond the borders of Tibet. Another popular lithograph depicted Hanuman, the monkey god, flying through the air and carrying a snow peak on his shoulders. This was an illustration of one episode in the Ramayana epic, when Hanuman was sent to the Himalayas to find a magical herb, which had the power to restore life. Having no time or patience to search for the sacred plant itself, he uprooted an entire mountain and brought it back with him.

Many of the villages and pilgrim centers in Garhwal acquired their names and significance from the epics. In Jaunpur, to the west of Mussoorie, lay a village called Lakhamandal, which was said to be the place where the five Pandav brothers in the Mahabharata were almost killed when their palace of wax was set on fire. This area was known for the practice of polyandry, and the people of Jaunpur traced their marital customs to the same five brothers, who shared a single wife, the beautiful and chaste Draupadi. Stories such as these made the mountains seem magical, and they became for me a dimension of the unknown, visible in the distance but a place to which all access was denied. The fact that the Himalayas were forbidden territory, beyond the Inner Line, made them all the more intriguing. I remember hearing tales of Roop Kund, a frozen lake high above the Pindar Valley. In summer, when the ice melted, you could see the bones of soldiers dressed in armor. These skeletons were supposed to be the remains of warriors who had fought with Zowahar Singh, the Rajput general who conquered Garhwal in the fifteenth century.

The Himalayas were also a place of strange plants and medicinal substances, found only in the upper elevations. I was told about shilajeet, a potent oil that seeped out of the rocks and cured all kinds of diseases, or jawalabooti, a species of grass that only grew above the tree line. Its roots were phosphorescent and glowed in the dark. Beyond Joshimath was a place called the "Valley of the Flowers," where the bhramkamal bloomed, the Himalayan lotus; its scent was so powerful it could put a man to sleep forever.

There were rare animals, too, like the musk deer. Its glands were more valuable than gold, and if a poacher shot one, he could clear all of his debts and live securely for the rest of his life. Monal pheasants and scarlet tragopans were found in the highest ranges, as were blue sheep, tahr, snow leopards, and perhaps even the abominable snowman. One of the valleys near Nanda Devi, the highest mountain in Garhwal, was said to be so inaccessible that only a few climbers had ever entered this sanctuary. The animals in the valley were unafraid of men, supposedly as tame as sheep.

The mountains of Garhwal had a spiritual lure for Hindu mendicants, like the man we met in Kulu. Along the rivers and near the centers of pilgrimage were hundreds of ashrams and dharmsalas where sadhus and swamis lived. During the winter months many of them came down out of the mountains to Rishikesh and Hardwar. A few of the sadhus remained in the snows all winter long, living in caves and crude huts with minimal supplies, gunnysacks of flour or rice and dal given to them as offerings by pilgrims. Six months of the year they lived in total isolation, having renounced the world.

One of the regular visitors at my aunt and uncle's home in Rajpur was Swami Abhishiktananda, a French Benedictine priest who had come to India as a missionary and became a mendicant. Though he remained a Christian, Abhishiktananda looked very much like a Hindu rishi in his saffron robes, with flowing beard and hair. I remember meeting him once or twice, and what struck me was his heavy French accent and his laugh, an unrestrained sound of pleasure that seemed so unlikely coming from this aging, ascetic figure. My uncle and aunt, as well as my parents, always spoke of Swami Abhishiktananda with admiration and affection. At that time there was a growing interest in Christian mysticism, and quite a few of the more liberal missionaries were involved in exploring the intersection of their own theology with Hindu beliefs and rituals.

Swami Abhishiktananda was one of those who seemed to have erased the lines of nationality and religion. He still celebrated communion, though he used water from the Ganga and chapatis instead of wine and wafers. For part of the year Abhishiktananda lived in a hut, or kutti, on the banks of the Ganga near Uttarkashi. The kutti was nothing but a single room, made of stones and mud. After the Inner Line was established, Swami Abhishiktananda took Indian citizenship so that he could continue to live in Uttarkashi and travel freely in the mountains.

∘   ∘   ∘

The government of India was sensitive about maps on account of the border disputes in Kashmir and the war with China. The only maps available from the Survey of India were large scale, one inch to twenty miles, which were printed with intentional inaccuracies. These were virtually useless for hiking because they only showed the motor roads and larger towns. If anyone tried to follow them they were likely to get lost.

Our family subscribed to *National Geographic* magazine, which arrived by sea mail, often six months late. If any issues contained a map of India it was always blotted out by the censor's ink. For a while the authorities also used a rubber stamp which said, "The borders of India, as depicted on this map, are neither accurate nor correct." The censoring of these maps made me feel as though they contained a secret power of their own, the intricate filigree of contour lines and borders like the creases on the palm of my hand.

My father had a collection of old maps, some of which he had inherited from his parents. Most of these were based on the original survey conducted by Sir George Everest, which was updated in the 1920s. A few of the more recent maps had been revised after the U.S. Air Force conducted aerial photography of the Himalayas during the Second World War. My parents had used these maps on many of their hiking trips before I was born, and several of them were torn and stained from being carried in rucksacks and duffel bags. Spreading the maps open on our dining table, I could see the pencil lines which my father had drawn along the routes they followed to Jumnotri, Uttarkashi, and Dodi Tal. The oldest of these maps, which was practically disintegrating, had been used by my grandparents on a trek from Mussoorie to Simla in 1917, only a few months after they arrived in India.

During the late forties and early fifties, my parents and my uncle Jim and aunt Barry went on several long hikes together. In those days there was no Inner Line to stop them, and they trekked back to places such as Dodi Tal, a tiny lake at the foot of Bandar Punch. My mother and father would tell me stories about Dodi Tal, a gemlike pool surrounded by deodar trees. The lake was full of rainbow trout, which they caught with safety pins tied to a string. A Gujar shepherd brought them fresh cream to eat with the wild strawberries that grew along the shore. There was an idyllic, imaginary quality about Dodi Tal, this place which my parents had visited long before I was born. I had heard so many stories and seen so many pictures of the lake that it felt as if I'd actually been there, even though I never took that trek.

On one of the maps my father drew the Inner Line with a red felt pen, a crooked boundary that marked the limits beyond which we were not allowed to go. The line extended from Ladakh and Lahaul Spiti in the west, across the mountains north of Kulu and Simla, through Chakrata and the Jumna Valley, over to Darasu on the Ganga and farther east, below Chamoli and Joshimath, into the mountains of Kumaon, where it finally ended at the border of Nepal. Tracing the Inner Line with my finger I would try to imagine what lay beyond that barrier of ink. We had heard stories of foreigners who tried to cross the line and were arrested. One time a group of students from Woodstock got lost and wandered into the town of Darasu by mistake. They spent the night in jail and were sent back by bus the following day with threats of being deported out of India.

In my junior year of high school I read a book by Heinrich Harrer called *Seven Years in Tibet*. Harrer was an Austrian mountaineer who was arrested by the British authorities in India at the beginning of the Second World War. After escaping from a detention camp in Dehra Dun, he hiked through the mountains behind Mussoorie. Disguised as a Hindu pilgrim, Harrer crossed the Tsang Chokla Pass above Gangotri and made his way to Lhasa, where he remained for the rest of the war, living in a Tibetan monastery.

This book suggested the possibility that I could disguise myself and cross the Inner Line. Reading that Harrer had used the juice from walnut husks to darken his skin, my brothers and I collected green walnuts from the trees at Jabbarkhet and rubbed them on our hands. The juice left a brownish stain, the color of iodine, which wouldn't wash off for several weeks. There were times when I was tempted to put walnut juice on my face and dye my hair to see if I could pass for an Indian. Looking at the maps, I planned different routes across the Inner Line, up the Aglar Valley, following the Bhagirathi and Alekananda Rivers, avoiding the larger towns and trekking along pilgrim trails into the snows, as far as Mount Kailas.

Another book I read in high school was Rudyard Kipling's *Kim*. Once again there was the journey up into the mountains, accompanying the Lama on his search for the sacred river. There was also the suggestion of forbidden territory, spies, and dangerous frontiers, as well as secret identities. Even though I was born long after the British Empire had collapsed, I couldn't help identifying myself with Kim, who was "country born" and grew up speaking Hindustani, playing on the streets of Lahore. A repeated theme in much of Kipling's writing was the possibility of "going native," the desire to disguise oneself as an Indian and blend into the sea of faces.

All of this comes together in my memory, the maps, the hikes to Nag Tibba and the gorge at Seraghat, stories of shilajeet, the walnut juice, musk deer and images of a blue god meditating on the Himalayas, those "eternal snows." There are times when I still dream of crossing the Inner Line, imagining myself as a boy of sixteen, with a canvas rucksack, climbing a winding trail—it could be the path from Agora to Dodi Tal or the mule track from Guttu up to Khatling Glacier—it doesn't matter which route exactly. All I know is that ahead of me there is that point beyond which I am forbidden to go, yet I keep climbing, the leather straps digging into my shoulders, a numbness in my fingers because the weight of the rucksack cuts my circulation. My feet blister where my socks have gathered up at the toe and the sweat stings my eyes. As I reach the crest of the ridge, Bandar Punch is there above me, larger than I have ever seen it before, like a giant iceberg, sloping down from the sky, and suddenly I realize that I have already crossed that line and there is no one here to stop me as I continue upward, above the tree line now, the last of the silver birches behind me, their ragged bark fluttering in the wind, a glacial scree of rocks over which I scramble, leaving the path completely, climbing now without restrictions, free of borders, free of maps and diagrams, free of ghosts and gods, throwing off my rucksack so that I can leap from one boulder to the next until I finally reach the snow line and plunge my face and hands into the cold, moist whiteness that melts against my skin.

NO OBJECTION TO RETURN

Walking through the bazaar one evening on our way home from a movie at the Rialto Cinema, my father and I were accosted by a group of young Punjabi men. They were obviously tourists who had come up to Mussoorie for a holiday and I could tell that they had been drinking. The four of them were in a lively, uninhibited mood, their arms slung around each other. Seeing us, two foreigners coming toward them, they veered across the street and blocked our way.

"Good evening," said one of the tourists, speaking in English and swaying drunkenly. "Excuse me please . . . Are you Englishman or are you hippie?"

We did not answer him, and brushing past, my father and I continued on, ignoring the irritating sound of their laughter. In many ways there was nothing unusual about this encounter—we were often stopped by tourists in Mussoorie trying to strike up conversations, "Which country, please?"—but this man's question angered me. Perhaps he thought that my father was the Englishman and I was the hippie, though neither of us really looked the part. What annoyed me most of all was his assumption that a foreigner could represent only one of two things, the remnants of a colonial past or the recent influx of world travelers in search of Eastern mysticism. Why else were we in India?

The townspeople of Mussoorie knew that we came from Woodstock, but as far as the tourists were concerned, we were just another curiosity, one of the many unexpected sights that they discovered in the hills. During the tourist season, which ran from the end of April to late October, the bazaar was filled with holiday crowds from the plains, families with children carrying balloons and toys, newlywed couples on honeymoon, and groups of revelers who went from one restaurant to the next, carousing along the Mall at night. This was the time of year when the shopkeepers and hoteliers made their money. As soon as the temperatures started to rise on the plains the tourists began to stream up to the hills, and the Mall Road was choked with rickshas and ponies carrying people back and forth to scenic spots—Lal Tibba, Gun Hill, Company Gardens, Happy Valley, and Kempty Falls.

At Woodstock we used to joke about the tourists all the time. Many of them had never been up to the mountains before and they were terrified by the precipitous heights, clinging to each other as they walked along the paths. We made fun of the honeymoon couples, timidly holding hands as they promenaded along the Mall, or posing for romantic pictures with the snow mountains in the background. They looked uncomfortable and self-conscious, the brides in their silk saris with gilt embroidery, the grooms swaggering about with walking sticks, shirts unbuttoned to the waist. Mussoorie had a thriving cottage industry, producing walking sticks. At least ten different shops competed with each other, selling every kind of cane imaginable, each of them elaborately carved and varnished, with ornate handles and metal tips. The tourists carried their walking sticks wherever they went, twirling them around with a jaunty air.

During the height of the season we avoided going into Mussoorie because it was so crowded. Sections of the bazaar were closed to traffic, but other areas were jammed with cars, parked along the edges of the road. Sometimes the hotels were so full that tourists couldn't find a room and had to sleep in the havaghars, open pavilions along the Mall. There was always a shortage of water during the summer months and the storage tanks at the top of Landour Hill were siphoned off to supply the restaurants and hotels. The whole town was turned into a fairground with loudspeakers blaring film tunes, Ferris wheels and merry-go-rounds, hawkers selling cotton candy and roasted corn. In the early seventies a cable car was installed on Gun Hill and lines of tourists waited for hours to get a ride. Most of these visitors preferred the crowded chaos of the bazaar to the quiet pathways of Landour, flocking to the cinemas and cabarets, billiard halls and roller-skating rinks. With their transistor radios and gaudy fashions they seemed uninterested in the mountains and the forests, unaware of the natural beauty that surrounded them.

The tourist season tapered off in the monsoon and by the first week of November the town was virtually deserted, the restaurants and souvenir shops boarded up for winter and all but a few hotels closed for business. The Mall was empty and silent except when it snowed in January and busloads of tourists came up from Dehra Dun. They were often unprepared for the cold, walking through the snow in plastic sandals, bundled up with shawls and blankets. During the winter my brothers and I would go sledding near Lal Tibba and the tourists often asked us to pose with them in photographs, as if we were some sort of exotic creatures who lived in the snow. Occasionally we got into snowball fights with groups of rowdy college students who started pelting us from above and calling us names.

There was an underlying tension between Woodstock students and the tourists in Mussoorie, particularly when we went out for dates with our girlfriends in the bazaar. The young men made remarks or nudged the girls as we walked past. There was an expression in India, "Eve teasing," which included anything from catcalls and whistles to pinching a woman's breast. Foreign women, in particular, were seen as fair game. If I was by myself, I could ignore the comments that were made, the occasional insult and derisive laughter, but if I was walking with my girlfriend the harassment took on a different tone and I felt the need to answer back. Most times if I said something in Hindi that would be enough, but once in a while it led to arguments and fights.

I looked upon the tourists as intruders who came up to Mussoorie for a week or two, then went away. Unlike the townspeople, whom I knew, these interlopers, with their pestering questions and constant stares, reminded me that I was a foreigner. Even though I was born and raised in Mussoorie they made me feel as if I didn't belong in the town. The most common word for foreigner in Hindi was "angrez," which actually meant Englishman, though it was used for anyone who had white skin. Once in a while the tourists called us "firangis," an Urdu word, originally Persian, which was used to refer to the Portuguese who came to India in the fifteenth century. Both of these terms carried a hint of animosity but they were not as bad as "lal bandar," which meant red monkey, or "chitta gandu," white butt-fucker. Most of the tourists minded their own business or were mildly curious, but it was the groups of young men, the "loafers," who called me names. They assumed that I didn't understand what they were saying and this made it even worse, the casual slurs and comments whispered under their breath. I resented their insults and obscenities, but more than that it was the sense of alienation that I hated, a feeling of being excluded and set apart.

•   •   •

Mussoorie had five cinemas and two of them, the Rialto and the Picture Palace, showed English movies as well as Hindi films. Both of these theaters had been built in the forties and there was a dated, tawdry atmosphere about them, even though their names suggested the romance of the silver screen. The carpeting in the aisles was threadbare and the curtains on the doors were stained and torn. Just below the screen was a line of red buckets filled with sand in case there was a fire. We had a choice of four different prices for tickets, the cheapest being the one-rupee seats right up in front, five rows of plywood chairs that creaked whenever you moved. The Rs. 1.75 seats, where I usually sat, had coiled springs under the plastic upholstery and they were only slightly more comfortable. The last ten rows at the Rialto cost Rs. 3.50 and beyond that were the box seats for five rupees. I only sat there once, with a girlfriend I was trying to impress. The red velvet cushions were worn smooth and there was a curtain to pull across for privacy during intermission.

At Rialto, before the trailers started, they always played the same three or four songs over the loudspeaker. One was the Beatles' "Hard Day's Night," another was Cliff Richard's "Congratulations and Celebrations," and the third was "Bernadine," sung by a crooner I didn't recognize. The fourth song was "Come September," by the Ventures, which eventually got so scratched that the refrain kept repeating itself until the projectionist remembered to shift the needle. While waiting for the movie to begin we would order tea or soft drinks from the refreshment stands outside that sold potato chips dusted with chili powder, Cadbury's chocolate bars, and mango papad. During the film waiters came around with flashlights and collected the teacups and empty bottles from underneath our seats.

Most of the films we saw were British and American productions, as well as a few Italian movies, dubbed in English. They changed once a week, and in front of the Picture Palace and the Rialto there were displays of stills and posters for the coming attractions. We had very little choice as to what we watched; one week it would be a Dean Martin comedy, while the next it might be Richard Burton and Elizabeth Taylor in *The Taming of the Shrew*.

Most of these films were released in India several years after they first came out in England and America. The prints were often very poor and sometimes the projectionists got the reels mixed up. After the lights dimmed we would be shown a government of India newsreel, black-and-white documentaries produced by the Ministry of Information and Broadcasting. Most of these films contained pictures of Indira Gandhi laying the foundation stone for a new hospital or inspecting progress on the Bhakra Nangal Dam, shots of water flowing through penstocks and turbines generating electricity, coal mines and oil refineries. Public Sector projects were highlighted to show that the country was well on its way toward modernity. During the wars with Pakistan there were also scenes of tanks racing across the desert in Rajasthan and fighter jets careening overhead. Most of the newsreels were nothing more than propaganda glorifying the Congress Party and its achievements.

The movies began with a brief shot of the censor's certificate, a large stamp in one corner with the letter U for universal and A for adults. The ratings really didn't matter because the ticket sellers and ushers never turned us away for being too young, and the adult pictures were so thoroughly censored that there wasn't much chance of our innocence being corrupted. The offensive scenes of nudity and lovemaking were cut and spliced without any effort to provide continuity. One moment a couple would begin to embrace, and seconds later the scene shifted abruptly to an unrelated conversation or car chase, leaving us uncertain what had happened in between. I remember going to one film which was so badly cut that the story made no sense at all, a sequence of unrequited moments patched together like a frustrating dream.

The Bridge on the River Kwai was one of my favorite movies, with Alec Guinness as the stubborn British colonel captured by the Japanese. David Lean's films were always popular, and *Lawrence of Arabia* used to be shown at the Rialto at least once a year. Most of the school would troop down to watch it, our favorite lines already memorized: "The secret is not minding that it hurts," or "Thy mother mated with a scorpion!" These films appealed to my schoolboy fantasies of heroism, the hard-boiled British stereotypes of courage and fair play. Whether it was Peter O'Toole in the role of T. E. Lawrence or Charlton Heston playing Chinese Gordon in *Seven Days in Peking*, these were the colonial champions whom we idolized. When the James Bond movies arrived in Mussoorie they reinforced these British myths, and added a sexual tension that eluded even the most diligent censors.

Most of the American films we saw were slapstick comedies, often with Laurel and Hardy or the Three Stooges. One that I remember particularly well was called *Those Magnificent Men in Their Flying Machines*, which I went to see several times at the Picture Palace, where I also watched Doris Day and Rock Hudson in *Man's Favorite Sport*. Many of the best films produced in America during the sixties and seventies never reached Mussoorie because the Indian government began to restrict Hollywood movies on account of foreign-exchange regulations and trade disputes with Washington. There were a couple of Westerns that came around each year, *How the West Was Won* with Jimmy Stewart, and John Wayne in *Rio Bravo*. The other film which we watched again and again was called *MacKenna's Gold*, a B grade movie that ended with Styrofoam boulders rolling into a canyon. The only reason for its popularity was that the censors failed to cut one sequence in which the heroine swam naked in a turquoise pool of water.

During high school I also began to watch Hindi movies, and I saw everything from historical romances like *Pakeezah*, with Meena Kumari, to the Dev Anand thrillers *Jewel Thief* and *Johnny Mera Naam*. While the Hollywood pictures offered imagery and story lines that took me back to America, Bombay films opened up a whole new aspect of India which I had never experienced. Even though I understood the language and could follow the dialogue, much of the context was unfamiliar. These movies required a considerable suspension of disbelief, with characters breaking into song at regular intervals and convoluted plots that were full of coincidence and melodrama, but most Hindi films also portrayed the day-to-day lives of the urban middle class. Many of them were family sagas about Hindu households in which the customs and traditions were exaggerated and romanticized—respect for elders, stereotypes of noble fathers, chaste wives and sacred mothers, heroic sons and wicked uncles who repented in the end.

Anand was one of the first Hindi films I ever saw, starring Rajesh Khanna, Sharmila Tagore, and Amitabh Bachan. It was a simple, wholesome story, the details of which I can't recall, except that the movie included romance, humor, friendship, and cancer— I do remember that the doctor gave his diagnosis in English, "lymphosarcoma of the intestines." For me the most intriguing part of the film was to see the relationships within a Hindu family and to feel that I was able to watch the characters interacting without being self-conscious of my own foreignness. In the obscurity of the cinema, with the lights turned off, I could observe what was happening without my own presence trespassing on the scene. This was a part of India that I had never seen up close and I found it fascinating, the household gods and family rituals, as if I were looking through the keyhole of a culture which I barely understood.

At the end of every film, the audience would stand up for the national anthem, "Jana Gana Mana," which was played as soon as the credits stopped rolling. The Indian tricolor appeared on the screen, flapping in the breeze, the same grainy black-and-white imagery from the government newsreels. It didn't matter whether the movie I had watched was an English picture or a Hindi film, *The Dirty Dozen* or *Hare Ram Hare Krishna*, I stood there dutifully until the final strains of the anthem ended before filing out the doors.

·   ·   ·

In 1970, my cousin Tom returned to India after dropping out of Yale. He worked for a year as the social activities director at Woodstock and helped out at the boys' hostel. Like all of us, Tom felt a strong affinity to Mussoorie, and he used to tell me that he had no interest in going back to the United States. There was a determined, almost zealous, conviction in his voice when he said that India was the place where he belonged. More than anyone else in our family Tom felt the need to identify himself with the country of his birth. After his return he decided to become an Indian citizen and give up his American passport.

While he was working at Woodstock, Tom got interested in Hindi films and applied to the Film and Television Institute in Poona, where he studied to become an actor. There was a romantic, reckless quality about Tom's life, and my brothers and I looked up to him as someone who was pursuing a goal that we all admired. Even before he graduated from the Film and Television Institute, we were convinced that he was going to become a hero, a star of the Indian screen, and we were glad to play the role of his sidekicks, or chumchas, as they were called in Bombay slang. Whenever Tom came up to Mussoorie for a visit, we would head off with him to the bazaar and watch the latest Hindi movie. Afterward we'd wander home in the dark, along the Tehri Road, singing film songs at the top of our lungs, "Zindagi, ek safar, hai suhana. . . . Jahan kal, kya ho, kisney jana!"—Life is a journey of bliss. . . . Who knows what will happen along the way! We memorized the dialogue from all the films, particularly the action movies, in which there were characters called Jackie and Tiger. My youngest brother, Andy, was the best at doing imitations of villains like Prem Nath or Pran, twirling an imaginary mustache and giving a thumbs-up sign, repeating the words, "Done, boss!"

After he graduated from the Film and Television Institute, Tom moved to Bombay and got his first part, in a movie called *Charas*, starring Dharmender and Hema Malini, both of whom were at the height of their stardom. My cousin played the role of an Interpol agent who was trying to break up a drug-smuggling ring. In the final scene, he and Dharmender shot it out with the villains in an underwater cavern, full of motorboats and drums of oil that kept exploding. Soon after *Charas* was released our extended family went to see the film, taking up the entire back row of the cinema. Every time Tom appeared on the screen we cheered and whistled, excited by his debut. At intermission, when the lights came on, every single person in the audience turned around and looked at us. The cinema hall was packed and we were the only foreigners in the theater. Sitting there with all of those eyes upon us I felt embarrassed and exposed. A few minutes earlier, with the lights off and the movie running, I had been completely absorbed in the spectacle on the screen, but now that we were being watched by several hundred people I wanted to crawl under my seat and hide.

At the beginning of his career Tom continued to play the part of a foreigner—European police inspectors, international villains, and British colonials. He always spoke his lines of dialogue in Hindi but remained an outsider on the screen. Within a year or two Tom became enough of a celebrity to be recognized on the street, and whenever he came up to Mussoorie tourists would stop him and ask for autographs. It took a few more years before he was finally cast as an Indian, in Raj Kapoor's blockbuster, *Ram Teri Ganga Maili*. For him this was a moment of pride and affirmation, an acknowledgment that he could finally take on the role for which he had been rehearsing all his life.

Tom officially became an Indian national after eight years of waiting for the government bureaucracy to process his application. Before it was finally granted he had to go to the U.S. consulate in Bombay and renounce his American citizenship. A lot of people, most of them outside the family, tried to persuade him not to do it, but he went ahead anyway, and I could understand his reasons. It was something which I myself had seriously considered, even though I didn't share the same convictions as my cousin. For me there had always been a sense of ambivalence about my nationality and I was unwilling to commit myself to one country or the other.

* * *

As foreigners in India we had to register with the police and inform them of our whereabouts. The Foreigners' Regional Registration Office was located in Dehra Dun, near the district courthouse. Every year we had to get our residential permits renewed, a tedious and time-consuming process. Forms had to be filled out in triplicate for each member of the family and these were submitted to the FRRO with photographs and passports. S. L. Mark, the liaison officer for Woodstock, took care of most of the paperwork, carrying our documents up and down the hill to Dehra Dun. He was the most patient man I ever knew and handled all of the residential permits and visas for the foreigners at the school, as well as income tax and other bureaucratic formalities.

From time to time we were required to appear in person, and Mr. Mark would drive us down to the FRRO. The police inspectors who worked there were surly and suspicious, with bloodshot eyes that betrayed hostility. Cigarettes smoldered in the saucers of their teacups, a cloud of blue smoke circling the room, as the blades on the ceiling fans turned listlessly overhead. The policemen sat behind steel desks, which were piled high with files, stacks of paper held together by rusty straight pins or tied up with knotted twine, dog-eared folders into which our applications disappeared. Sometimes we would have to sit for half an hour before the policemen acknowledged our presence. Every step in the process involved red tape. Affidavits had to be attested by a notary who sat outdoors, under the banyan tree near the courthouse, with a ledger, a cashbox, and an assortment of rubber stamps in front of him. Next to the notary sat a clerk who sold stamp paper and cyclostyled forms. Our papers had to be countersigned by the district magistrate and his judicial assistant, whose offices were inside a sprawling bungalow, a maze of shadowy rooms, opening one upon the other. Extra copies were demanded, without any explanation, and Mr. Mark would rush out of the courthouse to the paan wallah at the corner, who had a photocopying machine hot-wired into a streetlight, where he produced hazy copies of our documents for fifty paisa a page. All of these papers were then carried back to the FRRO and the inspectors looked them over with meticulous care. If they found any inconsistencies the forms were handed back for resubmission and the process had to start again. Nothing was simple at the FRRO and the inspectors engaged in a constant game of harassment. Besides the missionaries there were many others who came and went from this office, Tibetan refugees, tourists who wanted to extend their visas, hippies who had lost their passports. The policemen treated all of us with disdain.

Our files were kept in dusty metal cabinets which stood like barricades around the office. The wads of brittle paper grew thicker every year we lived in India, scrawled over in blue ink and smudged with dozens of rubber stamps. Over time our papers had been handled by so many different clerks and officials that they were torn and falling apart, patched together with strips of cellotape and glue. In my senior year at Woodstock I read *The Trial* by Kafka, and I had no difficulty understanding the frustrations and paranoia of the characters, after dealing with the FRRO. Our applications were filed away, illegible receipts were issued for documents and fees, passports were returned, but I couldn't help feeling that these visits were inconclusive. Even though Mr. Mark would always try to reassure me, a nagging doubt remained that one day my residential permit would be rejected. This was what I feared the most, the thought of being expelled from India.

Perhaps if we had been willing to pay a bribe our paperwork would have been handled more efficiently, but our Puritan values, or more likely the fear of getting caught, kept us from doing this. India's bureaucracy suffered from rampant corruption and I'm sure that a couple hundred rupees—"speed money" as it was called—would have moved things along. As it was, the renewal of our permits remained perpetually under consideration and in our passports there was a stamp which read "Residence Application Pending." Every year we would apply for another residential permit and the cycle began again, without any of the officers actually giving us permission to remain in India.

Leaving the country was almost as difficult as getting our residential permits renewed. Whenever we went on furlough each of us would have to get what was called a "No Objection to Return." This was a document that was issued by the FRRO, after approval had been granted by the Home Ministry in Delhi, which allowed us to travel out of India and return within a year. If we were going to be away for three months or less there was a simpler process, called a "Return Visa," though both documents involved a series of application forms in triplicate as well as several visits to Dehra Dun.

.   .   .

During the winter of 1971, our family spent a short two-month furlough in America. We visited my grandmother in California and saw other family members in Ohio and Pennsylvania, but most of our time was spent meeting with alumni groups in different cities across the United States. As principal of Woodstock, one of my father's jobs was to raise development funds for the school. In addition to teaching English, my mother was also working as the editor of the alumni magazine, *The Quadrangle*, and compiling address lists for WOSA, the Woodstock Old Students Association.

This time we weren't in America long enough to really get homesick but I don't remember enjoying our furlough very much. For the first couple of weeks my brothers and I overdosed on television and junk food but the novelty soon wore off. I also got tired of attending Woodstock reunions. We flew from city to city: Los Angeles, San Francisco, Seattle, Denver, Chicago, New York, Washington, and Philadelphia . . . twenty-eight flights within the space of five weeks—the aerial equivalent of driving across the

country, coast to coast. At each city we were met by former Woodstock students, faculty, and retired missionaries who had lived
on the Landour hillside. My brothers and I knew very few of these
people, though I had heard some of their names. Most of the
alumni were from the forties and fifties, but one or two recent
graduates sometimes showed up, faces that I recognized. The
reunions were held in the basement of a church or the auditorium
of a retirement home, and the format was almost identical wherever we went. A potluck supper was set out on folding tables,
bright yellow chicken curry that tasted like stew, pots of lentils
which had been boiled into a glutinous paste, overcooked vegetables laced with mysterious spices and served with sticky clods of
rice or tortillas, a poor substitute for chapatis. At best, these meals
reminded me of the food in the Woodstock cafeteria.

After dinner my father gave a talk and presented a slide show
explaining the new building projects that needed funding. Every
time he showed a picture of the school there would be an audible
sigh of nostalgia from the audience and gasps of pleasure at photographs of the snows. He would talk about the student recruit-
ment program and the rising number of international students.
Children of alumni were encouraged to apply and everyone was
asked to donate money to the school. I had heard this talk so many
times that I often sneaked away into another room until it was finished, the last slide clicking through the projector and the lights
switched on.

Attending these reunions made me aware of a scattered frater-
nity of people in America who had shared the same experiences of
Landour, a network of names and addresses that were listed in *The
Quadrangle*. Toward the end of the program my mother would make
a pitch for subscriptions to the alumni magazine and ask everyone
to write down his name and address. Some of the alumni had been
classmates of my father and others had been at Woodstock when my
parents taught there, right after they were married. Many of them

dressed for the reunions in Indian clothes, saris that kept losing pleats, Gandhi caps, and muslin kurtas several sizes too small. There was a lot of shrieking and hugging, people trying to talk in Hindi or "Babu English," jokes and stories about the school and hillside. One of the attractions of these gatherings was that nobody needed to explain himself to any of the others in the room, with none of the awkward questions that strangers asked about Mussoorie.

Underneath the conviviality and laughter there was a depressing side to the Woodstock reunions, the shadows of an irretrievable past. Many of the alumni had not gone back to India since graduation and this was a part of their lives which had been cut short. Many of them expressed regret and sadness because they could not return. As I listened to their broken Hindi I wondered if someday I would also forget the language. So many of these people seemed to be living in a kind of afterlife, holding on to those transient memories of Woodstock but separated from Mussoorie forever. Traveling from one reunion to the next it felt as if we were visiting groups of émigrés who had been exiled from their homeland. I was disturbed by their sense of loss and separation as well as the sentimental bonds that tied them to each other.

The reunions always ended with the singing of school songs:

Everywhere we go
People want to know
Where we come from
So we tell them,
We're from Woodstock,
Mighty, mighty Woodstock. . . .

Song sheets were passed around for those who couldn't remember the words, and we sang "The Hiking Song," "The Bells of Mussoorie," and "Shadows," which was saved for last, a few frail voices carrying the tune and everyone else joining in on the refrain:

Woodstock, known over all the land,
Woodstock, sung of on every hand.
Woodstock . . .
Here many chances of learning we find,
Building the body and training the mind.
Forward! aim at the better goals;
Onward! find what the future holds;
Upward! rugged and steep though the pathways may be,
Palms come from striving you know.

Toward the end of January, after we had attended more than a dozen reunions in towns like Goshen, Indiana, and Newton, Kansas, my parents realized that I had endured enough. My friend Scott Bunce had left India with his family the year before and moved to Michigan, where they were settled. It was arranged that I would visit him for a week, while my parents and brothers continued touring the country.

After one of the reunions in Philadelphia, I was put on a Greyhound bus and headed off to Michigan by myself. It was an eighteen-hour ride, with a change of buses in St. Louis. Though I tried to sleep, I couldn't make myself comfortable and the coach was overheated, smelling of cigarettes and damp upholstery. The other passengers were sprawled in their seats or sat staring into the passing darkness beyond the window, like myopic zombies in a trance. Several times during the night we stopped at different bus stations that looked identical, twenty-four-hour coffee shops, where the same glazed doughnuts seemed to orbit on revolving trays and the neon glare was bright as a supernova. I was afraid to get out of the bus for fear of being left behind.

At some point I must have fallen asleep, for I woke up to the viscous dawn seeping through winter branches and piles of snow plowed up in drifts along the highway. Inside the bus it was warm as an August day in India, but outside there was a polar landscape, bleached white hills and distant barns that looked like igloos. I had no idea where I was, somewhere in Ohio or Indiana. The names of the cities on the highway signs were unfamiliar. At the next bus station I built up enough courage to get down and buy one of the doughnuts I had been eyeing all night, as well as a cup of coffee.

By the time Scott Bunce and his father met me in South Bend, I felt as if I had left the known world behind. The snow was deeper than I'd ever seen before and some of the houses which we passed were buried up to the windowsills. It was good to see Scott again and the two of us talked about our friends at school. He and I had spent most of our childhood together in Mussoorie, collecting snakes and beetles during the monsoon, or hunting birds with air rifles. With all of the snow outside there was no possibility of doing those kinds of things and we spent most of our time indoors, listening to music and talking about Mussoorie. The day after I got there his parents drove me out to see Lake Michigan, which was completely frozen. The icy wind was so strong that I could barely stand as I stared across a pale wasteland of blowing snow. Along the shore were jagged ridges of ice, waves that seemed to have frozen just before they broke against the rocks. Everything in sight, the trees and boulders, was coated in a transparent film of ice, and I couldn't imagine how anyone would choose to live in a place like this.

■　●　●

The first short story I ever wrote was about my trip to Michigan. It was called "Going Greyhound," and I started it for an English class when I got back to Woodstock. Though I rewrote it several times over the next couple of years I finally tore the story up and threw it away. There wasn't much of a plot but I worked hard on my descriptions, the doughnuts in the coffee shops, the smell of damp upholstery inside the bus. By this time I had started reading Hemingway and I tried to imitate his dry, laconic style. The only other thing that I can remember about my story was that the main character was running away from home, though it wasn't clear where he was going.

Before I started writing stories I had been trying my hand at poetry for a couple of years, encouraged by my mother and my cousin John, both of whom were poets. When he was in high school, John used to compose stanzas of free verse on the blank pages of hymnbooks in Parker Hall. He graduated from Woodstock in 1965 but the poems remained, and every time I attended chapel services I used to look for the penciled verses on the flyleaf of the hymnals. While the rest of the congregation was singing "A Mighty Fortress Is Our God," I would try to decipher my cousin's faint scribblings, cryptic poems about madness and desire. John was the first person to introduce me to the poems of Allen Ginsberg and John Berryman, most of which I didn't understand, though I tried to untangle the knotted passions in their verse.

The idea of becoming a writer intrigued me, and my ambitions for a career as a naturalist had been set aside after I nearly flunked a course in chemistry. Hemingway remained my idol and I read all of his books, enjoying the masculine bravado of his battle stories and the hunting and fishing tales, such as "The Snows of Kilimanjaro" and "Big Two-Hearted River." In my own romantic fantasies, I saw myself as one of the heroes in his books, a lone white hunter in the African bush or a member of the lost generation, drinking absinthe at a Parisian café and shooting pigeons with my slingshot to feed myself. These images had little to do with my own experience, yet they suggested a familiar sense of alienation, the dislocated perspectives of a nomadic life. Earlier I had resisted the idea of being a foreigner, but reading books like *The Sun Also Rises* and *A Moveable Feast* I began to realize the appeal of identifying myself as an expatriate.

Virtually everything I wrote in high school was later thrown away, sheaves of poems and nearly a dozen stories. Some of these were set in India and most of them centered around journeys, including one about an airport transit lounge. The characters that I created were transients of one kind or another, and much of what I wrote was autobiographical, though I changed the names of people, towns, and places to maintain the guise of fiction. My stories were full of invisible borders and erased identities, false passports and relationships that would soon be left behind.

GANGA

During one of the earliest epochs of Hindu mythology the gods performed a series of rituals to lure the river Ganga down from the sky, but they were afraid that the force of her waters would destroy the earth. The only god who was strong enough to absorb the shock of her descent was Siva, who had taken the form of a sadhu, or mendicant, and was meditating in the Himalayas. After some persuasion, he agreed to let the river fall upon him, and as Ganga spewed from the clouds, she landed on his topknot and flowed through the matted locks of his hair. In this way the world was saved from destruction and Ganga brought life and fertility to the land.

Garhwal was the watershed of the Ganga, fed by many tributaries, including the Alekananda, the Bhagirathi, the Mandakini, and the Jumna, all of which had their own mythology and lore. At the sources of these rivers were the temples of Jumnotri, Gangotri, Kedarnath, and Badrinath, presided over by Siva and other deities of the Hindu pantheon. The confluence of each tributary was considered auspicious and all along the river there were shrines and

temples, pilgrim sites and bathing ghats where devotees could sub-
merge themselves in the purifying waters of the Ganga. In addition
to worshiping the river as a goddess, Hindus believed that when
they died their ashes should be immersed in the river so that their
physical remains might be carried downstream with the current
and eventually swept out to sea. Both as a metaphor and as a part of
nature, the river washed away all past identities and represented the
cyclical flow of life and death.

When I was nine years old I nearly drowned in the Ganga, at a
place called Shivpuri, fifteen miles upriver from Rishikesh. This
was probably the closest I ever came to dying when I was a child,
and the experience left me with a lingering fear of water and a
sense that in some strange way my destiny was linked to this river.
Even though I went swimming in the Ganga many times afterward,
I still had nightmares about being sucked away by the current, of
going under and feeling the whirlpools pulling me down into the
gray-green depths of the water, the round shapes of rocks on the
river bottom sliding underneath me as I flailed my arms and legs,
unable to reach the surface.

During the spring of 1966, when I was in fourth grade, my
brother Joe and I were in boarding together at Ridgewood. Over
the Easter weekend, the two of us were invited to stay with Aunt
Barry and Uncle Jim at their home in Rajpur. My cousin Dean,
Uncle Dave's eldest son, was studying at Woodstock for a year and
he was a class ahead of my cousin Tom. Both of them were in the
senior boys' hostel, and after the morning chapel service on Good
Friday the four of us headed across the valley below Midlands, hiking down the old walking road to Rajpur. It felt good to get away
from Ridgewood and we ran most of the distance, about eight
miles, arriving at the Christian Retreat and Study Center in time
for lunch.

The next day we set off early for Shivpuri, which was about a
two-hour drive from Rajpur. There was no town or village there,
only a roadside temple and a dharmsala where pilgrims could stay

the night. A small stream entered the Ganga at this point, on either side of which was a crescent-shaped beach, where the river turned a broad S curve between the mountains. At its widest point the Ganga was about seventy-five yards across, narrowing into a stretch of rapids just below Shivpuri. Uncle Jim parked the jeep at the side of the road and we carried our picnic baskets and towels down to a sandy spot along the shore. It was a bright day, though the air was cool, and the warm sand felt good beneath my feet. As soon as we set up our picnic spot, my uncle headed off downstream with his fishing rod to try his luck in a pool below the rapids.

Aunt Barry had assigned Joe and me to each of our cousins, since neither of us could swim. Dean was responsible for me and Tom was told to look after Joe. Changing into our bathing suits, we headed up the river to a shallow inlet about two hundred yards away. Getting there we had to wade across the stream, which was not very deep, cascading over the polished rocks. The inlet was protected from the main flow of the river by a spit of sand, safe enough for Joe and me to go in up to our waists. For half an hour we splashed about near the riverbank, while Tom and Dean swam out a ways and let themselves be carried downstream by the current, fifteen or twenty feet from shore. The snow-fed waters of the Ganga were full of silt, a milky gray color and bitterly cold. Every few minutes Joe and I got out and lay on the sand and rocks to warm ourselves.

During the monsoon, the Forestry Department floated timber down the river. Most of the wood was pine or deodar, cut into eight-foot sleepers and squared off on all four sides. When the water level in the Ganga dropped, many of these logs ran aground, and there were dozens of sleepers at Shivpuri, scattered about on the shore. After they got bored with swimming my cousins came up with the idea of building a raft. Dragging the heavy logs into the shallow water, we laid eight of them side by side and put two more across to keep them in place. It was not a very sturdy raft and the logs kept shifting about but it was buoyant enough to carry Joe and me.

By this time we were getting hungry and decided to float back down to where Aunt Barry was waiting at our picnic spot. While my brother and I sat on the raft, Tom and Dean swam alongside to keep us near the shore. After we had gone a short distance, Joe got nervous and jumped off, scrambling onto the riverbank. I wasn't aware of any danger until we came to the stream, its clear, swift current spilling into the murky waters of the Ganga. Suddenly the raft began to follow a different course, and even though my cousins tried to steer me back to safety, I found myself heading out into the middle of the river. The current was deceptively strong and both Tom and Dean had to finally give up and swim to shore, while I was carried away downstream. Not knowing how to swim, I dared not jump off the raft, even though I knew it was heading for the rapids.

By this time Joe and my cousins were running down the beach, shouting to alert Aunt Barry. All of this must have happened in less than a minute but my memories of the event move slowly, frame by frame, more like a slide show than a film. I could see the cliffs on the opposite bank gliding past me, as if I was stationary and it was the mountains that were moving. Standing on the raft, I felt completely paralyzed, with the rapids coming closer, the furled white crests of the waves and the water plunging over submerged rocks. Already the sleepers beneath my feet were starting to break apart with the uneven motion of the current.

The sound of the river was so loud I couldn't hear the others calling to me, but from their gestures I knew they wanted me to jump. Tom dived into the river once again and started swimming toward me, about fifty yards away. I hesitated for a few more seconds, then threw myself into the Ganga, frightened and bewildered. As I went under, the cold shock of the water sucked the air from my lungs. My eyes were closed but when I finally surfaced everything seemed very bright, as if I were looking straight into the sun. There was water in my mouth and up my nose. The river lifted me for a second or two and I caught a breath, then I went down again, the opaque current churning all around me. The rounded, almost human forms of rocks slipped by as I turned over once, then twice, tumbling like an acrobat. Again I came up to the surface and this time I could see the shoreline racing past. I was choking now, trying to cough up the water I had swallowed, even though there didn't seem to be any air remaining in my lungs.

At that moment I felt Tom grab me by the shoulder, and both of us went under, our white legs kicking in the gray-green water. The rocks beneath me seemed much closer and we bumped against them as Tom struggled to pull me back up to the surface. A few seconds later, I realized that my aunt was holding me by the other arm. My muscles felt limp and I began to lose consciousness, as if I had been separated from my body. Aunt Barry and Tom were finally able to drag me onto shore, only a few yards upstream from the worst of the rapids. The next thing I can remember is lying on the warm sand, gagging and throwing up mouthfuls of Ganga water.

Half an hour later, by the time I had recovered, Uncle Jim came up the riverbank carrying a six-pound mahseer. He hadn't realized what was going on but told us that he'd seen the raft colliding with a rock, just above the pool where he was fishing. He said that the rapids had hurled the sleepers about like matchsticks and if I had stayed aboard there wasn't a chance that I'd survive.

•   •   •

In 1970, Lieutenant Colonel Morris Mehta, who had recently retired from the Indian army, joined Woodstock as a dorm supervisor at Ridgewood. I had heard from my father that he was an expert fisherman and I was eager to meet him as soon as he arrived. Over the next few years, while I was in high school, he became a close friend and mentor, with whom I went fishing on the Ganga many times. The Colonel was a stocky Anglo-Indian man who had served as an artillery officer in World War II, fighting in the Sahara. He was proud of being a "gunner," as he called himself, and told me stories about Cairo and the North African campaign. At times he could be crusty and temperamental, with a military brusqueness in his manner, though he was also immensely generous with his time and spent hours teaching me the finer points of fishing and how to make my own homemade lures. Fishing tackle was difficult to find in India and very expensive, but Colonel Mehta made most of his lures himself, which he designed specifically to catch mahseer. In the basement at Ridgewood we set up a workshop, with a small lathe on which I learned to turn out wooden plugs. We painted these and attached brass lips to make them move through the water like a minnow. The only part of the lures that we had to buy were the treble hooks that Colonel Mehta ordered through Dewan Brothers' shop in Dehra Dun.

The Colonel's favorite fishing spot was Byasghat, about forty miles upstream from Rishikesh. At this point the motor road climbed two thousand feet above the Ganga before descending to the town of Dev Prayag. We had to park our jeep near a tea shop at the side of the road and hike three miles into the valley, crossing a deep gorge, over which there was a treacherous suspension bridge. From here it was another two-hour walk along the pilgrim trail to Byasghat, a small village at the confluence of the Nayar River and the Ganga. There was a forest bungalow at Byasghat but Colonel Mehta preferred to pitch his tent on the riverbank, just below the confluence. Each year he would try to schedule his arrival at Byasghat while the mahseer were coming down the Nayar after spawning. He used to tell me that if we timed it right, there were so many fish in the river you could walk across "the blighters' backs." All of them were ravenous with hunger and ready to bite at anything we tossed into the water. The largest fish that Colonel Mehta caught was over seventy pounds, a "bloody grandmother," as he called it, so strong that it had straightened all three tines on a treble hook.

As I worked away at my lures, sanding and painting the torpedo-shaped plugs, attaching split rings and hooks, I kept anticipating the moment when I would accompany Colonel Mehta on our first fishing trip to Byasghat. Two other schoolmates were working with me, Johnny Warren and Malcolm Wilson, all three of us dreaming of the giant fish that we would catch. Woodstock was in session during September, right at the end of the monsoon, but we had a holiday for Mahatma Gandhi's birthday during the first week of October. Setting off after school, we drove to Rishikesh, then up into the mountains, past Shivpuri, where I had almost drowned six years before. By the time we parked our jeep and hiked down to the suspension bridge, it was already dark, and our flashlights showed the broken boards and rusted cables that sagged dangerously under our weight. Everything was exactly as Colonel Mehta had described it, and by ten o'clock we pitched our camp on the sandy shore. Though we could barely see the Ganga in the darkness, the rushing sound of the current filled the valley, a deep primordial roar.

In the morning we saw that the Nayar was running clear and well below the high-water mark. Even before we had wet our lines, Colonel Mehta was pessimistic and said that we had arrived too late. Most of the mahseer had already moved down the Ganga after spawning and we had missed our chance. For the next four days we fished the confluence of the Ganga and the Nayar but the only thing we caught was a five-pound mahseer which Johnny Warren landed on the first day and a kalabans that was foul hooked. Each morning the Colonel woke us up at dawn and we went out and "flogged the river," from six o'clock to lunchtime and then from three in the afternoon until sunset. As my frustration mounted I began to wonder if my bad luck was a result of the curse put on me by the sadhu at Satya Narayan, when I caught my first mahseer. Colonel Mehta tried to keep our spirits up by telling us stories of fish he'd caught on earlier trips and pointing out landmarks at

GANGA

Byasghat like the black rock, an enormous boulder in the middle of the Ganga which was barely visible above the swollen current. He also told us about the legendary fisherman, Baby West, who used to travel all the way from Calcutta to Byasghat every year and set up camp for a month. Baby West worked for the Indian Railways and some of the villagers still remembered him. They said he was a huge man, weighing at least two hundred kilos, and they claimed it took a mule to carry all of his tackle boxes up and down the hill.

Returning to Mussoorie empty-handed, we continued making our lures and dreamed of catching a monster fish. Colonel Mehta loaned me a couple of books to read, *Circumventing the Mahseer* and *The Rod in India*, which only added to my obsession. The following year we took several fishing trips to a more accessible place on the Ganga, called Phulchatti, about five miles upstream from Rishikesh. The first time we camped in a dharmsala, a pilgrim shelter, but a sadhu who was staying there objected to our fishing and Colonel Mehta got into an argument with him. After that we always took our tents to Phulchatti and camped on the sand.

Along the banks of the Ganga we saw a number of cremations taking place, a procession of villagers carrying a bamboo litter with a corpse wrapped up in a shroud. Driftwood and dry branches from the nearby forest were collected and piled on top of the body, and sleepers that washed ashore were sometimes added to the pyre. The orange flames would rise up brightly amid the bleached white rocks and sand, smoke drifting into the mountains on either side. If we were camped downwind, I could smell the charred odor of burning flesh and bones. Unlike the elaborate rituals performed on the burning ghats in Hardwar, where logs of sandalwood were burned and priests poured ghee into the flames, these were simple cremations. Instead of chanting prayers the mourners sat around on the sand and rocks, waiting for the pyre to burn down to ash. Often the villagers would leave the fire smoldering overnight and return in the morning to immerse the ashes in the Ganga. Several times, while fishing at dawn, I came around a corner on the riverbank and found the remains of a funeral pyre, the last embers still glowing and a wisp of smoke trailing out across the water.

Occasionally there were bodies in the river, too, the corpses of sadhus, who were not cremated but simply weighted down with stones and cast into the Ganga. While fishing we had to keep an eye out for the corpses as they floated past. Joe once hooked a body and had to cut his line. The skin on the floating corpses was the same color as the water, a soapy gray. Their arms and legs moved listlessly with the current and the dead bodies lay facedown, as if peering into the depths of the river. Sometimes I would try to picture my own body drifting downstream with the current, staring sightlessly at the submerged rocks. The corpses often washed ashore, particularly when the water level in the Ganga dropped. One evening, just before dusk, I was climbing over a pile of boulders below Phulchatti, trying to reach a fishing spot, when I jumped down onto a narrow finger of sand and heard an angry buzzing noise. A swarm of flies rose off a decomposing corpse that was wedged between the rocks. The smell was nauseating and the bones were visible through the rotting skin and flesh. I ran from there as if I'd seen a ghost.

We didn't have much luck at Phulchatti though we did catch a couple of small mahseer on spoons and spinners. Eventually Colonel Mehta and I decided to try Byasghat one more time, and on this occasion we reached the confluence before the water level in the Nayar had fallen. The Ganga was full of silt and the black rock was completely submerged. The monsoon rains were still coming down, and we had to dig trenches around our tents at night to keep from being flooded. For the first two days we had no luck at all and Colonel Mehta began to speculate that the mahseer were feeding at night because there was a full moon.

I was so desperate to catch a fish that I was ready to try anything by then, and as the moon came up over the ridge, I picked up my rod and set off down the riverbank. Colonel Mehta and the others headed upstream toward the confluence. The moonlight gave the river an eerie sheen and the water was a pale, translucent color, while the round white rocks on the shore seemed to glow. Being alone, I felt uneasy as I stepped into the current, wading into the water up to my waist to avoid getting snagged on the rocks. My tennis shoes sank into the sand and the freezing water swirled around my legs.

The lure I'd chosen was a homemade plug which had lost its outer coat of paint and was mostly white. I figured that it would be visible underwater, in the moonlight. Bracing myself, I cast out into the Ganga, just upstream of the black rock. As soon as the plug hit the water my fishing rod was bent with the force of the current and I reeled in slowly, feeling the lure wriggling through the turbulent water.

On my fifth cast I let the plug go down a little deeper, lowering the tip of the rod, when suddenly I felt a violent strike and almost pitched forward as the drag on my reel began to whine. Struggling to raise the rod, I gave out a whoop of excitement which was drowned by the roar of the current. The mahseer began its first run and all I could do was keep from being swept away. It felt as though I had hooked the river itself. I was using an eight-foot surf casting rod and a heavy saltwater reel that held about 250 yards of line with a breaking strain of twenty pounds. The drag was set as tight as possible because of the swiftness of the current and the limited stretch of river we were fishing. About 300 yards downstream the Ganga curved around a sharp cliff and there was no chance of following the fish beyond this point.

The line on my spool was disappearing rapidly and I waded out of the river. As I began to walk downstream, reeling steadily, the mahseer finally stopped its run. I could still feel the weight of the fish, and after I had retrieved about 150 yards, the mahseer ran again. I could see the monofilament stretched taut across the river, shedding beads of water in the moonlight. Within a couple of minutes the fish had gone beyond the cliffs and my line was now rubbing against the rocks. There was nothing I could do except to wade out into the river once again and try to keep the fish from breaking free. The Ganga broadened at this point and the water was shallow for thirty feet or so, after which the bottom dropped off steeply and I dared not go too far. The mahseer had paused again and leaning into the current, I began to pump the fish upstream, raising the rod above my head, then lowering it as I reeled in, gaining a few yards at a time.

To my left, I noticed there was a quiet backwater along the near side of the cliffs, a still, unruffled pool. It took me at least a quarter of an hour to coax the fish away from the rocks, but as soon as I felt that I was safe the drag began to scream again, as the mahseer made its final run. Fortunately, instead of going toward the cliffs, it turned into the backwater, where I felt a surge and saw my fish for the first time, turning over on the surface. The moonlight reflected off the mahseer's gold and silver scales, which looked like plated armor. By now the fish was exhausted, played out, and she came in easily, rolling onto one side as I reached down and slipped my fingers into her gills. The plug was hanging out of one corner of her mouth. As I tried to raise the fish out of the water, I could barely lift her onto shore. The mahseer was almost four feet long, and when we weighed her the next morning, she tipped the scales at forty-seven pounds.

By this time Colonel Mehta and the others had grown worried because I hadn't returned. In the distance I could see their torches flashing across the rocky shore as they came to search for me, afraid that I had drowned. There was no way that I could shout to them above the rushing sound of the Ganga. Dragging the mahseer over the rocks, I was shivering with cold and my shoulders ached from the strain of landing the fish. At that moment I felt a sense of elation and regret. Every minute or so the fish slapped its tail against my legs, tensing itself in the throes of death, and there was a part of me that wanted to release it back into the river, to watch it disappear into the milky current. The bright beams of the torches were coming closer now and I still had a chance to let it go. The mahseer's eyes were bulging and its mouth opened and closed, the gills moving against my fingers, as it tried desperately to breathe, drowning in the moonlit air. I could smell the odor of the fish and feel its slick scales against my skin. Standing there in the moonlight, waiting for the others to find me, I felt an overwhelming sense of apprehension and fear.

. . .

There were sections of the Ganga where we were not allowed to fish, especially near the bathing ghats in Hardwar and Rishikesh where pilgrims fed the fish. Schools of mahseer hovered around the temple steps and as soon as anything was thrown into the water you could see a churning of fins and tails, as the fish fought over scraps of bread or handfuls of puffed rice. The largest mahseer were five feet long and must have weighed a hundred pounds. Some of them were so tame that they would swim between our legs and take the food right out of our hands. Every time we crossed the footbridge at Laxman Jhoola, on our way to Phulchatti, I would look down at the river to see the mahseer swarming around the ghats, and there was always the temptation of casting a lure into their midst.

On either side of Laxman Jhoola, lines of beggars sat shoulder to shoulder, holding out their bowls for coins. Many of the pilgrims made a point of putting money in each of the bowls, five- or ten-naya paisa pieces that the beggars rattled about as they called out blessings for those who gave them alms. Distributing money to beggars was considered a means of gaining merit in this life, a form of insurance against being reborn as one of them. Near the tea shops above Laxman Jhoola was a man who changed money for the pilgrims, recycling the five- and ten-naya paisa coins, which he collected from the beggars at the end of the day. As middleman he took a commission on all transactions, ten paisa out of each rupee, sorting the coins into neatly counted piles. Most of the beggars were lepers and their features were shrunken, noses flattened and faces disfigured by the disease. Their hands were often reduced to stumps, which were bandaged with rags and covered with sores. Some of them had no legs at all and they were pushed about on crude wooden carts. Whenever they saw us coming the beggars began to howl and wail, like mourners, pleading with us to give them money. Some of them reached out to touch our feet as we walked by, calling us "Lord" and "Master," "Blessed One" and "Saint." To cross the bridge at Laxman Jhoola we had to walk a gauntlet of at least a hundred beggars holding up their deformed limbs and crying out in unison in hoarse, beseeching tones.

I never gave the beggars any money, partly because there were so many of them that I wouldn't have known where to begin. Begging was something that I had experienced all my life in India, people coming to the window of our car and holding out their hands for money, children, women with babies, men with crippled limbs, and old people, their eyes blinded with cataracts. As foreigners we attracted more attention than others and the beggars pleaded with us, "Bhooka! Bhooka!"—Hungry! Hungry! My parents had always refused to give the beggars money because they felt it was demeaning and only encouraged them to continue begging. As a child I accepted this logic, though it didn't make things any easier and I was troubled by the anguished voices and the expressions of desperation in their eyes. Whenever beggars came to the window of our car or stopped me on the street, I would wave them off and try to look the other way, but some of the beggars were so persistent that I almost wanted to pay them to leave me alone. In India, poverty was an unavoidable fact of life and even though we may have become hardened to it, the beggars were impossible to ignore. They forced us to look at their deformities, as if to make us understand the inequities of life and the extremes of human suffering.

The name, Rishikesh, meant gathering place of the rishis, another word for sadhus. The town was full of mendicants, especially during the winter months, when the shrines up in the mountains were closed because of the snow. Even though these rishis had renounced their worldly identities, many of them were eccentric characters. Some were draped in beads and amulets, with rings on their fingers and bracelets on their arms. Others carried bamboo staffs surmounted with metal tridents or decorated with tinsel and saffron pennants. The sadhus came in all ages, from arthritic old men who could barely walk, to sturdy well-fed youths, their dark hair oiled and gleaming in the sun. Some daubed their skin with ashes and smoked chillums of hashish, while others carried conch shells and the spiral horns of black buck, through which they blew a single note to announce their presence. My cousin Marty told me once of a sadhu she met on the road to Rishikesh who hailed her as she was passing by. Raising his hand in a gesture of blessing, he shouted: "One foot up. One foot down. I'm on my way to London town!"

In many ways, the streets of Rishikesh were a form of a religious theater. There were devotees of Rama and Krishna, singing and dancing in ecstasy, mad sadhus ranting at the roadside, shouting the many names of god. Some of the rishis sat in meditation under roadside pipal trees or offered to read your palm and tell your fortune. A few of them wore sunglasses, carried plastic briefcases, and had printed business cards, while the Naga Babas wore nothing at all, parading through the streets with their genitals exposed. Rishikesh was full of exhibitionists, holy men who ate razor blades and broken glass, street performers who lifted eight-pound metal shots with their eyeballs and swung them around their heads. At Chotiwalla's restaurant, where we often stopped for lunch, there was an obese young man whose skin was painted blue. He sat and watched us as we ate, with a disconcerting smile on his face, a look of corpulent beatitude. There was always an element of the grotesque in Rishikesh. Walking up to Phulchatti one time, we passed a woman who was dressed as the goddess Kali, her hair teased into a black mane that reached to her waist, her face painted red and black, and her tongue, which was hanging out of her mouth, impaled with a silver trident.

During the sixties and early seventies a number of Western hippies or freaks came to Rishikesh and added to the spectacle. Many of them put on the saffron robes of sadhus or discarded their clothes completely. On one of the beaches above Laxman Jhoola I remember meeting an American sadhu who was sitting cross-legged on the sand, wearing only a G-string around his waist. He chatted with us for a while and said that he used to work for Boeing in Seattle, building jumbo jets, before he was laid off. Some of the hippies came to Rishikesh for the hashish and other drugs which were freely available, searching for chemical rather than spiritual bliss. One day, while I was sitting at a tea stall near the bus stand, there was a wasted-looking Englishman who was hallucinating on something. He was staring at a calendar on the wall, with a picture of Hema Malini dressed as a cabaret dancer, and he kept saying, "Jesus Christ! Jai Guru Dev! Jesus Christ! Jai Guru Dev!" At Phulchatti I met a Frenchman who said that he had eaten nothing but green onions for the past six months and claimed that he never felt cold. On another fishing trip we discovered a group of foreigners living in a cave across the river from our camp. Two of them were women who spent most of their time sunbathing in the nude, and Malcolm Wilson and I cursed ourselves for not bringing a pair of binoculars.

The most respected ashrams in Rishikesh were the Divine Life and Sivananda ashrams, though probably the most famous one was founded by the Maharishi Mahesh Yogi, where the Beatles came to seek enlightenment in 1968. The town of Rishikesh had once been a quiet place of meditation and tranquillity, surrounded by forests and mountains, but with the construction of motor roads into the mountains it had become a crowded, overpopulated town. During April and May, busloads of devotees traveled through Rishikesh on their way to visit the sources of the Ganga at Badrinath,

Joshimath, Kedarnath, and Gangotri. Most of these shrines were accessible by bus or car and very few of the pilgrims used the old walking trail that followed the course of the river.

The town of Hardwar was twenty miles downstream from Rishikesh, at a place where the Ganga flowed through the Siwalik hills and out across the plains of North India. One of the holiest sites for Hindus, Hardwar was also a city of ashrams, bathing ghats, and temples, where Brahman pundits kept family genealogies going back several hundred generations. Every twelve years the Kumbh Mela was held in Hardwar. Considered the most auspicious time for bathing, this festival attracted millions of pilgrims to the town.

Har-ki-pairi, a temple built on a platform in the middle of the river, was the most popular attraction for pilgrims in Hardwar. During the monsoon, which corresponded to the month of Sravan in the Hindu calendar, devotees from towns all across North India came to Hardwar and collected Gangajal, sacred water, carrying it home in brass vessels hanging from bamboo sticks balanced across their shoulders. At times there were so many pilgrims walking along the road that traffic on the main highway between Hardwar and Delhi had to be diverted. Gangajal was considered the most pure and sacred element, used for rituals and worship in temples and household shrines. Hardwar was also where British engineers built the headworks for the Upper Ganges Canal, diverting most of the river into a network of irrigation channels that flow across the Doab.

During one of many field trips we took to Hardwar and Rishikesh, a group of my classmates and I went to see a sadhu who was said to have entered a state of samadhi or complete detachment from his body and the world. He was sitting cross-legged, with his eyes closed, in a cement tank that was being filled by a trickle of Gangajal from a plastic hose. One of his disciples told us that when the water filled the tank the sadhu would be submerged. Being in a state of samadhi, the holy man did not need to breathe and could stay alive underwater for several days. Later that afternoon, when we came back, the water level had barely reached the sadhu's navel. His disciple, an earnest young man in a yellow dhoti, promised us that if we returned at midnight the tank would be filled. Unfortunately we couldn't stay to watch this miracle, as we had to catch our bus back to Mussoorie.

. . .

During the winter of 1973 I took a trip to Banaras with Bud Skillman. He taught chemistry at Woodstock and was originally from Kentucky, a Baptist missionary who had been at the school for six or seven years. Bud was a restless, bearded man who always seemed to be searching for something beyond the physical world. He had a friendly, earnest manner and a forceful voice. One time he preached in Parker Hall and even without a microphone he shook the rafters with the hellfire rhetoric of a tent revival meeting. At the same time, Bud was interested in Hindu mysticism and used to tell me that someday he was going to walk off into the mountains and become a sadhu. He used to spend a lot of time talking with me, trying to come to terms with Hindu concepts like moksha (supreme joy) and maya (illusion). I'm sure that Bud would have made a good sadhu because he enjoyed philosophizing. He once told me about a book he'd read, *Jesus Died in Kashmir*, which put forward the theory that Christ had become a wandering mendicant instead of dying on the cross, and that he eventually found his way to India during the last years of his life.

The two of us traveled to Banaras by train, riding third-class in an unreserved carriage. We wanted to see how little money we could spend and planned to stay in dharmsalas wherever we went. It was the kind of travel that appealed to me, a journey without fixed dates or destinations. We got to Banaras the following day and found a dharmsala attached to a temple near the railway station. Most of these guesthouses allowed pilgrims to stay free of charge, though it was expected that we would give a donation to the temple when we left. On the walls of the ashram there were slogans in

English and in Hindi: "God Is Great," "Duty Is Your Destiny," and "Regularity Leads to Purification of the Soul." The main idols in the temple were of Rama and Sita, lifelike figures with brightly painted clothes, standing in a marble alcove. Not far away was a smooth stone lingam, the phallic symbol of Siva, embedded in a cement yoni, a stylized version of the sexual organs of a goddess. One of the attendants showed us to our room, a simple cubicle with two string cots and a window overlooking the courtyard of the temple. It was pleasant enough but later that night we found that the temple played religious hymns over a loudspeaker until midnight. After that we finally fell asleep but were awakened at four o'clock with the bellowing of a conch shell and the clash of cymbals as the morning prayers began.

Banaras is one of the most important cities along the Ganga, a place where millions of pilgrims travel every year. It is known for its temples and bathing ghats, as well as the cremation grounds where hundreds of bodies are burned each day. I had never been there before and Bud showed me around the city, taking me from one temple to the next. In many ways it was no different from other towns I knew in North India but there was a distinctive atmosphere, the intensity of religious fervor combined with an easygoing lifestyle. Like Hardwar and Rishikesh, the city attracted droves of sadhus as well as plenty of hippies. An English couple were staying next door to us at the dharmsala and they recommended a Chinese restaurant nearby where we could eat. Bud and I wandered over there at dusk and found ourselves surrounded by other foreigners. The owner of the restaurant was a Nepali and the food was terrible, sweet-and-sour paneer and eggplant chow mein. The Rolling Stones were playing on the music system—"I can't get no satisfaction"—and the air was thick with hashish smoke. The conversations all around us were in different languages, French and Spanish, German and English. Most of the hippies were dressed in a version of Indian costumes, with turbans and lungis. One of the freaks in the booth beside us was a German transvestite, obviously a man, but wearing a sari. He had put sindhoor in his hair and had a bindi on his forehead, pretending to be a Hindu bride. Before we left the restaurant he got into a fight with his companion and they started shouting at each other in German.

After dinner Bud and I decided to have a paan to get rid of the taste of sweet-and-sour cornstarch. Banaras is famous for its paan, and Bud ordered one with tobacco while I asked for a meetha paan. Several years earlier I'd tried a tobacco paan and almost threw up the minute I put it in my mouth. The fresh green leaves were laid out with a flourish and moving his hands like a conjurer the paan wallah added the ingredients, smearing the paan with red paste and placing cardamoms, betel nuts, and anise in the center. For Bud he put a pinch of perfumed tobacco and for me a spoonful of treacle, flavored with rose essence and mint. Each of these was then folded into a packet and handed to us with a ceremonious gesture. Walking back to our room in the dharmsala through the dimly lit street, we fell silent as we chewed our paan.

Early in the morning the following day we took a boat ride on the Ganga, floating past the ghats. Some of the pyres were already burning and we could hear the temple bells ringing all across the city. The water was a muddy brown, flecked with silt and carrying with it a garland of marigolds, charred pieces of wood and straw. The Ganga at Banaras seemed so different from the river that I had known upstream, the mountain torrent with its swift, tumultuous rapids. Here it was sluggish and lapped the shore with gentle waves. Our boatman poled us out into the center of the current and we drifted slowly past the lines of temples where pilgrims dipped beneath the surface of the water and rose up with their hands folded in a gesture of supplication to the rising sun.

SHIKAR

As I headed down the path to Patreni, the smooth crepe soles of my boots skidded over the loose rocks. Even though it was just past noon, the day seemed to be coming to a close, cold and gray, the December clouds shifting above the mountains like tectonic plates. There was a depressing stillness, the oak leaves hanging limp in the winter air, a musty odor of dried ferns and moss, the repeated wailing of Himalayan barbets deep within the valley. The temperature had dropped below freezing, and stopping at the spring above Jabberkhet, I had to suck at the ice to get a drink. Blowing into my cupped hands for warmth I looked down at the lines of terraced fields about a mile away. The ripening cholai was a rusty orange and the newly planted wheat was just beginning to sprout. The thatch-roofed huts and cowsheds at Patreni seemed almost invisible in the opaque light. Threads of woodsmoke drifted above the village, slowly unraveling on the breeze.

Less than an hour before, I had finished my last midterm exam in U.S. history. After handing in the essay answers to my teacher,

Mr. Hilliard, I ran home and picked up my rucksack. I was glad to be out of school, leaving behind the restrictions and routines, textbooks and papers, the exam questions which had seemed so pointless—comparing the Monroe Doctrine to the Big Stick policies of Teddy Roosevelt.

The town and school had disappeared behind a shoulder of the ridge. The trail cut back sharply through a stand of deodar trees and descended to the deserted fields below. Beyond the fields was a charred ridge, burned by the forest fires that summer. A few of the chir pines remained, crooked stakes driven into the blackened hillside. Walking along the trail to Patreni I felt a sense of loneliness and separation. Most of my classmates would be going down the hill by bus the next day and traveling by train to their homes on mission compounds in different parts of India—Calcutta, Ratlam, Baroda, Ludhiana, Delhi. Their trunks were packed for the winter holidays and a sense of excitement and anticipation engulfed the school, the hurried farewells, final papers and exams, lines of coolies carrying luggage down the hill.

The leather straps on my rucksack cut through the layers of my canvas jacket and the weight made me lean forward to balance myself. There was nobody else on the trail; the dairymen and their mules had already gone into town delivering milk. They would not return until the evening. Across the valley, I could hear the jangle of cowbells and the calls of children herding cattle. The plaintive cries of the barbets continued, mournful and melodic.

A sharp wind had picked up and I could tell a storm was coming. Still half a mile from Patreni, I heard a sound that made me stop, a low rustling noise that grew steadily louder, blotting out all other sounds. I started to run as the first hailstones began to fall, hitting the back of my head and stinging my ears and face. There was no cover near the path where I could take shelter as the storm gathered force. The noise of the hail was all around me now, a muffled cannonade. The pellets of ice turned the trail white and made my boots slip at every step. Twice I almost fell and the second time, when I put out a hand to steady myself, my fingers were so numb with cold I couldn't feel a thing. The wind kept changing direction, hailstones pelting into my face and tearing at the weeds along the edges of the path. I tried to bunch my neck into the collar of my jacket and pulled the sleeves over my fists. The hail rattled off my rucksack like buckshot and ricocheted against my legs.

There was a violence to the storm that seemed almost vindictive, as if the sky were taking its revenge upon the earth. The noise was deafening and I began to panic, running blindly along the trail, my eyes winced shut against the driving ice. I felt disoriented and afraid, unable to recognize any of the landmarks on the trail. There was no place to hide, no protection from the storm. As I reached the edge of the fields at Patreni, everything looked different, bleached white, the sky a blowing whorl of hailstones.

Ahead of me, I could just make out the shape of the oak tree that grew at the center of the village. Dil Das's chaan was twenty feet above the trail, and as I scrambled up the steep khudside, my boots skidded out from under me and I fell heavily onto my knees. Picking myself up I pushed open the thatch door of the chaan and blundered through. I heard the buffaloes shifting nervously but could see nothing in the dark, still blinded by the whiteness of the hail. A dog growled at the far end of the shed and I could just make out the glow of firelight. There was a rich, sour smell of straw and urine. The lumbering black shapes of the buffaloes moved about in the shadows, the sweep of their horns and the rolling whites of their eyes. Brushing past them I moved toward the fire.

Dil Das was seated on the floor near the hearth, with Rani Devi, his wife, and their daughter Gurra. Tulsi, one of Dil Das's uncles, was also in the chaan. They greeted me and laughed as I shrugged off my pack and brushed the hailstones from my hair and out of the creases in my jacket. Kneeling by the fire I put my palms toward the flames. The smoke stung my eyes and a few stray hailstones dropped into the hearth, sputtered and hissed. Still winded from my run and the battering of the storm, I inhaled the familiar odors of the chaan, the animals and woodsmoke, wet thatch and cow dung.

"You should have waited until after the storm," said Dil Das, raising his voice over the rattle of the hailstones outside.

"It only started when I was at Palli Khala," I said, adjusting the sticks to make the fire burn brighter. My fingers had begun to thaw.

"This is early in the year for hail."

"The cholai will be ruined," said Rani Devi.

"And the new wheat," said Dil Das. "Finished."

"Do you think we can still get down to Kholdighat this evening?" I asked.

"Stay here the night and leave in the morning," said Rani Devi. "With this hail it will get even colder."

"The storm should stop soon enough," said Dil Das, lighting a bidi with the end of a burning twig.

We spoke a mixture of Hindi and Garhwali. Rani Devi added a few more sticks to the fire and drew aside the lid of a degchi that rested on the clay hearth. She added a measure of milk and several spoonfuls of sugar to the tea. As it came to a boil she lifted it off the fire and poured four glasses of chay. The steaming brass tumblers were passed around and I held mine by the rim so it wouldn't burn my hands. I felt a little warmer now, though my boots and jeans were soaking wet.

Now that my vision had adjusted to the darkness I could see Dil Das's features watching me, his unshaven, weathered face, the dark, attentive eyes. His cropped hair was covered by a woolen balaclava and he was wearing an old army jacket and khaki trousers. I didn't know how old Dil Das was, though I guessed he was nearly fifty. There was a youthfulness about him though, especially when he smiled, which made him seem much younger.

"So, your holidays have started now?" asked Dil Das.

"Yes, I took my last exam this morning."

"Did you pass?" asked Tulsi.

"I don't know," I said, shrugging.

"I hope he fails," said Dil Das. "That way, he'll stay another year and not go back to Am'rika."

"Do you have hailstorms in Am'rika?" asked Rani Devi.

"Sometimes," I said, though I wasn't really sure. "Mostly snow."

"Snow is not so bad. It doesn't damage the wheat."

Rani Devi was Dil Das's second wife. The first, whom I had never known, had died eight years earlier. Gurra was Rani Devi's only child, no more than four years old. Dil Das had an older daughter, Dharma, from his first marriage.

The tea had warmed me and after a few minutes I moved back from the fire and leaned against the mud walls of the chaan. Dil Das relit his bidi from the coals and began to tell about a hailstorm several years ago.

"The stones were that big," he said, making a fist. "The next day, when I went into the jungle, I found birds that had been killed by the hail, pheasants and whistling thrushes, knocked right off the branches, dead."

By the time Dil Das finished speaking the storm had stopped. There was an empty silence; even the wind had been stilled. We got up and went outside to take a look. The mountains were completely white, even the burned hill across the valley. The clouds were low and dark, like kneaded clay.

"If we're going, we should start," I said.

Rani Devi had come outdoors as well, standing barefoot on the carpet of hailstones.

"Why don't you stay the night?" she said. "You can leave early in the morning."

Dil Das shook his head.

"There won't be any hail at Kholdighat," he said.

"When will you be back?"

"Tomorrow or day after."

"And who is going to cut the cholai?"

"The hail has already harvested it for us," said Dil Das, laughing.

I went inside and opened my backpack to take out the shotgun, which I had broken down and wrapped inside my sleeping bag. I ran my hands over the double barrels to make sure that it was dry. Fitting the breech together I put the wooden clamp in place and snapped it shut. The gun had a familiar smell of oil and powder. It was an ancient twelve-gauge with Damascus steel barrels, which had once belonged to my great-grandfather, who was the sheriff of Richfield County in Ohio. My grandfather had brought the gun to India with him in 1916 and it had been passed on through the family. My great-grandfather had probably used the twelve-gauge for shooting squirrels though I liked to imagine that he had used it to gun down outlaws. Choosing two of the cartridges I had brought with me, I shouldered my rucksack and went outside. Dil Das joined me in a couple of minutes, carrying his own shotgun, a bolt-action twelve-gauge with a single barrel.

The hail had already started to melt as we set out along the path between the terraced fields. About a quarter of a mile beyond Patreni we joined the main ridge, on the other side of which was Chattarmani's house and fields. He and his brothers were Brahmans, while Dil Das and the others in Patreni were Harijans, or untouchables.

Most of the forest along the ridge was pine with very little undergrowth. Dil Das led the way and the two of us kept moving at a good pace until we reached Bhairav Ghatti. At this point there was a cut in the ridge, with open cliffs on either side, a scarred wall of rock dropping several hundred feet into the chir forest below. Just beyond Bhairav Ghatti the ridge rose up again as a low hill, rounded like a dome. There were a few pine trees growing on the lower slopes of the hill but all of them had been struck by lightning, their trunks and branches shattered. The hill was covered with long grass which had been flattened by the hail. Even though the trail circled around the lower part of the ridge, Dil Das headed up a goat path which zigzagged to the top. I leaned forward and grabbed at the wet grass to pull myself up the steep incline.

The clouds had lifted and from the top of the hill there was a clear view in all directions. Ahead of us I could see the Dehra Dun Valley and the Siwaliks beyond, like a corrugated reef. To the east the Tehri Hills unfolded, range upon range. Villages were scattered over the mountains, tiny clusters of slate-roofed houses and cowsheds, surrounded by terraced fields that looked like a series of uneven steps cut into the slope of the ridge. Dil Das turned and glanced back at me.

"Give me a coin," he said.

I reached into the pocket of my jeans and took out a four-anna piece. Dil Das held it in the palm of his hand, a silver sequin against his creased and callused skin. As I hugged myself for warmth, he walked through the long grass and stood a moment, silhouetted against the moving clouds, a dark, ungainly figure, holding his shotgun by the barrel. Looking eastward I could see Sirkanda Devi, a mountain peak with a temple at the top. It was several miles away but in the colorless half-light following the storm, the whitewashed shrine stood out like a beacon.

I watched as Dil Das leaned down and placed the coin in the wet grass. The villagers never cut fodder on this hill because it was considered a sacred place. Whenever Dil Das and I went hunting on the ridges below Patreni, we would stop at the hill and leave an offering for the goddess. Though I didn't believe that the coin would bring good luck, I couldn't see any harm in it. There was no temple or shrine on the hill, not even a cairn of rocks, only the view of Sirkanda Devi in the distance and a rustle of wind in the grass.

The only man-made object on the hill was an iron flail, a crude, misshapen implement, which Dil Das had showed me several years before. I searched in the grass and found it lying a few feet from where he'd placed the coin. The flail looked as if nobody had touched it for two or three months. The metal felt wet and cold as I picked it up. There was no rust on the surface though it was tarnished black. Dil Das claimed that the metal was a special iron alloy, which attracted lightning to the hill. The flail weighed about three pounds. The handle was eight or ten inches long, a rough forged piece of metal that flared out at one end, in the shape of a trowel. Attached to this were a dozen or more chains, several of which were broken. As I shook the flail to untangle the chains, it made a rattling sound. Dil Das had told me that if a person went mad or was possessed by one of the many bhoots and spirits that haunted the mountains he would come to this hill and beat himself with the flail to drive the demons from his body.

"Have you ever been possessed?" I asked as we made our way down the hill to the main path.

"Once, years ago. I was your age," said Dil Das. "I had gone to cut grass on the big cliffs below Chattarmani's fields when I felt something leap onto my back. I thought it was a bear or leopard but as I fell down the khud I could see nothing. The bhanchut almost killed me. I was able to grab on to the branch of a kingod bush to stop myself and I must have been unconscious for several minutes. When I opened my eyes the weight was gone from my back, though I could feel something inside of me, as if the bhoot was sucking at my heart. I ran all the way home and told my father what had happened. He made me come here and whip myself with the flail to exorcise the spirit."

"Did it work?"

Dil Das nodded and looked away toward the summit of Sirkanda Devi, silenced by the memory of that experience. I tried to picture him as a young man, whipping himself with the iron flail, the blood streaming down his back as the chains clawed at his flesh.

We continued down the ridge past Donk, a settlement of three or four chaans. An old woman was coming up the path with a brass water vessel balanced on her head. She stepped aside and greeted us cautiously. We had loaded our shotguns before setting out but there was little chance of seeing any game until now. The path descended through an area of scrub jungle, past a spring, and down to another saddle where there were deserted fields and a single chaan. Though I heard a covey of pheasant calling in one of the ravines, we did not see them.

By the time we reached the end of the ridge at Devi Dhang the light was beginning to fade and it looked as if we were going to have another storm. This was a place I often hunted, a broad stretch of cliffs that lay opposite the village of Chamasari, above the water mill and gorge at Seraghat, where I had camped with my classmates two years before. There wasn't much of a path and we skidded down a vertical slope, digging our heels into the grass. The foliage had changed, from pines and oaks to semla trees and cacti which grew at lower altitudes. The rucksack dug into the base of my spine and made me clumsy and unbalanced as Dil Das guided me across to a point from where we could see the cliffs. Moving as silently as we could, the two of us edged our way forward to an outcropping, from where the cliffs fell away to the stream, which lay five hundred feet below.

For half an hour we sat and watched the cliffs, our eyes picking over each stunted cactus, every shadow and tuft of grass, waiting for the mountain goats to show themselves. At last we heard a sound of rocks falling from above and Dil Das nudged me, pointing straight ahead. Two ghoral appeared, about a hundred yards away, like shadows moving across the face of the cliff. They were much too far away for us to fire at them and I wished I had my father's rifle instead of the shotgun. Their coloring made the ghoral almost invisible and only when they stopped and looked in our direction could I see the white patches on their throats. They had not seen us, but the ghoral seemed nervous, and within a few seconds they had disappeared. We waited at Devi Dhang for twenty minutes more, then climbed back up to the saddle and followed another trail that led us down to Kholdighat.

It was completely dark by the time we reached the deserted chaan near the stream. Gathering armloads of dry wood and kindling, we lit a fire and made some tea. I had a few supplies in my

rucksack, a kettle, a packet of tea leaves and sugar, powdered milk:
and a tin of luncheon meat, in case we didn't shoot anything.
There was also a half bottle of rum which I had hidden in the folds
of my sleeping bag.

The chaan at Kholdighat had been built by Dil Das's father and
for many years it was their winter home. When the weather turned
cold they would move their buffaloes down to the lower altitudes
for several months. During the past three years, however, no one
had lived at Kholdighat. Dil Das and his brothers had lost most of
their buffaloes, one or two of them killed by leopards, the others
sold to pay off debts. Their dairy operations had declined to a point
where only one brother, Ratnu, made a living selling milk. The
rest of them were virtually destitute, growing a few subsistence
crops on their fields and picking up day wages here and there. Dil
Das also distilled his own liquor in the village, which he sold ille-
gally, a potent brew known as "kacchi," made of raw cane sugar
and yellow raspberry roots.

We opened the luncheon meat and put the can in the fire to
heat. Dil Das had brought a few chapatis with him, rolled up in
newspaper. With the fire burning we were warm enough, though
one section of the chaan had collapsed and there was nothing but
straw on the floor. We opened the rum and each of us poured himself a drink. I added water from my canteen though Dil Das drank
his neat, swallowing the rum in a single gulp.

As we ate the luncheon meat and cold chapatis, Dil Das told
me stories about other Woodstock boys with whom he had gone
hunting. I had heard most of these tales before but each time they
were recounted something more was added. Dil Das began by telling
me how Ray Smith and he had shot a tiger on Pepperpot Hill, above
Kimoin. This was the only tiger that anyone had ever seen in Mussoorie and it was so heavy they had to get a dandie to carry it
home. Pouring himself another drink of rum, Dil Das told me
about hunting for ibex with John Taylor in the mountains beyond
the Rhotang Pass in Kulu and how he got sick with tuberculosis

after that trip and had to be put in the mission hospital at Ludhiana for three months. He also described duck hunting on the jheels near Delhi with Ernie Campbell, whom he called his shikari guru. Dil Das remembered all of their names—Bobby Fleming, Chris Appleby, and Dean Fasnacht, who was wounded in Vietnam and lost his sight. A few years earlier he had written Dil Das a letter telling him what had happened.

"I couldn't read the letter," said Dil Das, "so I took it to the school and Mrs. Kapadia translated it for me. Dean Fasnacht wrote that he was fighting in the war and a bomb went off and now he is blind. It's a terrible thing. . . . What is Am'rika doing there? What is this war in Vietnam?"

I started to explain that the war was over now and the Americans had pulled out, but Dil Das waved his hand impatiently.

"Dean Fasnacht and I shot a barking deer below the fields at Jabberkhet," he said. "You know, where the trail goes down to Bandar Chowki. In his letter he described the place and wanted to know if I still remembered that kakar. Of course I do. I never forget the animals that I've killed."

The person whom Dil Das remembered best of all was John Coapman, who graduated from Woodstock in 1946. The two of them were about the same age and they had grown up together in the forests around Patreni. After Woodstock, John became a professional hunter, taking wealthy clients on tiger shikars. Dil Das accompanied him on many of these hunts in different parts of India. I had met John Coapman several times, whenever he came back to visit Mussoorie. He was a large man, six foot two and weighing almost three hundred pounds. His parents had been Presbyterian missionaries and he was related to us by marriage—his sister Cleo was married to my uncle Dave. John sahib, as Dil Das called him, had done a lot of different things, one of those figures who was larger than life. For a time he had lived in Hunza, a remote Himalayan kingdom in northern Pakistan, where he was employed by the mir of Hunza, a Muslim prince. During the fifties

John was responsible for bringing Coca-Cola to India and worked as their distributor in Delhi for several years. In the early sixties he started Tiger Tops, a game resort and jungle lodge in the lowland forests of Nepal. Dil Das had worked at Tiger Tops for a couple of years and he told me that John sahib had cleared an airstrip in the jungle so that rich tourists could be flown in from Kathmandu. He described how they were carried from the airplane to the jungle lodge on elephant back, and lived in luxurious tree houses made of bamboo. Dil Das had been employed as a game guard and tracker searching out the tigers and rhinoceros to show the tourists. Eventually, John Coapman's partners at Tiger Tops took away his share of the company and he was forced to leave Nepal. From there he went to Kenya, where he built and ran one of the Hilton jungle lodges. While he was in Africa John Coapman sent Dil Das a set of pictures of himself posing with animals that he had shot on safari, eland and kudu, lion and zebra.

There was an irresistible romanticism to the stories I heard about John Coapman, a combination of Kipling's "The Man Who Would Be King" and Hemingway's *Green Hills of Africa*. Sitting in the deserted chaan at Kholdighat, drinking the last of the rum, I couldn't help but feel that there was something in this experience that I shared with all of the others who had hunted with Dil Das. He sat across the fire from me, a bidi smoldering between his lips, eyes watering in the woodsmoke.

"Steve dost, next summer you will graduate from Woodstock and leave Mussoorie, then who will hunt with me?" said Dil Das.

"I'll come back," I said.

"Maybe . . ." His voice trailed off. "If I'm still here. John sahib, Ray Smith . . . each one of them came here to hunt with me at Kholdighat. But all of them are gone. We had good times together. In those days there was plenty of shikar. Every weekend we would hunt for kakar and ghoral."

"Tomorrow we will shoot a ghoral," I said.

"Yes, if we are lucky. Look here, Steve dost," he said to me, the rum making him slur his words. "I have always been a shikari. That's what I was born to do. Whatever money my father made, our dairy business, I threw it all away for hunting. This business of shikar has ruined me."

Dil Das gestured toward the collapsed section of the roof, the empty stalls for cattle, and the vacant doorway of the chaan. Even though there wasn't any anger or accusation in his voice, I could tell that Dil Das held all of us accountable for his misfortunes. He had nothing left, only his debts, and two young daughters that he still needed to marry off. Behind each story that he told, behind our laughter, I could sense the sorrow and regret that lay hidden in his words.

That night I was awakened by a sound in the darkness. Having no watch, I tried to guess what time it was, seeing a few embers still glowing in the hearth and hearing a pygmy owlet calling somewhere up the ridge. My sleeping bag was warm and we had spread a layer of straw on the ground. For an hour or so I lay unsettled and disturbed, listening to the silence which encircled us, and then I fell asleep again. Just before dawn Dil Das shook me by the shoulder and handed me a mug of tea. Leaving our rucksacks in the chaan, we set off down the valley. It was cold enough that there was frost on the grass. My shotgun had no strap and the cold metal stung my fingers. In the faint light I could just make out the jumble of boulders in the stream. Several years before there had been a flash flood at Kholdighat and the water had risen almost to the chaan. Dil Das had been staying there that night and he had told me how the mountains shook as if there was an earthquake. When the flood subsided they found that the stream bed below the chaan, which had been twenty or thirty feet deep, was now filled with rocks and most of the paths had been washed away.

After going downstream for three quarters of a mile, we started to climb up a forested ridge. It was still too dark to see anything more than the profiles of the hills but from time to time we stopped and listened. At one point we heard a kakar calling on the opposite ridge, a shrill, barking sound that was repeated every fifteen seconds. The kakar was too far away for us to try stalking it, and after a few minutes the deer fell silent. There were birdcalls now, scimitar babblers and whistling thrushes, and from the deserted fields across the valley the cry of a black partridge, "paan bidi cigarette," and the chuckling whistle of kalij pheasant. I had put birdshot in the right barrel of the shotgun and LG in the left. Both cartridges were homeloads that my brothers and I had made.

After half an hour of climbing Dil Das crouched down beneath a pine tree that overlooked a wooded slope about fifty yards to our right. Beyond that was a section of the ridge where a landslide had sheered away most of the trees and underbrush, leaving an open gash of rocks and cliff. The two of us did not speak at all, as if the stories from the night before had drained our words away. The sky was getting brighter and trees and rocks were taking shape, the shadows receding. We still had half an hour before sunrise, and laying the gun across my lap, I wrapped my arms around my knees for warmth. We waited like this until the chir pines at the top of the ridge were lit up by the first rays, their green needles ablaze with light. No animals had showed on the slopes in front of us and Dil Das finally lit a bidi, stood up, and threw a rock into the ravine below. I held the shotgun ready in case something ran up the slope, but there was nothing.

We continued up the ridge, toward Moti Dhar, crossing the old mule trail to Dehra Dun. Most of the area was forested with pines, but there were oaks and other broad-leaved trees in the valleys and on some of the slopes. We did not meet anyone else along our route, though we came to a clearing where shepherds had camped a few days earlier, the ground littered with droppings and the stench of goats in the air. Circling the ridge we passed a small shrine in which there was a carved image of Nag, the cobra deity. Here we left another coin.

The area where we were hunting was part of the Moti Dhar forest block but we had no permit. Even though we were poaching there wasn't much chance of meeting a forest guard, and Dil Das knew most of them, supplying them with liquor from time to time. As far as he was concerned it was his forest as much as anyone's and he didn't care about licenses or permits. We hunted all morning and into the afternoon. Twice we saw ghoral but both times they were out of range, several hundred yards away across the valley. By the time we turned around the sun was so warm that I had taken my jacket off and wrapped it around my waist. Both of us had eaten nothing since the night before and we were exhausted.

Returning by the same route, we walked more quickly now, for there was little chance of seeing any game in the middle of the day. We passed the cobra temple and the shepherd's camp, talking quietly, trying to decide if we should spend another night at Kholdighat. Dil Das had planned to go back up the hill to Patreni and I wasn't looking forward to the climb. As we headed down the ridge, I was looking across at the scarred landslide to my right, when Dil Das suddenly reached out and grabbed my sleeve, pulling me down beside him and pointing toward the bushes on our left.

I had raised the shotgun to my shoulder even before I saw the ghoral, which was standing about forty yards away, partly hidden behind a barberry bush. Aiming at the base of its neck I fired the left barrel of the twelve-gauge. Dil Das had raised his gun as well but the ghoral dropped immediately and tumbled into the ravine. Twenty minutes later, after scrambling through the underbrush, we found the animal lying dead in a gully full of rocks. It was a large male, the size of a big goat, dark brown and gray in color, with six- or eight-inch horns. The two of us could hardly believe our luck, just when we were about to give up, and Dil Das kept thumping me on the back and pointing to the holes where the buckshot had left its mark. Using vines, we tied the ghoral's legs together, and I lifted it onto my shoulders. Heading down the trail to Kholdighat I could feel the animal's warmth against my back.

As soon as we reached the chaan Dil Das lit a fire and we gutted the ghoral with my skinning knife. Removing the entrails, I cut out the kidneys, heart, and liver. Both of us were starving and we decided to cook these before heading back up the hill to Patreni. One of Dil Das's rituals, whenever he killed an animal, was to swallow the gallbladder. It was extremely bitter and had to be cut away very carefully for fear of spoiling the rest of the meat. I watched him as he sliced the gallbladder free and held it in his bloodstained hand. Jokingly he offered it to me but I didn't have the courage.

"This will make you strong," he said, sliding it into his mouth like a raw oyster and shuddering for a second as he swallowed. We cut the rest of the internal organs into pieces and roasted them over the fire on sticks. The meat was tough and had a pungent, gamy flavor, but I was so hungry it didn't matter.

Shadows were already inching their way up the hill as we set off from Kholdighat. Following a shortcut up the ridge, which was used by grass cutters, the two of us took turns carrying the ghoral, while the other person shouldered both rucksacks and the guns. It was a difficult climb and even though the temperatures dropped as soon as the sun disappeared behind the ridge, both of us were drenched in sweat.

We reached Patreni after dark and by this time the dead ghoral had stiffened, so it was difficult to skin. We butchered it outside in the light of a kerosene lantern and each of the families from the village was given a portion of the meat. I saved one leg to take back home with me and Dil Das kept the rest. After washing the blood from our hands the two of us sat down in front of the fire. Rani Devi was tending a makeshift still and the chaan was filled with the sour odor of fermenting kacchi. Positioned above the fire was a large metal canister on top of which was balanced a brass water vessel. A clear plastic pipe emerged from one side of the canister and a thin trickle of liquor was flowing through this into an empty rum bottle. Tulsi, who didn't seem to have moved from the day before, was giving instructions as Rani Devi added twigs to the fire and tested the temperature of the water in the upper pot. When the bottle was three quarters full she removed it and put her hand under the pipe, letting the kacchi flow onto her fingers. Before I realized what was happening, Rani Devi stuck her hand in the fire and it lit up with a flickering blue flame. Shaking her wrist to put it out she smiled at me.

"You see, good stuff," said Dil Das, laughing, as Tulsi slipped a second bottle under the pipe.

Rani Devi filled three glasses with an inch or two of kacchi and handed them to each of us. The liquor was still warm and made my eyes run. Dil Das and Tulsi tossed theirs back in a single swallow but I drank mine slowly. It had a raw, smoky flavor and a bitter aftertaste but I could soon feel the warmth spreading from the center of my chest and down my arms and legs.

Dil Das poured himself another shot and grinned at me.

"Remember, dost," he said, "you won't find anything like this in Am'rika."

1974

One of my closest friends in high school was Kevin McConeghey, whose family lived in Rangoon. Both of us were interested in writing and we collaborated on articles for the school newspaper, *The Tiger*, including a satirical series called "The Mad Shikari." The main character was a bloodthirsty white hunter named Blast M. Ded, whose mission in life was to exterminate every species from the face of the earth. These stories were supposed to be ironic, the kind of black humor that appealed to us at that age. The Mad Shikari's faithful gun bearer was a man named Will and we had a recurring joke about "Fire at Will!" Once a week McConeghey and I used to sit together in the Senior Lounge or at the flagpole outside of Parker Hall and write up the latest episode, each one a little more horrific than the last—Blast M. Ded shooting partridges with a bazooka or slaughtering a circus full of animals with a Gatling gun. I don't think anyone else found these stories at all amusing but the two of us thought that every word we wrote was hilarious, perhaps because they contained a good amount of self-parody. The

Mad Shikari eventually got so gruesome that Ruth Unrau, our faculty adviser on the newspaper, told us to stop, and we wrote a final episode in which Blast M. Ded repented his ways and became an ardent conservationist.

McConeghey had an acid wit that could cut through any conversation and the two of us styled ourselves as cynics. He was at Woodstock for only three years and, unlike many of my other friends, came from a very different background than my own. His father worked for the United States Information Service in Burma and Kevin had studied at several international schools before coming to Woodstock. In some ways, though, there wasn't that much of a difference between growing up as a mish-kid or an embassy brat. We shared many of the same uncertainties and a sense of rootlessness that came from living between cultures. Our sense of humor was acerbic—some would have called it adolescent—but the ironies were laced with an edgy sense of detachment. Kevin could deliver one-liners that punctured the most serious discussions about religion or identity and in this way he and I kept our distance from the truth. At talent shows in Parker Hall the two of us used to do a facetious news report in which we made up scandalous stories about our teachers and our classmates, poking fun at everything from Bible Club to Wednesday night dances at the hostel.

In the fall of our senior year an American astronaut came to speak at the school, sponsored by the U.S. embassy in Delhi. He was traveling around India giving lectures about the NASA space program and exhibiting one of the moon rocks which had been brought back by Neil Armstrong and his crew. A special assembly was organized at the school and we were all expected to attend. The moon rock was going to be displayed in a glass case and the whole school had to file past, as if it were some sort of sacred relic. McConeghey and I got irritated by all of the fuss and ceremony, so we decided to boycott the assembly. The day before the astronaut arrived the two of us went off down the khud and got the largest boulder we could carry, an enormous chunk of limestone, which we placed at the head of the covered passageway leading up to Parker Hall. Underneath this rock we placed a sheet of paper on which we scribbled a note:

EARTH ROCK, DON'T FORGET IT.

Leaving this as a protest we sneaked off campus to Rai Singh's tea shop, where we had a cup of chay and waited until the assembly was over. As it turned out the astronaut took our protest in good humor and made a joke about it in his lecture, though the headmaster wasn't amused because we had skipped assembly and Kevin and I were restricted for a couple of weeks.

McConeghey introduced me to a variety of things that I had missed while growing up in Landour, including the music of Chuck Berry. Kevin played the harmonica, and in his hostel room he would turn up the volume on his record player and, leaning into his mouth organ, eyes closed and shoulders hunched, he would wail out an accompaniment to songs like "Maybellene" and "Hail, Hail, Rock and Roll." Despite our guise of cynicism the two of us were sentimental romantics at heart and when it came to girlfriends Kevin and I liked to pretend that we were wounded souls in a loveless world.

I was still reading a lot of Hemingway, *For Whom the Bell Tolls* and *A Farewell to Arms*. McConeghey, on the other hand, considered F. Scott Fitzgerald to be the greatest writer of the twentieth century, and during rocky periods in our junior and senior years, when both of us had been dumped by girlfriends, we would sit at Rai Singh's tea shop, looking out at the lights of Midlands and reciting the last lines of *The Great Gatsby*, as if they were a personal mantra.

Both of us took solace in dramatizing our emotions, though much of it was tongue-in-cheek. We affected a subversive attitude toward everything, a jaded, world-weary style that I assumed to be a writerly pose. Sometimes the two of us even pretended to be

Hemingway and Fitzgerald and imagined ourselves as members of a lost generation. McConeghey and I shared a page in our yearbook and we included a photograph of Hemingway and a quote from *Death in the Afternoon*. This was one of many literary gestures that we made in school, posturing as writers, even before we fully understood the implications.

The Woodstock yearbook was called the *Whispering Pine* and I was one of the editors. This involved an enormous amount of work, most of which we did ourselves, raising money on May Day and at the Woodstock Sale, taking photographs, proofreading the text, arranging the layout, and having the yearbook printed in time for graduation. For me the yearbook was an opportunity to piece together all of the images of Woodstock and Mussoorie that I wanted to preserve and carry with me when I left. Anitra Mansson, Steve Harper, and I took most of the photographs, pictures of monsoon mist filtering through the oak trees, the snow mountains from the Chukkar, Sports Day and basketball games, a rock lizard on a pushta wall, a time exposure of the lights of Dehra Dun, signboards in the bazaar—Kwality's restaurant, Omi Sweet Shop, Beekay Optical Works, a picture of a roadside stall selling fireworks. In many ways it was like a scrapbook, the names and images pasted together on each page, a collage of random memories.

My senior year at Woodstock was probably like any other American high school experience, a frenetic medley of activities and rituals leading up to graduation. Many of my classmates and I had been together at Woodstock from elementary school, and as we realized that we would soon be separating, there was an uneasy urgency to everything we did, as if our impending departure brought these rites of passage into sharper focus.

So many relationships had changed over the years; classmates that I played with at Ridgewood I hardly spoke to during high school. Scott Bunce had come back to Woodstock for his senior year and though I was not as close to him as I had been before, we remained good friends. Flirtations and romances flared up, then died away. New friends had arrived in recent years, while others had departed. By the time we graduated from Woodstock, the number of missionaries on the hillside had diminished and many of my classmates were from families who worked for international organizations or embassies. An increasing number of Indian students were also attending Woodstock and the school was becoming more diverse. At the same time, we were still part of a small, enclosed community and Woodstock was like an extended family, with all of the loyalties and squabbles, alliances and anger, love and bitterness.

The major event of the fall semester was the Junior-Senior Banquet, Woodstock's version of the prom. Swati Worah and I were "going steady" at the time and I remember that she got her nose pierced for the occasion. It was supposed to be a formal affair but nobody took the dress code very seriously. I wore an old suit jacket handed down from my cousin John, a pair of corduroy jeans, and a clip-on bow tie that I borrowed from my father. A few of the girls wore gowns, delivered at the last minute by Faiz the tailor on Mullingar Hill who was known for never having anything ready on time. The banquet was held in the ballroom of Hackman's Hotel, which had once been the fanciest establishment in Mussoorie, though by this time it was run-down and had a seedy, haunted appearance. Kevin McConeghey and I acted as the masters of ceremony, introducing the skits and other entertainments that followed the banquet, making wisecracks, and reciting Kipling, in overblown British accents, "Gunga Din" and "The Ballad of Boh Da Thon," which seemed to suit the colonial ambience of Hackman's Hotel.

Some of the high school faculty attended the banquet and our homeroom teacher, Graham Hilliard, was sitting at our table. He taught an advanced-placement U.S. history seminar, which I took with Kevin and five or six others from our class. The seminar met twice a week over coffee to discuss subjects ranging from Lord

Cornwallis's surrender to the Teapot Dome scandal. Mr. Hilliard, who was a brusque Canadian with a white goatee, had a reputation for being strict and dictatorial but in the seminar he loosened up and spent much of the time telling us about political shenanigans of the past. His most famous line, which we memorized immediately, was about Aaron Burr, whom he described as, "a shameless profligate, whose reputation for debauchery was unequaled in American history." The Watergate conspiracy had recently been exposed and I had been reading in *Time* and *Newsweek* about Richard Nixon and his cronies.

History had always interested me and during activities week, when each of the seniors did a special project, I wrote a paper on soldiers of fortune in nineteenth-century India. My interest in the subject was sparked by a book, *Sikander Sahib*, about James Skinner, an Anglo-Indian mercenary who fought for several native princes and was eventually recruited by the British to raise the first cavalry regiment of the Indian army. The direct descendants of James Skinner still lived in Mussoorie and they owned property in Barlowganj, including Sikander Hall, where a portrait of their ancestor hung on the wall. I was fascinated by the romantic, swashbuckling aspects of Skinner's life, but also by the fact that he was "country born." During his career, Skinner faced severe prejudice from the British because he was the son of a Scottish officer and a Rajput woman. His struggle for respectability, as well as his reconciliation of two separate cultures, made him an attractive figure for me to study. I got permission to do my research at the library of the Indian Administrative Academy, located at the other end of Mussoorie, near Happy Valley. They had a collection of old books and memoirs from the period, including a translation of Skinner's journals, which were originally written in Persian. Reading about colonial history I began to realize how my own presence in India was linked, in a peripheral way, to the British Raj. I too was country born, though unlike Skinner and his descendants, I could make no claims to the land. All of us were interlopers of a kind, and from what I read, it was clear that missionaries were as responsible for the spread of empire as the men at arms.

The application essay which I wrote for Wesleyan University was essentially an argument against the need for passports. Idealistically, I argued that the world would be a better place if we could shed our national identities and break free of territorial and cultural borders. In my essay I tried to make the point that patriotism was now obsolete. I'm not sure whether the admissions officers at Wesleyan were persuaded by what I wrote but I did get my early acceptance letter by the first week of December. I had never visited Wesleyan before and the only thing I knew about the college was that two of my friends from India, Woodman Taylor and Jeff Campbell, were already studying there. The brochures and catalogs, which had arrived in the mail, showed pictures of the campus, a row of neo-Gothic buildings overlooking the college green, cheerful students reading on the lawns, professors with earnest expressions leaning over their desks in an attitude of intellectual concentration, photographs of the cross-country team running through autumn foliage, a new arts center where Indian musicians played tabla and sarod. The catalog listed courses in African drumming, Chinese and Japanese calligraphy, creative writing, Introduction to Human Sexuality, Phenomenology, Myth and Symbol in Indian Asia, colloquiums on the Marquis de Sade and Metahistory. Wesleyan seemed much more liberal than Woodstock and in many ways I was eager to leave Mussoorie and get away from all of the restrictions that lay over me. But the thought of departure was frightening and at times it was almost unbearable to think that I would soon be moving way from India.

In the spring of 1974 our drama class put on a production of Archibald MacLeish's play *J.B.*, and I was cast in the title role. It was a serious and depressing script, based on the biblical story of Job. The play was directed by Bill Shryock, who was head of the theater department, a likable and flamboyant teacher who wore polka-dot ties and buckskin vests. He had worked as a professional actor in his younger days and liked to talk about his Broadway experiences. MacLeish's play stirred up a controversy on the hillside because it questioned the existence of God. Some of the more conservative missionaries were offended, even though *J.B.* presented an essentially Christian message about human suffering. The main character started out as a successful family man, part of the American dream, with a house in the suburbs, but suddenly his life began to fall apart. His secure and stable world collapsed around him and by the end he was reduced to rags and covered with boils. These sudden tragedies and disasters forced him to question his faith in God.

* * *

Our graduation ceremony was held in Parker Hall on June 28, 1974. The monsoon had just broken but the sun came out in the late afternoon as we gathered on the playground near the gym to have our pictures taken. B. S. Thukral, who owned a studio in Mussoorie, was the official photographer for all Woodstock events and he was there with several cameras around his neck. Our class had decided that we would wear Indian dress for the ceremonies. The girls were in saris or ghagra outfits made of colored silks. The boys wore Nehru jackets or achgans that buttoned up to the neck. We posed together as a group, all forty-five of us, lined up on the bleachers and squinting into the sun. Mr. Thukral took a series of pictures with smaller groups, fourteen of us who had been together in first grade, posing with Miss Schroeder, who had been our teacher twelve years before.

Parker Hall was decorated with bouquets of blue hydrangeas, and to the accompaniment of the processional from Mendelssohn's *Italian Symphony* our class walked down the aisle and took our places on the stage, while the rest of the school and families from the hillside filled the auditorium. Our graduation speaker was Bud Skillman, who had been particularly close to our class. I can't remember what Bud said in his speech or much of anything else about the ceremony, because I was trying hard to control my own emotions. There were trophies and prizes handed out. David Buckner was the valedictorian. A choral group sang a couple of songs, the school chaplain said a prayer, and finally we were given our diplomas by Dr. Miller, the chairman of the Woodstock Board. As I was called forward, he gestured to my father, who was also seated on the dais to the side of the stage, and asked him to give me my diploma. Taking the scroll of paper and shaking hands, neither of us could hold back our tears.

After the ceremony there was a reception line where all of the parents and teachers filed past and congratulated the senior class. I was too choked up to stand in line, and ducking out the side door of Parker Hall, I headed up the Zig Zag path to a secluded knoll near Redwood cottage. Here I sat down and wept, without holding back, the monsoon mist sifting through the rhododendrons and oaks. My tears came easily now, just as they had done when I walked down this hill to start first grade with Bagh Chand pulling at my hand. Twelve years had gone by and the hillside had hardly changed, the same trails and houses, familiar trees and plants. I was seventeen years old, almost an adult. It was time for me to leave, and yet the thought of going away from Mussoorie terrified me because I was afraid that I was never coming back. The mist was closing in around me and it was getting dark, the cicadas scraping out their tuneless cry. My hair and clothes were beaded with moisture, a heaviness in the air. Returning to Parker Hall I found it empty. The graduation crowd had moved down to the quad. I went into the bathroom near the library and washed my face before walking down the ramp to join our graduation banquet in the dining hall.

We celebrated for most of the night, leaving the banquet as soon as dessert was finished and heading off to scattered parties on the hillside. Though it rained a little, early in the evening, most of the night was clear. Clusters of students moved about in the darkness, gathering at Rai Singh's tea shop and other places, couples embracing in the shadows, the yellow beams of flashlights dancing through the trees, shouts and laughter, people getting drunk or stoned. We moved up and down the hillside, that treacherous Snakes and Ladders board, free at last of rules and expectations. Kevin McConeghey had brought a box of Burmese cheroots for us to smoke and we finished most of them during the night, passing them out to everyone we met. Malcolm Wilson, who had connections at the U.S. embassy in Delhi, had smuggled up a bottle of Jack Daniel's bourbon from the commissary. We visited the homes of several teachers, waking them up with our revelry and moving on, walking out the Tehri Road in huddled groups, sitting together in a circle at Fairy Glen, then heading up to the top of the hill for a final circumambulation of the Chukkar. Even though I wasn't as drunk as some of the others, who were throwing up and falling off the side of the khud, I felt a heightened, almost giddy sense of where I stood, the place itself, each lamppost on the Tehri Road where I had searched for beetles, the turning points on the cross-country course, the corner on the Eyebrow path where I caught the pit viper, the giant oak tree below Zig Zag, its mossy branches fringed with ferns.

There was an impending feeling of dispersal. These were the last few hours in which we were together, and then it would all be over. Jamie Gilmore was headed off to Canada. John Windsor to Australia. Sarita Ladia and Binayak Bannerjee to Calcutta. Bablu Kapoor, Nadeem Shafi, and Arun Arora were going to Delhi. Scott Bunce was returning to Michigan. Betsy Scott was on her way to North Carolina. Kirit Amin was flying home to Malawi. Kevin McConeghey would return to Rangoon and then start college at Oberlin in the fall. Manju Mehta was off to Mexico, where her father was the Indian ambassador; after that she would be joining Wellesley. Many of our classmates were catching flights from Delhi the day after graduation and they had taxis booked to pick them up at dawn. Malcolm Wilson and I stayed awake all night and at five in the morning we said good-bye to Kevin and Scott at the school gate, shouting farewells and staggering home, with dead cheroots between our teeth. We had pitched a tent in the backyard of Woodstock cottage so that we wouldn't disturb my parents when we came home and I remember the sun coming up over the Tehri hills as I crawled into my sleeping bag and fell asleep.

Malcolm and I were leaving in another couple of weeks. The two of us had made plans to fly from Delhi to Paris and tour around Europe on bicycles before heading back to America. For six or eight months we had been planning our travels, poring over maps of Switzerland, Austria, and Germany, searching through catalogs and trying to decide which kind of bicycles we should buy. I was looking forward to the trip because it provided a transition, breaking our journey, instead of flying directly from India to the United States.

A couple of days after graduation, we took a family hike to Deolsari and Nag Tibba. My cousin Marty was visiting Mussoorie and joined us with a friend from Bangladesh, where she and her family were living at the time. We set off along the Tehri Road and descended into the Aglar Valley from Seolkholi. It was a route I'd taken many times before, crossing the wooden bridge at Thatur and reaching Deolsari by late afternoon. The forest rest house was surrounded by deodar trees and about a hundred yards away stood an old wooden temple which housed a stone idol of the goddess. As we arrived at Deolsari I could see that the villagers were rebuilding the temple. Six or eight men were cutting huge deodar logs into planks, while others were removing the roof, which was rotted and covered with moss. The smell of freshly cut cedar filled the air.

That night, we lit a bonfire outside the forest bungalow and sat around it for an hour or two, talking and watching the sparks rise up with the smoke. We had our dogs with us, Schnapps and Chottu, and they had been sniffing around the bushes near the rest house, searching for pheasant and partridges, even though we hadn't brought our guns. The deodar forest was silent, the straight trunks of the trees reflecting the light from our fire, like a colonnade of pillars. All at once we heard a leopard start to call nearby, a deep, sawing noise that reverberated through the trees. The dogs looked up, listening intently, as the calling continued for five or six minutes. Nobody spoke, for the sound had an eerie, primal resonance, and I could picture the leopard moving through the lines of trees, a fluid shadow. He was less than a hundred yards away and when he finally stopped, Andy, Joe, and I got out our flashlights and walked up the hill to try and see him, though the leopard had long since vanished into the night.

. . .

I left Mussoorie a few days later, saying good-bye to my family at the bus stand near Picture Palace and riding a taxi down the winding road to Dehra Dun. It was raining heavily and landslides covered the road. Just beyond Kin Craig the other passengers and I had to get out and push the taxi over a wash of debris. I watched for the familiar landmarks along our route: the path to Bhatta Falls, where Mr. Goodwin gave us our first lesson in sex education; the bridge at St. George's College; and farther down the ridge, a deserted palace with tin spires and turrets which had once belonged to the maharaja of Nepal. We passed the limestone mines which had been gouged into the hill and continued on down to the toll gate, where busloads of tourists crowded around the tea stalls and the young boys sold lemons to cure nausea. I did not feel carsick that day, even though there was a hollow sensation in the pit of my stomach. I kept my eyes focused on the landmarks as they passed, the spring at the side of the road where my father often stopped to fill the Landmaster's radiator when it overheated, the deserted fields below Kulukhet, and finally, the lone tree hill. A few minutes later the taxi took the last hairpin bend at Kothal Gate and we turned onto the bypass road near Rajpur, leaving the mountains behind. I looked back through the rear window of the taxi and noticed an optical illusion that I remembered from other drives along this road. The Himalayas seemed to be growing larger the farther we drove away.

Malcolm Wilson and I stayed in Delhi for two days before we caught our flight to France. When we got to Paris one of the American embassy staff was standing near the customs gate with a sign that said, "Mr. Wilson/Mr. Alter." Malcolm's parents knew the chargé d'affaires in Paris, Galen Stone, who had arranged for us to be met at Orly Airport. The man from the embassy explained that Mr. Stone was out of town for a few days but took us to a hotel near the place de la Concorde, where they had booked a room. Before leaving us there he handed Malcolm an official-looking envelope. Opening it, we discovered that we had been invited to tea at the U.S. ambassador's residence that afternoon. Since we were planning to spend the next few weeks traveling by bicycle, the only clothes I had were shorts and T-shirts. Fortunately, Malcolm had an extra dress shirt and tie, as well as a pair of trousers that would fit me.

The embassy was within walking distance of our hotel, and when we got to the gate, I was awestruck by the scale of the building. It was like a palace, with a spacious courtyard and an imposing facade. The marine guard checked our passports and gestured for us to go inside. At the top of a broad flight of stone steps stood a footman in white jacket and gloves who led us inside. Walking into the residence was like entering a museum, with portraits of Benjamin Franklin and other dignitaries on the walls, a world so totally removed from Mussoorie and Landour that I could make no comparisons at all.

The tea party itself was stiff and formal. There were about eight people altogether, including the ambassador and his wife. Nobody really seemed to know why Malcolm and I had been invited but they were polite enough. We sipped our tea and ate our biscuits, answered questions about Woodstock and Mussoorie. One of the guests was an elderly woman from New York, who made a remark to me about American youth having lost the pioneer spirit. I didn't have the slightest idea what she meant and just kept nodding and smiling. Malcolm did a better job of taking part in the conversation and after tea the ambassador and his wife showed us around the residence, pointing out their favorite paintings on the walls. The two of us were the first to leave and as we were ushered out, the ambassador asked us to sign the guestbook in the hall. Picking up the pen to write my name, I looked at the entry above and nudged Malcolm with my elbow. There in a scrawling, imperious hand was the signature of the secretary of state, Henry Kissinger.

The next day we bought our bicycles from a Peugeot dealer near the Arc de Triomphe and rode them down the Champs-Elysées. I had never ridden a ten speed before and the traffic in Paris terrified me, as I kept trying to figure out the gears. Malcolm spoke a little French but I had no knowledge of the language and my only familiarity with the city came from reading Hemingway's books, which bore only a slight resemblance to the Paris we encountered. Cycling across to the Left Bank we looked for some of the famous cafés but they were all expensive tourist traps, where a glass of beer cost more than fifty rupees. We bought a cheap bottle of wine at a grocery store instead which we drank on the balcony of our hotel.

We had planned our itinerary before leaving India, looking over maps of Europe in the Woodstock library. From Paris we took a train to Basel, then cycled on to Zurich. Though I had stopped there with my parents on our first trip to America in 1962, I had no recollections of the city. Malcolm had brought a tent and for most of our trip we stayed at public campgrounds to conserve our money. Being summer, there were tourists everywhere and we had to pitch our tent in a line with dozens of other campers. Our first night in Zurich the couple in the tent beside us kept us awake until after midnight with the sounds of their lovemaking. When we woke up in the morning, around seven o'clock, I could hear our neighbor beginning to grunt again and his companion moaned in an exhausted French accent, "Non, Philip, non. It's too early in the morning."

The scenery in Switzerland was dramatic, though I kept telling Malcolm that the Alps didn't compare to the Himalayas. The roads were steep and we were carrying about fifty pounds each in our saddlebags. Going uphill we had to gear down to the point where our bicycles were hardly moving. On our way up to the Arlberg Pass, a group of Italian tourists went by in their bus, cheering us on. When we reached the top of the climb they were waiting with beer and chocolate, welcoming us like heroes, slapping our backs and helping me wheel my bicycle to the side of the road. After two bottles of beer and a slab of Suchard chocolate, I felt invincible. Going down the other side of the pass, we flew around the corners as if we were on a roller coaster.

We cycled an average of sixty or seventy kilometers a day, leaving Switzerland behind and passing through the tiny kingdom of Liechtenstein in only three hours. After crossing the Alps, most of the riding was easy, and we circled through Austria and into Germany. The only accident we had was somewhere in Bavaria, when I was coming down a hill and my front tire got caught in a railway track that crossed the road. The bicycle skidded out from under me and my left leg was badly scraped. Fortunately there was a café nearby where the owner administered first aid, comforting me in German and offering me a beer to ease the pain.

Malcolm was more interested in sight-seeing than I, and whenever we stopped at a campground, he would set off to visit a nearby castle or museum, while I guarded our tent and wrote letters and poems in my notebook. Already a little homesick for Mussoorie, I wasn't really interested in seeing the sights of Europe. At Innsbruck I bought myself a pipe and decided to take up smoking. Sitting in front of our tent, I practiced keeping the pipe alight and brooded over our departure from Mussoorie. In Munich we stayed with friends of Malcolm's family, sleeping in beds for the first time in two weeks. The daughter in the family and her boyfriend took us out to a beer garden in the evening, where we sat under the chestnut trees and tried to understand what was being said to us in German.

Eventually we ended up in Strasbourg, from where we took a train back to Paris. This time we stayed with Galen Stone, who lived in an expensive neighborhood near the Eiffel Tower. When we arrived at his house, it was early evening and he was sitting in front of the television set. As we came in, he nodded solemnly and gestured for us to sit down. I could see a picture of Richard Nixon on the screen, his lips moving, but the words inaudible because of the commentator's voice in French. I hadn't seen a newspaper in several weeks and had no idea what was going on, but once he had finished listening to the newscast, Mr. Stone explained that the president of the United States had just resigned.

· · ·

The next day I arrived in Boston and Janet Wien, my father's cousin, was there to meet me at Logan Airport. She had agreed to be my guardian while I was in America, and I stayed with her for the next three weeks, before college opened. Janet had a house in Belmont which she shared with a close friend of hers, Emilie Farnsworth. I had met both of them several times before, while we were in America on furlough. They made me welcome and the weekend after I arrived they took me up to Emilie's summer cottage in New Hampshire, on an island in the middle of Lake Winnipesaukee.

After traveling for the past few weeks it felt good to stay in one place for a while, though I got restless soon enough. Hitchhiking to Portland, Maine, I visited my cousin John, who was living there, and after that I thumbed my way up to Montreal for a couple of days, crossing the border and coming back. I spent a lot of time writing, working on a short story called "Cicadas," which was set in the monsoon. Learning that I intended to be a writer, another friend of Janet's, Eleanor Vorhees, gave me a manual typewriter that had been sitting in her basement for a couple of years. It was an old Olympus, a heavy secretarial model, with bauchy keys and a carriage return that looked like a gearshift. I liked the feel of it, however, and copied out the poems which I had written while traveling through Europe, sending these to my mother. She had written me a couple of letters, addressed to the American Express offices in Munich and Paris. There was also an aerogramme waiting for me at Janet's house, in which my mother described the monsoon storms which had brought down landslides on the Tehri Road.

Wesleyan was scheduled to open right after Labor Day and I was eager to get started with college. I took a Greyhound bus to Middletown, leaving my bicycle behind but carrying the typewriter and my two saddlebags. Riding into Middletown along Route 9, I recognized the arches on the bridge over the Connecticut River from a picture in the admissions brochure. The town itself seemed quiet and unexciting, the sidewalks deserted in the warm afternoon. The ticket agent at the Greyhound station gave me directions to the campus, which she said was only half a mile away. I didn't want to spend the money on a taxi but I couldn't lift the two saddlebags and my typewriter at the same time. Carrying the bags for a short distance, I left them on the sidewalk and came back to get the typewriter. In this way I ferried my luggage, at intervals, until I finally reached the campus. By the time I got there my shirt was drenched in sweat and I was cursing the heavy typewriter. At one point I even thought of abandoning it at the side of the road, but I kept telling myself that if I was going to become a writer, I had to carry it all the way.

At the freshman registration tables, on the lawns outside North College, I was given the key to my dormitory room. New students had been arriving throughout the day and there were people moving in all directions, carrying suitcases and boxes. I found my dorm without much trouble, a two-story building on Foss Hill, with a long corridor down the middle and rooms opening off both sides. Unlocking the door, I found an empty space, with a bed, a chair, and a desk. A built-in cupboard filled one wall and facing this was a large window overlooking a grassy courtyard. I had a single room with a door that connected to my neighbor on the right, which I locked immediately. Setting the saddlebags on the floor, I opened the packet of orientation materials that I had been given, a sheaf of papers, forms to fill out, letters welcoming me to Wesleyan.

Most of the other students on my hall were freshmen and many of their parents were there to help them move into the dorm, carrying desk lamps and stereos, toaster ovens and boxes of books, posters for the walls and rugs for the floor. Excited voices filled the hall, and going past one of the doors, I saw a mother making a bed and a father assembling a table fan. There was a bewildering sense of chaos, like being in a railway carriage that was about to leave, except that none of us were going anywhere. Closing my door, I lay down on the striped mattress and caught my breath, my arms still sore from carrying the saddlebags and typewriter. In the room beside me I could hear furniture being moved about and someone shouting instructions. The bare white walls of the room, the gray linoleum floor, had a spartan, monastic feeling.

My trunk of clothes and other belongings, which had been sent by sea freight from India, would not arrive for another month or two. The only possessions that I had brought with me were packed inside the two saddlebags, three or four changes of clothes, a pair of jeans I'd purchased in Boston, running shoes, my spiral notebooks, a wad of letters, and my passport. For bedding I had a lightweight sleeping bag, which I took out and spread on top of the mattress. Unpacking my bags, I put my clothes in the cupboard. The Olympus typewriter sat on the desk, its white keys grinning at me.

At that moment I felt completely alone. None of my classmates knew my name or where I came from and nobody had noticed my arrival at the dorm. It was as if my identity had been erased, though I knew that soon enough I would be forced to explain myself, facing a familiar barrage of curious questions. For the time being, however, I felt a comforting sense of anonymity, the overwhelming emptiness of negative space.

EPILOGUE

Already the memories were coming back, shaping themselves into stories that I would tell again and again, recounting the names and places, arranging and rearranging the incidents so that they fit together in the hollow of my mind. Some of these were written down, as I picked at the keys of my typewriter, stringing lines of fiction across the page—imperfect memories, looped like Christmas lights around the branches of a tree.

The process of forgetting had begun as well, erasing the edges of an image to heighten the contrast, the way I learned to mask a negative by waving my fingers through the beam of light from an enlarger, blurring the margins of a photograph. I forget who taught me that. I forget who taught me how to knot my shoelaces, the simple things one does each day. It must have been my mother but I can't remember. I know she taught me how to read. I learned touch typing from Leona Cressman, who used to stand at the front of the classroom with a ruler, beating out a steady rhythm on her desk like a drum major, as I poked at the keys, J J J . . . K K K. The

quick brown fox jumped over the lazy dog. I can still remember
that sentence even though I have forgotten the Bible verses that
I memorized, the names of the apostles, the Ten Commandments.
Thou shalt not . . .

There were lies I had to live with—a leopard I once saw, or may
have seen, or didn't see but said I did, in the ravine below the
garbage dump at Ridgewood, its pug marks pressed into the pale
gray ash near the incinerator, a movement in the bushes, the alarm
calls of kalij pheasant. I was alone and nobody was there to question what I saw or didn't see, the story told so many times that I
convinced myself it must have happened.

Sometimes it was so much easier to lie.

"Where are you from?"

"Boston . . . but my mother is English."

There are stories I haven't told, about my brothers, the rocket
that Andy built, made of cardboard tubes, with a bamboo stem,
fueled by a mixture of charcoal, sulfur, and saltpeter—the recipe
for gunpowder which my father taught us, handed down from his
childhood. Andy set up a launchpad at the edge of our yard and
aimed the rocket in the direction of Mullingar . . . but this is his
story to tell, not mine.

I could have written about Joe wrestling in Dehra Dun, Kan-
tha Pahalwan, the dirt akhara near the police lines, the drummer
gathering the crowds and after the bout, how my brother was
carried around the ring, spectators pressing rupee notes into his
hands, how the policemen from the Foreigners' Regional Registration Office recognized us and offered Joe a tumbler of milk to
drink, mixed with ghee and almond sharbat, a gesture of reconciliation . . . though once again, he is the person to tell that story.

The three of us used to run together along the Tehri Road,
training for cross-country, starting slowly up the hill from Woodstock Cottage, past Eastwood Gate and above Fern Oaks, the gradient becoming gradually steeper, taking the corners single file,
leaning into the sharp turn below Pine Point, from where we could

see the Tehri hills cloaked in shadow, half an hour until sunrise, the air thin and cold, our lungs tugging at our ribs, legs working harder now to keep the pace, knees up, arms swinging loosely, tireless at that age, three brothers, unbeatable in the half-light of a September dawn, the road winding into the cusp of the ridge, into the bend of an elbow, into the curled palm of my hand, breathing steadily in unison as we rounded the shoulder of the hill below Sun Cliff, turning back into the moist declivities, the gully which ran from Oakville down to Dhobighat, muscles tightening with the strain, tendons stretched—running like antelope spooked by the wind, knowing every turning on the road, the bend above South Hill and the level stretch below Ashton Court, the electric wires overhead like lines of music, the call of a whistling thrush, an oak branch in the shape of a treble clef, racing against each other, yet running together, trading the lead as we headed downhill to Jabberkhet, the rubber soles of our Bata sneakers slapping the tarred surface of the road, accelerating down the slope, matching each other stride for stride.

We could run forever, beyond Flag Hill, beyond Bhattaghat and the Peephole, where the snows appeared through a cut in the ridge, beyond the city limits, climbing all the way to Tibri, unwilling to stop, the milestones and furlong markers slipping past, the sound of village drums in the distance, marking time, crossing valleys in a single stride, hurdling across the ridges, leaving Landour far behind.

ACKNOWLEDGMENTS

In the process of writing this book I have come to realize the profound uncertainties of memory, and I have relied on a variety of sources to corroborate what I remember of my childhood. Certain names have been changed and in one or two instances the chronology of events has been adjusted to provide a more coherent narrative. For confirmation of historical and geographical details I have consulted Percival Spear's *A History of India, Volume 2*, Gurmeet and Elizabeth Thukral's *Garhwal Himalaya*, and Ruskin Bond and Ganesh Saili's *Mussoorie and Landour*. I have also referred to Gurmeet Thukral's photographic book *Woodstock School*, which contains a brief history by Lois Deckert. *Ophrysia*, the field notes of the Woodstock Natural History Society, provided helpful information regarding the flora and fauna of Mussoorie.

I would like to thank Allen Peacock at Henry Holt, who first suggested this book to me and gently twisted my arm until I finally agreed to write it. Jill Grinberg, at Scovil Chichak Galen Literary Agency, has offered encouragement throughout, listening patiently to the anxious ramblings of a novelist confronted with the dilemmas of nonfiction. Alan Lightman, Director of the Program in Writing and Humanistic Studies at MIT, urged me on in this endeavor and arranged for a travel grant so that I could return to Mussoorie during the summer of 1996. My thanks to him and to Philip Khoury, Dean of Humanities and Social Sciences at MIT. Anita Desai's support and guidance has always been reassuring throughout the ups and downs of writing. I am also grateful to Kit and Joe Reed for more than twenty years of friendship, conversation, and advice. Scott Bunce, Kevin McConeghey, and Malcolm Wilson allowed me to pester them with questions about our years at school, elements of which are best forgotten. Though I am grateful to them and many other friends from Woodstock, the responsibility for any errors, exaggerations, and omissions is entirely mine.

Members of my family have been extremely supportive in this project, and I would like to thank Marty and Lincoln Chen for their boundless generosity. Barbara Alter, my aunt, helped me reconstruct aspects of our life in India, while my brothers, Joe and Andrew, have always let me steal their stories without complaint. My parents, Ellen and Robert Alter, assisted in many ways, not only reminding me of names and dates but sharing perspectives on the subtle nuances of Landour. Their tolerance for my opinions and beliefs has always permitted me the freedom to write without constraint. Most of all, however, I am grateful to my wife, Ameeta, who has put up with the self-absorbed preoccupations of my work; she and our children, Jayant and Shibani, have patiently given me the time and space to finish this book.